BOOKS BY J. FRANK DOBIE

A VAQUERO OF THE BRUSH COUNTRY

CORONADO'S CHILDREN

ON THE OPEN RANGE

TONGUES OF THE MONTE

TALES OF THE MUSTANG

THE FLAVOR OF TEXAS

APACHE GOLD AND YAQUI SILVER

JOHN C. DUVAL: FIRST TEXAS MAN OF LETTERS

THE LONGHORNS

GUIDE TO LIFE AND LITERATURE OF THE SOUTHWEST

A TEXAN IN ENGLAND

THE VOICE OF THE COYOTE

THE BEN LILLY LEGEND

THE MUSTANGS

TALES OF OLD-TIME TEXAS

Tales of Old-Time Texas

J. FRANK DOBIE

Tales of
Old-Time Texas

Illustrated by
BARBARA LATHAM

Little, Brown and Company

Boston   *Toronto*

DEDICATION

*Indebted to many storytellers, I dedicate this book to certain ones
who have helped make it and have added to my life. Several of them
are dead. All grew up on the soil, and not one was ever incorporated
into the machine age, with its jargoning power to make people de-
pend on canned amusements. They cultivated the art of interesting
themselves and others. They were and are individuals in the best
sense of the word, never confounding dull conformity and greedy
exercise of the "profit motive" with individualism. Only three of
them ever added up any profits. Their gusto, their generosity of
spirit, and their prodigal delight in sharing stories and characters out
of experience freshens me as I set down their names:*

BILL (W. H.) KITTRELL, *who never fools himself;* ROCKY REAGAN
and ASA JONES, *bedrock cowmen, horsemen and borderers;* ELOJIO
JUAREZ, *joy-giving vaquero of thorned ranges;* RAILROAD (R. R.)
SMITH *and* W. M. LONGWORTH, *masters of repose—"The dreamer
lives forever but the toiler dies in a day";* WES BURTON, *never running out of hope even when nothing else is left;* MRS. BRUCE REID,
of birds and wild flowers; JIM BALLARD, *looking with serene irony
through pretenses and etching characters with what they said;* H. B.
PARKS, *tenacious rememberer, silent sufferer, tonic laugher;* CAPTAIN
DAN SMITH, *whose love of living outquivered the palsy that gripped
him.*

911475

Introduction

Now that I have gathered together these tales of my land and people, they seem inadequate. Put down on paper, they lack for me the zest, the reality, the flavor that I drank in as a listener to the original tellers. Print for the eyes of strangers evaporates the humanity with which a tale told in genial companionship is saturated. Some wit has said that the translation of prose from one language to another is a betrayal; of poetry, an assassination. The translation of *telling* into *printing* always changes a tale; it may improve it — in the way Shakespeare turned an Italian melodrama into *Romeo and Juliet*; but the process of transplanting can easily wither earthy freshness. I have none of the scientific folklorist's reverence for the oral original of a tale — unless the original is masterly; it generally needs bettering. My custom is to try to tell a tale as the original teller should have told it. Any tale belongs to whoever can best tell it. When I reflect on where and how and when and with whom I heard rollicky old Bigfoot Wallace's yarn of his hickory-nut armor, and then read my printed version, I remember an incident in the life of Sir Walter Scott. He had ridden low and ridden high taking down ballads from the lips of people in his "ain countrie." After he printed them in the *Border Minstrelsy*, he took a copy to an old woman of the Highlands. "Thank ye, sir," she said, "but they were made for singing and nae for reading." The best tales told by accomplished nonwriting tellers are made for telling and nae for printing.

The one quality in most of these stories that satisfies me is their failure to be "action-packed." The tempo of the earth is not the tempo of action. The tempo of the earth-dwellers to whom I have been listening for many years is the tempo of growing grass, of a solitary buzzard sailing over a valley, of the wind from the south in April, of the lengthening of a tree's shadow on a summer afternoon, of the rise and fall of flames in a fireplace on a winter night; it is the tempo of a staked horse grazing out from camp in darkness, of a coyote greeting moonrise, of a bobwhite making dawn more serene, of a lizard in the sun waiting for a fly, and of cows chewing their cuds after they have drunk; it is the tempo of a ranchman sitting on the front gallery and looking for hours and hours into space with latent hope for a cloud. This is not to say that folks who belong to the earth do not vivify action. They do, but somehow, in the phrase of Reed Anthony, cowman, they always appear to have "ample time." They may hum, but their humming is not the humming of industry. They may be propertied, but their minds are not on drilling the guts out of the earth, damming up rivers, laying pipelines across continents, converting the elements into bombs to annihilate nations. They may run, but they have a genius for soaking in and oozing out.

One time a buzzard was circling around and around, as deliberate as thought or greed in chiseling the features of a human being, when a hawk came sweeping by.

"Brother Buzzard," the hawk paused to say, "you'll never get anything to eat lazing around up here this way. Come with me and we'll catch something."

"Thank you, Brother Hawk," the buzzard said, "but I await the will of God."

And the buzzard kept sailing and sailing, high and unhurried, while the hawk rushed on his way. After a while he streaked back.

"Still waiting, I see," he said.

"Still waiting on the will of God," the buzzard said.

The buzzard sailed on in majestic repose and the hawk streaked on with rapine intent. A third time their paths crossed.

"Old Slowpoke," the hawk taunted, "I'm going to show you something. You see that sparrow away down yonder sitting on a sharp stob of a dead post oak?"

"Yes, I see the sparrow on the sharp stob and I see a thousandlegs inching along on the ground right under him," the buzzard said.

"Well, watch me get meat," the hawk said.

"Good hunting, Brother Hawk," the buzzard answered. He just kept on sailing and awaiting the will of God.

The hawk stretched out for a dive at the sparrow. He folded his wings and shot through the air like a guided missile. Just as he approached his target the sparrow darted and the hawk, by some error, hit full against the sharp stob. It went clear through his side and into his heart. He fluttered on the stob a minute and then fell lifeless to the ground beside the inching-along thousandlegs.

Meanwhile the buzzard was still circling slow and even, but his circles soon grew shorter in diameter and he spiraled downward until he lit on the ground beside the dead hawk.

He had awaited the will of God.

That buzzard had the tempo of the tales in this book — tales that belong to a patch of roasting ears guarded from bears by an old hound, to contemplators of tracks made by the unseen Wild Woman of the Navidad, to Colonel Abercrombie sitting in the shade of a chinaberry tree waiting for a mole to pop out of the ground, and to many another representative of long-gone life.

It is better to have a just sense of values unsatisfied than to have a cheap sense of values fulfilled, and so I have left Roy Bean out of this book. There are more yarns about him per-haps than about any other Texas character, but he was essenti-ally a publicity-hunting impostor and vulgarian, and striving to make a hero out of him only adds to the hardupness of Texas for heroes possessing the elements of nobility. I could have put Pecos Bill in also. His name was unknown until Tex O'Reilly, a newspaperman, put him into the *Century* maga-zine (October, 1923), claiming him as a folk character. Later, when somebody else wrote a book about him, O'Reilly sued for money on the grounds of plagiarism, claiming that he had in-vented Pecos Bill. He had. Now all the school children at Pecos, Texas, can tell Pecos Bill yarns — most of them as me-chanically constructed as the totals out of an adding machine. They represent the typical American tall tale, which is little more than an adding machine product. I have told tall tales here about northers, sandstorms, and the like, but I'm bored with the Roy Bean–Pecos Bill sausage-links.

Classifying all traditional tales as "tall" shows the debasing effect of jargon on the perceptive faculties. Properly, a tall tale is one of sheer exaggeration. It is usually short of wit and de-void of humanity. It is tolerable only when it brings out charac-teristics of situation, place, person or some other subject. The most ingenious tall tale ranks below any good anecdote of char-acter, though the almanac-minded manufacturers of humor have driven the character anecdote off the air and out of films in favor of their product. Anecdotes about Abraham Lincoln are as traditional as "Barbara Allen." I considered putting a selection of anecdotes about Sam Houston, Brit Bailey, Pamela Mann, W 6 Wright and other Texians in this book, but they didn't seem to fit. (*Texian*, along with *Texican*, was used before *Texan* became common. The name still carries a kind of out-of-the-old-rock connotation.)

Jokes, laws, songs, stories, all forms of human expression except those bedded deep in human nature and truth, become obsolete. Thirty-one years have passed since I brought out as contributor and editor — with the help of Bertha McKee Dobie, who still "o'erlooks each line" — *Legends of Texas*. It soon went out of print. I took from it whatever legends about lost mines and buried treasure were worth taking and wove them into *Coronado's Children*; then for a long time I kept on expecting to revise and extend the remaining material. When I finally came to write the present book, I found that what had once interested me — more historically than narratively — now bored me. For changed me as well as for changed times, the sentimentality of lover's-leap stories has become inane; the saccharinities of miracles and pious doves wither the intellect; the sacerdotal humbuggery of the Lady in Blue and other borrowings from the Middle Ages denies the fact that imagination and reason are integrated. This generation is not, of course, less sentimental, less credulous or more realistic than preceding generations. It is merely the directions taken by sentimentality, credulity and unrealism that change. Anybody who can believe that Formosa is China can believe anything: that the stars are the forget-me-nots of the angels or that screw worms can be "talked" out of cows by quoting a verse from Isaiah. Unadulterated superstition is the lowest and dullest form of folklore. Imaginative power, not superstition, makes Hamlet's ghost harrow up thy soul and translates Queen Mab of the fairies into a reality a thousand times realer than any female of the human species pictured in a thousand Sunday newspapers.

Well, I have gone in one canyon and come out another. The way to spoil a story is to talk about it rather than tell it.

J.F.D.

Contents

xvi Contents

Part One

Corn Dodgers and San Jacinto Corn

"H IS bread it was corn dodgers," went a song of pioneer times. After Stephen F. Austin had located many colonists in Texas and acquired many thousands of acres of land, he wrote: "I am still very poor, living on coffee made out of parched corn, cornbread, milk and butter." At that, Austin had two articles seldom found on the tables of settlers. Travelers among them habitually remarked on the constancy of cornbread and the lack of milk and vegetables. Fruit, except wild berries, plums and grapes, was virtually unknown.

It used to amuse me when we rode up to a house at night and called for a meal, to hear the woman sing out to a boy, "Run to the field and bring two or three ears of corn. I want to make some bread for the gentlemen's supper." So we had to wait until the corn was gathered, ground, kneaded and baked. I suppose this is the true method of living from hand to mouth.

The quotation is from *Trip to the West and Texas,* by A. A. Parker, Esq., who crossed into Texas in December, 1834. Even cornbread he sometimes found scarce, for beef could be "raised with less trouble than corn." At only three places during his travels did he find wheat bread. Many of the householders, he recorded, "are what our northern people would call indolent." Occasionally he rode up to a good farm or large plantation with fine herds of cattle and a comfortable dwelling, but the typical homestead was a one-roomed log cabin wherein a family slept and fared on "cornbread, meat and sweet potatoes." Parker stopped at "some places where they had twenty or thirty cows but no butter, cheese or milk." He did not find butter "at half the places" where he called and "obtained cheese only once in Texas." He verified the old saying that Texas had "more cows and less milk than any other country on earth." Frederick Law Olmsted, whose illuminating *Journey through Texas* came twenty years later, found cornbread and salt pork the unrelieved fare morning, noon and night.

According to a grandma tale, verified in essentials by documentary evidence, the first corn crop raised by English-speaking people in Texas depended on a pointed stick and a hound. Grandma and her family came in an ox wagon, along with two or three other families, all bound for homesteads near the mouth of the Colorado River, where the schooner *Lively*, commissioned by Stephen F. Austin, was to land farm tools and supplies from New Orleans.

Grandma and her sister walked behind the wagon nearly all the way, in company with a milk cow. In the heavily loaded wagon was a sow. One morning the family awoke to find a litter of six pigs with the sow. Then the sow died and the pigs were left orphans. At night Grandma and her little sister took them into their pallet and there the pigs slept warm. They drank some of the cow's milk. The weather was turning cold, but by day the jolting in their box helped to keep them warm. Every night they slept in the pallet.

About Christmas the family reached the mouth of the Colorado River, but the *Lively* had not arrived. The men built a cabin and, while they waited for the ship that was never to come, they hunted. The people ate venison for bread and bear steak for meat. Sometimes they had honey out of trees. They had a little corn, but they were keeping it to plant.

Now, the Colorado River bottom was covered with a heavy growth of reed cane. One day the dogs ran a bear into this canebrake and the boys set it afire. The cane popped and roared like guns in a battle. When the fire was out, the land where the canebrake had been was a clean field, covered with ashes and as loose and mellow as plowed ground.

Then Grandma took a sharp stick and punched holes in the ground, making rows, and her sister dropped a grain of corn in each hole, covering it with her foot. In a few days the corn was sprouting. Under the spring sunshine it grew an inch a day and was truly beautiful. But the ground was also covered with shoots of cane, coming up from roots not burned. The planters had neither plow nor hoe, but every morning they took sticks and went into the field and knocked down all the tender cane shoots. They did this until the corn was big enough to shade out the cane.

Then when the roasting ears began to make, bears and coons began to eat up the crop. Grandma tied an old hound in the middle of the patch. He'd bark and howl all night and scare the varmints away. The family ate fresh corn, roasting the ears in ashes. Even before it was hard they were making cornbread of it. That summer they got farming implements from the East, and thereafter the colonists usually had plenty of corn, but they had not come from a wheat country, were not now in a wheat country, and had no money to buy imported wheat flour.

Captain Jesse Burnam, the first settler up the Colorado River, and his family went for nine months without bread of any kind. One day, he related long afterwards, "a man from lower down the country came up and told me he had corn that he had planted with a stick. There were no hoes nor plows in the colony. I gave him a horse for twenty bushels and went sixty miles after it with two horses, and loaded eight bushels on them. I walked and led them back home. I had prepared a mortar before I left home to beat the corn in, and made a sieve of deerskin stretched over a hoop with holes punched in it. I always had young men about me for protection, and they would generally beat the corn. Then we would have to be very saving, and were allowed only one piece of bread around."

In 1827, Noah Smithwick, on his way from Kentucky to take up free Texas land, stopped at Burnam's place just as "corn was in roasting ear and the people feasting. They boiled it and fried it and roasted it, either by standing the husked ears on end before the fire and turning them till browned all around or burying them husk and all in hot ashes — the sweetest way green corn was ever cooked."

No other man of the colonies set down in writing so many details about ways of living as Noah Smithwick put into his reminiscences. The corn, he wrote, was of "the large, soft, white Mexican variety." People would flatten an old piece of tinware, often a leaky coffee pot that had been ripped open, on an ax-hewn board and punch it full of holes. The punched-out tin served to grate still-milky grains of corn from an ear rubbed over it. Bread from the grating was "very rich and sweet, if a bit heavy."

There were no mills, and after the corn was hard it had to be pounded into grits. "A sound tree was cut off three or four feet above the ground, and the stump was hollowed out by alternate burning and scraping until it would hold about a peck of shelled corn. Then a long pole with stone or iron pestle attached to the butt end was swung into the fork of an adjacent tree," so that

the pestle when lowered would pound down into the stump mortar. This contrivance was called mortar and sweep. It took less manpower to work the sweep than to hammer down directly on the corn in the mortar. The meal into which corn was thus pounded was not fine. "Often without sifting or salt, it was mixed with water and baked. The bread tasted delicious to people who had gone breadless for months. When cold weather came on the people cooked huge kettles of lye hominy."

Old settlers used to tell how a boy who had been given a flour biscuit put a coal of fire on its back to see if it would crawl. He thought it was a little terrapin. According to gossipy Noah Smithwick, an early settler named Martin Varner managed to get together enough money or pelts to buy a barrel of flour. Mrs. Varner made a batch of biscuits, which were "as heavy as lead and hard as wood. When they were done she set them on the table. The boy looked at them curiously, helped himself to one, and made for the door with it. In a few minutes he came back for another." The father stepped out to see what he was doing with the rarities. The youngster had punched a hole through the center of each biscuit, inserted a stick for an axle, and had the wheels ready for a toy Mexican cart. "Cartwheel" was a jocular nickname for biscuit. Even where flour biscuits could be afforded at all, they were a Sunday treat. In the Hallett household at Hallettsville, they were called "Billy Seldom," while the unvarying cornbread was called "Johnny Constant."

One time a family living on a creek was giving a wedding dinner — in the middle of the day — for their daughter and her groom. They were putting the big pot in the little one and were having not only flour biscuits but pound cake, golden with egg yolks and butter.

The cake was baked and sliced and on the table, when a settler named Bullock who lived at the very head of the creek — away up above the last fork, where the owls mated with chickens — came along. He and his family had not been invited to the "infare," as they lived out of reach. He did not belong to the company anyhow. His hair looked as if he used it for a napkin and had not had the bear grease washed out of it for years. His buckskin clothes were "cured" not only with tallow rubbed in to turn water but with the blood of butchered animals and all variety of dirt. Yet it would never do to let him go on without dinner.

"Now, Mr. Bullock," the hostess beamed, "I know how far it is on up to your home and how bad the road is and all that, but you have just got to eat something before going on. It's ready and you won't have to wait until all this crowd gets settled. Come right in."

Mr. Bullock washed his hands and face in a washpan on the back gallery, dried on the common towel, lumbered into the big hall, and sat down in a broad rawhide-bottomed chair near a great plate of sliced pound cake. Soon plates of fried chicken, fried venison, beef roasted over coals, bowls of mustard greens and potatoes, jars of mustang grape preserves and jelly from wild dewberries, and other good things were within his reach. There was plenty of butter and gravy too, next to the golden brown cornbread.

Mr. Bullock began peeling drumsticks at about a bite and a half each. He ate a piece of cornbread sopped in gravy and then he tried a slice of pound cake spread with butter. He sampled venison and approved of the beef, but a combination of fried chicken, pound cake and butter was evidently what his system called for. After he had consumed two or three pieces of pound cake the hostess moved the cornbread nearer to him.

The yellow corn from which it was made gave it a rich look, but Mr. Bullock was too deep in pound cake, butter and fried chicken to notice it.

Now the hostess was truly alarmed. Mr. Bullock had let his belt out a notch. It was a wide belt encased in rattlesnake skin. He appeared to be really settling down to business when he took it off and hung it over the back of his chair. While he was uncinching himself the hostess ran out the back door and into the kitchen, a room separate from the main house, and returned with a platter of biscuits — flour biscuits.

"Oh, Mr. Bullock," her voice came with an anxiety that anybody else would have noticed, "do have some biscuits. We don't have them very often, you know, but I have just finished a big baking of them."

"No thank you, ma'am," Mr. Bullock, who had resumed operations on the pound cake, responded. "You jes' save them there biscuits for the company. This here yaller bread is good enough for me."

Then he "blowed" some coffee in a saucer and swallowed it with another slice of "yaller bread."

The day after the battle of San Jacinto, April 21, 1836, while General Sam Houston lay on a pallet under a great live oak near the battlefield, Santa Anna was brought to him as a prisoner. Almonte, Chief of Staff under Santa Anna, joined in the talk.

"You talk about reinforcements, sir," Houston said to him, raising himself up. "It matters not how many reinforcements you have, you can never conquer freemen." Then, taking from his pocket an ear of dry corn which he had carried for four days, only a part of it consumed, he held it up and said, "Sir, do you ever expect to conquer men fighting for freedom whose general can march for four days with one ear of corn for his rations?"

The un-uniformed Texas soldiers were crowded around the group, and at the exhibition of the corn and the sound of Houston's dramatic words, they gave a yell of approbation.

"Give us that ear of corn," one of them said. "We'll plant it and call it Houston corn."

"Certainly I'll give it to you, my brave fellows," Houston said smiling. "Take it along if you care anything about it and divide it among yourselves. Give each man a kernel as far as it will go, and take it home to your fields, where I hope you will long cultivate the arts of peace as nobly as you have shown yourselves masters of the art of war. You have achieved your independence. Now see if you can make as good farmers as you have proved yourselves gallant soldiers. But do not call it *Houston corn*. Call it *San Jacinto corn*, for then it will remind you of your own bravery."

Accordingly the corn was distributed and later planted. Thus biographers of Sam Houston began telling the story at least as early as 1855. Marquis James in *The Raven* (1929) follows precedent in adding, "Thousands of tasseled acres today boast pedigrees that trace back to the San Jacinto ear."

In 1935 I published this story in newspapers over Texas, asking any reader who might know of any San Jacinto corn growing in Texas to inform me. I received one reply — and one only. Although it confirms the Sam Houston gesture, it hardly confirms the claim that "thousands" of acres of corn can be traced back to the San Jacinto ear. The letter came from W. A. Craddock, now dead, then living at Spur, Texas. It follows.

"My father, John Robert Craddock, later appointed by Sam Houston as captain of a company of Texas rangers, was present as a guard when General Sam Houston showed Santa Anna the ear of corn and told him, 'You cannot hope to conquer a people whose general and men can march three days on a ration of one ear of corn.' My father got a few grains and took them to his brother-in-law, Gabriel Jackson, who had a large plantation on the Brazos River in Burleson County. It was too late to plant the corn that season, for my father was not discharged until May 30. Therefore, the corn was carefully kept until the spring of 1837. It thrived, and for many years thereafter was grown on Gabriel Jackson's plantation.

"After serving in various Indian campaigns and as captain of the rangers, my father married and in 1850 opened a farm on Little River in Bell County. He secured some of this corn, planted it, grew it, and called it Sam Houston corn. I suppose he improved it by selection. When I first took notice of it, about 1870, it was indeed a wonderful corn. He had two kinds, both nearly snow-white. One had broad, flat grains, which he called 'gourd seed'; the other had long, slim grains, which he called 'shoe-peg.' But he called both varieties Sam Houston corn. I could write a book on its many kinds of goodness — as roasting ears, as lye hominy in the big iron pot, as pone bread in skillet, as ash cakes cooked in wet shuck under hot coals, as corn dumplings cooked with turnip greens in 'pot licker,' and as rockahominy, which was corn parched and ground and then perhaps sweetened — about the same thing as Mexican *pinole*. This was one of the most concentrated and easily carried foods known to man.

"I never knew Father to put a lock or bar on his cribs, and to all who needed bread the invitation stood out: 'Come and help yourself, for it is Sam Houston's corn.' He always loved Houston and stood by him in opposing secession. He died in 1891. I do not know if anyone after his death preserved the Sam Houston corn as a distinct variety."

If so, it's not through an agricultural experiment station, where everything is hybridized. But in a kind of sequel to the Sam Houston corn story scientific horticulture has had a part.

A few days before his death, in 1906, Governor Jim (James Stephen) Hogg, the great commoner among Texas governors, said: "I want no monument of stone or marble, but plant at my head a pecan tree and at my feet an old-fashioned walnut, and when these trees shall bear, let the pecans and walnuts be given out among the plain people of Texas, so that they may plant them and make Texas a land of trees."

Pecan and walnut were planted at the grave in the State Cemetery at Austin and cared for. In time they bore. About 1934 the Department of Horticulture of Texas Agricultural and Mechanical College began saving the nuts — such as could be rescued from worms, squirrels, coons and boys — to plant and grow into small trees for distribution. The walnuts have not grown and many pecan plants after being uprooted and shipped did not live. Now the pecan nuts are given out for planting. On courthouse squares and school grounds, in churchyards, parks and other public places in many counties over Texas, Jim Hogg pecans are helping "make Texas a land of trees."

The Wild Woman of the Navidad

It happened one day about noon, going towards my boat, I was exceedingly surprised with the print of a man's naked foot on the shore, which was very plain to be seen in the sand. I stood like one thunderstruck, or as if I had seen an apparition; I listened, I looked round me, I could hear nothing, nor see anything; I went up to a rising ground to look farther; I went up the shore and down the shore, but it was all one; I could see no other impression but that one; I went to it again to see if there were any more, and to observe if it might not be my fancy; but there was no room for that, for there was exactly the very print of a foot, toes, heel, and every part of a foot; how it came thither, I knew not, nor could in the least imagine.

THUS reads Daniel Defoe's description of the most famous human track in the literature of the world. In any solitary land a man will be surprised, interested, fearful or wildly glad at the glimpse of another human being; at the sight of a mere track of an unknown fellow creature he will be filled with wonder and curiosity.

For years the Wild Woman of the Navidad was the talk and the mystery of the Texas colonies. Sometimes the unknown was called "the wild man." Again, two and even three of the track-leaving but never-seen beings ran together. Many theories and speculations arose as to their origin. Stories spread about Africans who had run away from the Bowie brothers while they were buying slaves from the pirate Lafitte on Galveston Island at a dollar a pound and driving them inland, about escapes from blacks smuggled into the country by the outrageous Monroe Edwards, about a certain man from a cargo of raw meat-eaters landed on the Brazos who escaped with a stolen knife and months later was trailed to the Navidad, and about other runaways.

To settlers living against the deep woods and dense brush along the Navidad River no explanation was conclusive. One of them, Samuel C. A. Rogers, decided in his old age to write down the story that nearly everybody he knew was interested in. His record has here been amended as to punctuation and the like, but not as to language or detail.

"A great many persons [he begins] has requested me to write of the wild man, as he was called, but I have my reasons for not doing so. First, I am a poor scribe and do not like to write. Secondly, there is so much mystery connected with the doings of the wild man that my statements would be naturally disbelieved. Yet what I am going to relate is as true as Sam Rogers is my name. . . .

"In the spring of 1845 when going to my work one morning I discovered the tracks of three persons who had been near the house the night previous. The smallest track was of a bare foot that could have worn a No. 4 shoe; the second track was larger, one of the feet that made it being bare and the other shod; the third track was made by feet that must have required No. 9 or No. 10 shoes. The makers of these tracks had not done anything wrong; indeed, all they did for a good while was cause wonder and surprise.

"At this time my household consisted of my wife Lucinda, our little son John, a hired man by the name of Hall, Franklin Rogers, and myself. Lucinda wanted a new dress. Calico was then very scarce, and a lady who could dress in neat new calico belonged to the A-1 upper ten circle. Lucinda had a spinning wheel. The waters of the Sandies had a great many fish. Well, we men promised Lucinda the calico for her dress if she would spin thread for us to make a fishing seine with. She put in time after her housework was done, and when we came home from the field we would spin too, I carding the rolls of cotton and Hall and Franklin operating the wheel. In time we got our seine completed, and the way we hauled fish out of the creek would astonish anybody who knows that stream today.

"Then one morning we found the seine cut and half gone. I had just killed a four-year-old beef so as to sell his hide for a dollar and send to Matagorda for lead sinkers to put on the seine. Now the whole thing was a loss. The only clue we had were the tracks of the wild people. Hall said he was going to watch the next night, and if they came for the other half of the seine he would catch at least one of them with the dogs. Franklin Rogers said, 'Damn them wild people; if we can't catch or kill them, they will break us up.' I have been sorter religious for a great many years and I did not curse. The wild people did not come back, for a while at least.

"Meantime Lucinda had not been paid for her calico dress. There was no calico about, but finally some came to Texana, and I got the money to pay for it. Two of our milch cows died and their hides brought a dollar apiece. We had thought of buying coffee with the hides, as a trader at Texana was giving two pounds for a hide — but we could not get coffee and calico both. Then, as no more milch cows died, we had to kill six steers to make out the eight dollars. Lucinda did not like the dress after all, as it was curtain calico stamped with large flowers.

"Well, for nearly two weeks we did not miss anything more,

and we had become reconciled to the loss of the seine. Then one morning Hall rushed back a-raring and pitching and cursing from the bottom field, where he had gone to plow. I was astonished, for he was a member of the Presbyterian Church; I had heard Methodists curse and had heard Baptists curse, but had never heard a Presbyterian before. 'The damned wild people,' he said, had taken one of his trace chains; the grass was growing so fast it would soon have his crop; he couldn't plow without traces — and then the way he did curse! But we substituted a lariat for the chain, and Hall went on plowing and made a good crop of cotton, corn, and potatoes.

"The potato patch was the cause of his doing more cursing, for, after the potatoes got large enough to eat, the wild people would slip into the field nearly every night and gravel them up.

"The unknown folks had been around us nearly a year. Then we missed the tracks of the big one and the little one. I must say that I felt a little sorry that the one that made the small tracks was gone without my ever finding out who it was or what had induced the person to live such a life. I spent many nights watching but could never get a glimpse of any of the three wild ones. Most people supposed that the little tracks were made by some female. What became of the two missing wild ones was never known. Franklin Rogers and others thought they had died from sickness, as there was a great deal of rain that year and even among people protected from the weather there was much sickness.

"But the tracks of the one remaining wild man continued to appear. When corn was in roasting ear he would come nearly every night to get a supply. Once I had an old Irishman cutting hay in the cornfield. He usually rode to it and tied his horse while he worked or slept. One morning Franklin Rogers and I saw the old man riding towards us like the devil beating tanbark. He was screaming, 'Mr. Rogers, get your gun! The wild man is in the field!' We went and saw where a bear had broken down some corn. Then the Irishman admitted that he had been asleep, had awakened at a noise near him, and, seeing a black creature standing, had taken it for the wild man. After that he would not go to the field without a dog or without a book and 'one of the gloves of Saint Mary' given to him by a priest in Ireland. He could not read a line, but he was sure that the book and glove would keep him from harm as long as he had them with him.

"One morning about this time I missed a handsaw that I had been using the evening before and had left out in the yard. Two years later it was delivered to me by Russell Ward after he and his brother Lafayette Ward had surprised the wild man in the bottom. In fleeing, the wild man dropped a kind of basket or trunk that was very curiously woven. This contained a shirt of mine, a novel, a Bible, and many other articles taken from the house. The shirt had been torn and then the rent sewed up as skillfully as any woman could have sewed it. Thread and needles both made by the wild man were among the curiosities in the trunk.

"The wild man had been scared, but he did not leave the country. He kept coming to our premises. One morning after we had kept watch all night we saw tracks in the yard and garden that plainly showed he had been right at us. Russell Ward then proposed that all the neighbors collect and hunt out the bottoms. Eight of us met at the junction of the Navidad River and the Sandies and searched all day without seeing anything. Afterwards we found two different trees in which the wild man had made his home while the bottoms were covered with water. One of them was a live oak that forked about thirty feet above the ground. This fork formed a kind of flat place on which he could lie down and sleep and also build a small fire to cook whatever he had to eat. I climbed the tree myself, which was not difficult to do, as it did not grow straight but inclined considerably."

At this point the narrative of Samuel Rogers breaks off abruptly, without coming to an end. The whole story, however, was written out by a contemporary of Rogers, Martin M. Kenney. With a few minor interspersions and some changes in language, it follows, without quotation marks.

In the late 1830's settlers on the lower Navidad began seeing the barefoot tracks of two human beings but never the persons who made them. The size of the tracks indicated that one was made by a boy and the other by a girl or woman of delicate feet. The two sometimes invaded the sweet potato fields and sometimes helped themselves to a few ears of corn, but seemed to avoid any mischief and took only something to eat.

At first they were thought to be runaway slaves, but their gentle nature did not fit desperate runaways. Moreover, the size of the mysterious tracks demonstrated that they were not made by Negroes, and the makers of the tracks avoided Negroes as well as whites. After the runaway slave theory had been rejected, it was supposed that the unknown ones might be some wandering remnant of Indians; this conjecture was favored by the smallness of the feet. Yet the conduct of the wild beings seemed foreign to Indian character. Indians would not have been so secluded; they would have committed more mischief — or less.

The most probable conjecture seemed, for a while at least, to be that the unknowns were lost children who had become separated from their friends during the hurried retreat of the settlers from the invading army of Mexico in 1836 — the Runaway Scrape, as it was called. The children, it was supposed, had become so alarmed that, believing the whole world hostile, they in innocent ignorance avoided all mankind. But there were grave objections to this theory also. If the supposed lost children had been old enough to maintain themselves in the wilderness, they would not have lacked the discretion to make themselves known when their friends returned. Altogether, the riddle remained unsolved.

After some years the larger track was no more seen, but the small, slim track kept on appearing. Then a party of hunters noticed some bones protruding from a pile of sticks and leaves in the woods and uncovered a naked human skeleton. The hunters were not anthropologists; to them the skull belonged to some member of the human race; they did not know whether white, black or red, male or female. But people speculated and concluded that the larger of the two strange recluses had probably been a man and that when he died his mate gave his body, with sticks and leaves, the best burial she was capable of giving.

About the only places the small track was seen for a long time was in sweet potato fields, where the strange being frequently came by night and, after grappling a few potatoes, went away as stealthily as she came. From the impress of the fingers left in the mold it was judged that the hands were small and slim; and from the tracks, which were only a span long, it seemed certain that the author of these little depredations was a woman, and not of the black race, whose feet are large and flat. The track-maker was now called "the Wild Woman," though some called her "It."

Curious to know what manner of being she was, some young

men set a watch at a potato patch where there were signs of her recent depredations. As she was harmless and possibly ignorant of speech, they planned to seize her with their hands, and for this purpose they concealed themselves between the high ridges of the potato vines and waited in silence. At a late hour she came, and as near them as they had expected. The night was dark, but they could see the shadowy form. It was slim and apparently unclothed, but the color could not be distinguished. They sprang out to seize her, but, though they were active young men, she was more agile still, and bounded away as silently and quickly as the flitting of a shadow, and was instantly lost in the darkness.

For a long time she was not heard of. But at length fresh signs of her appeared in a manner that heightened curiosity. The settlers were obliged to keep vigilant and fierce dogs to protect the houses and domestic animals against beasts of prey. Trained to battle with bears, panthers, and other wild animals, the dogs were a trusted security against the clandestine approach of man as well as beast. The houses of the early settlers were constructed on the general plan of two log pens connected by a wide hall, open at both ends, all under one roof, shade and ventilation being the chief requisites in the southern climate. If a pen were large enough it could be partitioned, each sub-pen, or room, opening into the hall. Saddles, ropes and other horse-gear hung from pegs or antlers on the sides of the hall; guns were stacked in the corners of the rooms or rested in racks over the mantels and doors, ready for instant service; the settlers, skilled in the use of weapons, were scarcely less vigilant than their dogs. Thus guarded, they felt secure from prowling beasts and confident that human marauders would not be foolhardy enough to try to steal into their houses. In the summer time the doors and windows stood open day and night, and all wayfarers coming in good faith were welcome.

To one such house, on a bright moonlight summer night, when everything was still and the inmates were asleep, the Wild Woman came and entered, stepping over dogs, it would seem. What search or exploration she made was not known, but she entered the dining room, in which there was an open cupboard containing a plate of meat and a loaf of bread. She took part of the meat, and, breaking the loaf in two, took one half and left the other; and with this mute explanation of her motive, she departed as silently as she came. Not a dog whimpered, and the people of the house were none the wiser until morning, when this excusable theft excited their curiosity and compassion. But they wondered at the dereliction of the dogs.

The unknown one did not return to that house for a long time. But she soon entered another house of the same style, guarded by particularly vigilant dogs. In this her search was extended, as shown by the things she moved; but it was also obvious that her motives were not venal. There were gold watches hanging over the mantel, where she moved bottles and powder flasks, and she must have seen them, as the moonlight came bright through the windows. There was silverware in the cupboard, but she took only some scraps of food, taking, as before, only half and leaving half; and she effected her departure without disturbing man or dog. She afterward entered numerous houses in the same manner; not a dog would notice her. The Negroes became superstitious about her. They called her "that thing that comes."

One winter it was found that she was more or less regularly taking corn from a crib. The amount she took was trifling, but here seemed an opportunity to capture her and satisfy curiosity. All that needed to be done was to watch, and when she entered the crib to close the door. The watch was kept for several nights without results, a man staying inside the crib near the door, ready to close it. One night he had fallen into a doze when the rustling of corn shucks awoke him. The "thing" had come. He had only to push the door and call the people. But horror seized him. The thought of being shut up alone in the dark, even for a few moments, with the mysterious creature was accompanied by a sudden dread that he could not control. In his fright he cried out, and before he could move a limb the creature was gone with a single bound through the door into the enveloping night.

The compassion of the people arose with their curiosity. The poor creature was welcome a hundred times to what she took in her little forays, harmless to others but so dangerous to herself. Every means was used to communicate with her. Diligent search was made in the canebrake and in great hollow trees, some of which afforded almost a house. But all in vain; she avoided black and white alike, and no signs of her dwelling could be found in the dark forests where she roamed like some wild animal. Sometimes no sign of her would be seen for months or even years, and the people would cease to think of her; then suddenly she would appear with some trick, if it might be so called, more curious than any preceding.

On one of the plantations the woodworkers' tools, essential to the early settlers, were kept under an open shed where there was a rough workbench. From this the owner missed his handsaw, drawing knife, and some other tools. At first he suspected some petty thief. But several weeks afterward the tools were all found returned to their places, the handsaw scoured and polished as bright as a looking glass. What could this mean? It must have been the work of the Wild Woman. The polish put on the saw was wonderful. No one knew before that this familiar metal was susceptible of such a gloss, nor did anyone know the process by which it could be effected. Why did the woman take these tools? Was she building a hut or fixing her residence in some hollow tree? Was she making weapons, a raft, a boat? For any imaginable purpose the assortment she took was incongruous, deficient, or superfluous. Why did she return the tools so soon? What could be the meaning of the curious but useless pains she had taken with the saw blade? Was there some symbolic meaning, or message? Thus speculation ran.

A little later, a neighbor missed a log chain. His Negro teamster asserted that "dat thing what comes have tuk it." But a chain twelve feet long weighing thirty pounds or more —what use could the wild creature have for it? The owner said that if he ever "whipped a nigger for being a fool," he ought to "skin" the teamster. Not long afterward, the Wild Woman did come to his house and made the usual round among unconscious watchdogs and sleeping people to her usual prize, the cupboard, where she found a pan of milk, two loaves of bread, a plate of butter, and other food. She took half the plate of butter, dividing it neatly, took one of the loaves, poured half the milk out of the pan into a pitcher, and, taking the latter, departed. Two or three weeks afterwards, upon awakening one morning, the family found the pitcher standing on the bare ground before the door and the log chain coiled around it. The chain was scoured and polished as bright as the saw had been. To bring this chain and coil it before the door would seem to have been necessarily a somewhat noisy operation, but the dogs had taken no notice.

The people ceased to wonder at the recusancy of the dogs; it had become an established phenomenon. For seven years or more this strange creature had haunted the country, and all sorts of dogs and several generations of them had been tested. They seemed mysteriously insensible to the presence of the Wild Woman.

Her next exploit surpassed all and set curiosity on tiptoe. A farmer had a hog fattening in a pen near his house. A bear attempted one night to take it off, but the dogs seized the beast and after a severe fight killed it. The combative spirit of the dogs was so raised by this occurrence that they kept a lively watch, especially on the hog pen; and expecting every night to be treated to another bear fight, all were fiercely alive to the slightest alarm. One night during this state of matters, the Wild Woman brought a poor hog out of the woods and put it in the pen, then took the fat one out, making off with it safely, and not a dog barked or growled. The farmer said that he would have killed every dog on his place if he had thought they were at themselves when "that thing" swapped hogs with him. There was but one explanation possible: she had bewitched both hogs and dogs. There was no use in fattening the new porker; the Negroes would not have eaten a mouthful of it short of starvation. During several years "the thing" repeated this mysterious performance at numerous places. The substituted hog often bore a neighbor's earmark.

Trailing the Wild Woman with dogs should be easy now, for surely she could not carry so heavy a burden as a fat hog any great distance. But the dogs always lost the trail as soon as the people following were left out of sight. When the hog-taking achievement had ceased to be a wonder, some hunters came accidentally upon one of her camps, and here was material for fresh curiosity. There were piles of sugar cane, which abounded in the neighboring fields. Much of it had been cut into short lengths and chewed; hence it was evident that she knew the use of a knife. There were some curious strings twisted of the outside bark of the cotton plant. There were no signs of fire and no implements. A secret watch was kept on the camp for some time, but the creature did not return. Sometime afterwards, fresh signs of her having been seen, a general hunt was resolved upon. Dogs were procured that had been trained to follow runaway Negroes. They came upon the trail and pursued eagerly enough; but the trail led through ponds of water abounding in the swamp and soon put the dogs at fault.

A long time followed during which she was not heard of; then her camp was found again at a considerable distance from the former one; she had removed to another section of the country. This new camp revived curiosity. At it were several things of her own manufacture, baskets and a curious snare made from the fibrous bark of the cotton plant, seemingly intended to catch rabbits or other small animals. There were several articles taken from houses, a spoon, some table knives, and a cup. There was no clothing; her bed was moss and leaves; and there had been no fire. But what excited most curiosity was several books, and these had been kept dry. In one of the books was a letter of old date, containing tender sentiments and addressed to Miss ———. One of the books was a Bible, and in it were the names of the members of a well-known family in the neighborhood.

What then? Could this strange being read? Was she some too high-strung heart that had been so overstrained or embittered in the buffets of the world as to renounce human society and resolutely for many years keep herself secluded in the shadows of the forest? Had some wild romantic sentiment prompted her to seek the savage life of the woods with a companion, and then, having lost him, had she vowed to live so strange and rude a hermitage? And after so many years was the aching heart seeking solace in the company of old books? Or was she seeking for one book only, taking volumes at random in the dark until the light of morning should reveal the title — one book with a promise, a light, a solace for one human soul contained by no other? Such were a few of the questions and conjectures evoked by discovery of the books. The matter got into the newspapers.

Sympathy and curiosity rose together. If the creature could read, why not write her letters and place them where she would be most likely to find them? Letters plainly written in simple language were posted at her recent camp and other places entreating her to make herself known. Home and friends were offered her.

This serious drama was not without a comic side-scene. An eccentric old bachelor in the country by the name of Moses Evans had been nicknamed "The Wild Man of the Woods." Since there was now a veritable Wild Woman of the woods, wits invented a match. Several love letters, partly in verse, over the signature of "Moses Evans, the Wild Man," addressed to the unknown Wild Woman, were, with purported replies, published in Texas newspapers and copied over the United States. Meanwhile the serious letters posted on trees and out from the camp of the poor recluse remained untouched, and nothing occurred to indicate that she understood them.

By this time a general resolution had grown up that the riddle must be solved. A systematic and cautious plan was adopted. A number of hunters formed extended lines and drove through the woods with leashed hounds, while others, well mounted and provided with lassos, took stands. Several fruitless hunts were made, but late one evening the hunters became satisfied that the woman was in a neck of woods running out into a prairie about a quarter of a mile wide. The men with the lassos took positions along the edge of this prairie while others drove through the skirts of woods with the hounds. It was night before the men were well arranged, but a bright moon shone. Men accustomed to hunting with hounds can readily tell by the nature of their cries what kind of game they are pursuing. Scarcely were the men at their posts when the hounds raised a cry never heard before. They were following the track of some strange creature. Presently the breaking of little sticks and the hurried rustling of the brush near one of the lasso men announced the approach of something. A minute later it bounded with a light and flying step into the open prairie in the bright light of the moon.

It was the Wild Woman. She ran directly across the prairie in the direction of the main forest. The man nearest her when she ran out rode a fleet horse, and it needed all his speed to catch up with the object of pursuit. But the horse was so afraid of the strange creature that he could not be urged within reach of the lasso. Three times he came up but each time shied to right or left too far for his rider to throw, while the flying figure each time turned her course to the opposite hand and ran with the speed of a frightened deer. They were now nearing the black shadow of the great forest, which was projected far on the plain. Spurring his horse with angry energy, the pursuer came this time fairly within reach and threw his lasso; but at the instant of throwing, his horse shied as before, and the rope fell short. In an instant the pursued creature was in the shadow of a vast forest and further pursuit was useless.

One piece of knowledge, at least, had been gained: the rider had a good look at her as they ran together for several hundred yards across the prairie. She had long hair that must have reached to her feet while she stood but that flew back as she ran. She wore no clothes, but her body was covered

with short brown hair. The rider did not see her face, as she was between him and the moon, so that whenever she turned toward him her face was in the shadow. Once or twice he thought he caught a glimpse of wild eyes as she cast a frightened glance over her shoulder. She had something in her hand when he first saw her, but she dropped it either from fright or to facilitate her escape. After the chase this was sought for and found. It proved to be a club about five feet long, polished to a wonder.

A long time passed without anything further being seen of her. She seemed to have disappeared. But during the severe winter of 1850, when a great sleet fell and snow covered the ground, a camp was found in the brush of a tree that had recently blown down in the tangled thicket of a canebrake. At this place there were large piles of sugar cane, much of it chewed. There was a rude bed of moss and leaves, but no sign of fire. There was the strangest set of snares, made like those found before, of the bark of cotton stalks, but these were much more complex. The tracks in the snow were numerous and a span long. A watch was set, but the creature had taken alarm and did not come back.

The winter passed, and, some fresh signs being seen, another great muster was made; then, equipped with horses, hounds, and ropes, the pursuers made a favorable start on the track. The men took up stations in line and closed in from all sides. In the last resort, as was expected, the creature climbed a tree and was soon looking down with a frightened stare at the troops of baying dogs and the up-gazing men. Instead of the hair-covered female glimpsed by moonlight on the prairie, they saw, now, only a runaway African man cowered in the tree. The wild creature they were pursuing had, it seemed, by accident or design crossed his trail. The dogs, taking the latter scent, had been misled. Now the hunters could remember that the cry of the dogs changed during the chase, and it was thought that by going back in time the trail might be recovered.

But this Negro was somewhat of a curiosity himself, and they stopped to investigate him. He was entirely naked, an unknown condition for runaways. The hunters bade him come down, but he made no sign of obeying. They asked him to whom he belonged, but he made no answer. They threatened him, but he did not seem to understand. To frighten him into obedience they pointed guns at him, pretending that they would shoot him, but he motioned with his hand for them to desist and go away. They then climbed the tree and took him down by force. He trembled, but said nothing.

While looking at him they observed his feet and hands. Could it be, after all, that this was the wild being who had so long evaded the sight of man? They led him through a muddy place to see the track he made. It was measured and found to agree with the measure often taken of the strange wild one. The man was kept confined for some time, and the news of his strange capture was published far and wide. But no owner came forward nor could anything be learned concerning him.

At length a wandering sailor came that way who had been at a Portuguese mission on the coast of Africa; he knew the captive's tribe and spoke enough words of his barbarous language to learn his history. The African had as a boy been sold by his parents for "knife and tobacco" to slave traders, who had him with many others for a long time in a ship at sea. They came at last into a river. Here they were landed and kept for some days in a large house, where they had plenty of sugar and sugar cane. He and another, a grown man of his tribe, made their escape and wandered for a long time in the woods, crossing a great many rivers and prairies; he did not know how many. Often they were nearly starved to death, but his companion, skillful to throw the club, had as often taken some animal with which they sustained life. At length they came into the section of the country where he afterwards remained so long. They saw the people passing about, and they saw that some of them were Negroes, but were afraid of their clothes; they feared that the Negroes were cannibals. His companion died after several years, and ever since he had been alone.

As he was now a man in middle life, he had probably been brought across the sea between 1820 and 1830. His small feet received some explanation. It appears that there is a tribe on the west coast of Africa, perhaps more than one, characterized by very small feet. We learned from the savage what we did not know before: that there is a certain hour in the night, which varies somewhat with the moon, when the most watchful dogs are sunk in insensible sleep, and then a man may walk among them and step over them with impunity. His most extraordinary feat of exchanging the hogs was very simple, but if made known it might get somebody into trouble.

He was advertised as a stray Negro and sold on public account. The purchaser turned him loose among his other Negroes, and he remained in his new home. The Wild Woman was never afterwards heard of. Public curiosity died away; the abolishment of slavery put an end to runaways in the woods; only dimming tradition remained.

Other mysterious tracks and "wild men" passed into legend over the Texas frontiers and kept on appearing in some places long after frontiers had disappeared. The tradition was common throughout the South, and various romancers worked — and overworked — it into fiction.

In the seventies a tiny footprint that Texas rangers connected with the Pegleg robberies in the San Saba country gave them the same concern that a mysterious sign accompanying a series of murders might give a Chinese detective. Some years later lonely campers in the Big Bend country would awake in the morning to see tracks of moccasined feet leading to and from the vicinity — apparently of a man and a woman. But, no matter how good as trailers the campers were or how persistently they followed the trail, always the tracks ceased to lead on; after having been traceable for miles, they would vanish as completely as if the makers of them had taken wing. "Big Foot and Little Foot have been here," a cowboy might say upon stirring the ashes of his camp fire in the morning. But who made the big and the little tracks could never be found out. The treaders did no mischief. Finally these vanishers amid the solitudes ceased to be, even in tracks.

The Dream That Saved Wilbarger

O NE cold night soon after he came to Texas, Bigfoot Wallace was sitting in the warm cabin of a settler down the Colorado River when a stranger wearing a strange-looking fur cap entered, stood bent over the fire a few minutes, and then removed his headgear. At sight of the raw-looking, hairless scalp thus exposed, Bigfoot Wallace broke the social code against asking questions.

"My friend," he ventured, "excuse me, but what is the matter with your head?"

"I have been scalped by the Indians," the stranger replied.

He was Josiah Wilbarger. He customarily wore his hat, even at the dinner table, from the pre-dawn hour of rising until bedtime, when he put on a nightcap. The story of his scalping and of the dream that saved his life has been told in homes of old-time Texans and kept also in print for more than a hundred years. It is one of the best-known historical legends of the land.

In 1830, Josiah Wilbarger, lately from Missouri, located on a headright survey along the Colorado River about ten miles above the crossing of the *camino real*—the royal road, as the Spaniards called it—between San Antonio and Nacogdoches. His nearest neighbor was thirty miles or so down the river.

Two years later his friend Reuben Hornsby built, with slave help, a double-log cabin up the river, nine miles below the present city of Austin, and moved into it with his wife Sarah and eight children. Although separated by several miles, the families were close neighbors. The names Wilbarger Creek and Hornsby's Bend fix permanently the locations of these two outposts of colonization.   **911475**

Early in August, 1833, Wilbarger went up to Hornsby's to join a party of men scouting for headrights. The Hornsby home had already become a kind of land's-end headquarters. After spending the night, Wilbarger, in company with four men named Christian, Haynie, Standifer, and Strother, set out to explore to the northwest. On Walnut Creek they sighted a lone Indian, who ran and escaped into the cedar hills.

After the chase the party turned homeward. Near Pecan Spring, as the place was later named, they halted to noon. Wilbarger, Christian, and Strother unsaddled their horses and hobbled them to graze; the other two men staked theirs with the saddles on, merely removing the bridles. While the men were eating, they were without warning fired on by Indians, who had skulked up in the brush and timber. Some of the Indians had only bows and arrows. The white men got behind trees, which were small, and returned the fire, but soon Strother received a mortal wound and a ball broke Christian's thigh. With an arrow through the calf of a leg and a flesh wound in a hip, Wilbarger dragged Christian behind a tree. About this time an arrow went into his other leg. Haynie and Standifer now made for their saddled horses. As they mounted, Wilbarger started running toward them, calling upon them to wait. They saw him pitch headlong to the ground. Then they saw "fifty Indians" rushing for his scalp. They got away and reached Hornsby's house in safety.

There they told how they had seen the savages scalping their dead comrades and heard them yelling the blood yells. For the present, all the men agreed, the dead would have to care for the dead. The Indians were in such force and had met with such success that they might well be expected to attack the Hornsby outpost. A rider was sent below to carry the tidings to the Wilbarger home and to summon help.

At last the house was still and Sarah Hornsby fell asleep. About midnight she jumped awake from a vision as sharply defined as the peaks of clouds under sheet lightning. She shook her husband, speaking so loud that the men in the other room of the house heard.

"Wilbarger is not dead," she cried. "I saw him in a dream. He sits under a large post oak tree, naked, covered with blood from wounds, scalped. But he is not dead. I saw him plainly."

Reuben Hornsby soothed his wife. He tried to pacify her by going over the details related by the two survivors. He laid the dream to overwrought nerves. She quieted down and went back to sleep.

But about three o'clock she sprang from bed, more excited and intense this time than before. "I saw him again," she cried. Her husband could not pacify her now. She threw a dress on, lit a candle, aroused all the men.

"As sure as there is a God," she repeated, "Josiah Wilbarger is alive. He is alive out there, all alone under a large post oak tree. His only covering is the blood from his own wounds. He is scalped, but he lives, suffering tortures, hoping and waiting for help."

"But —" started to explain once more one of the men who had left Wilbarger.

"But me no buts," Sarah Hornsby went on with rising voice.

"I saw him as plainly as I now see you safe and sound in front of me. If you are not cowards, go at once or he will die."

"I'll say it again as I have already said it many times," the escaped man now got his word in. "I saw Wilbarger shot down. I saw at least fifty Indians around his body. They were even then lifting his scalp. They never leave a victim breathing."

"I don't care what you saw," Sarah Hornsby retorted. "Maybe you were too busy running to see anything straight. Anyhow, I have had the last look. I know that Wilbarger is alive. Go. Go at once."

There was no arguing, but Reuben Hornsby now pointed out that if he and the other men left before the expected recruits arrived from below, she and the children would be in grave danger.

"Never mind me," this wife flared. "I and my children can take to the dogwood thicket and lie hid. Go, I tell you, to poor Wilbarger."

She was a little, black-haired, black-eyed woman of pure Scotch blood off a plantation of traditional refinement in Mississippi. She sang Highland ballads, read the Bible to her children, and taught them to read the box of books she had hauled in an ox wagon all the way to Texas. One time when all the men were gone from her home in Hornsby's Bend she dressed in man's clothes and showed herself armed with a rifle in order to scare off lurking Indians. Another time while her husband was away she sent two of her boys at milking time to bring in the cows from the wild rye that stretched out from the house like a field of wheat. From the window — for there was never a relaxed minute at this habitation in the wilderness — she, gun in hand, watched them. Then, powerless to give aid, she saw a band of Indians raise up with a yell behind the boys, but the boys got into the house unharmed. Another time she saw savages kill two young men hoeing in the field; then after dark she and her young sons buried them. In time she buried one of her own sons and another youth who were fishing in the river when Indians killed them.

Against such resoluteness Reuben Hornsby and the other men could not now stand. Still, they refused to leave until daylight, by which time the recruits from below were expected. Sarah Hornsby made coffee, cooked breakfast. Daylight comes early in August. With it came the expected reinforcements. Then the searching party prepared to ride.

"Take these three sheets," Sarah Hornsby called. "Two to bury Christian and Strother in. One to wrap around Wilbarger.

You will have to bring him home on a litter. He cannot ride a horse."

This part of her prophecy alone proved erroneous. The men went to the campsite where the Indians had attacked the day before. They shrouded the bodies of Christian and Strother, from whom all clothing had been stripped. After much search, late in the afternoon, they sighted a red-hued figure under a big post oak tree. An advance rider, mistaking him for an Indian, called out, "Here they are, boys!"

At this, the figure rose up, saying, "Don't shoot. It is Wilbarger."

His body was caked with blood. The only particle of his clothing that had been left by the Indians was a sock. This he had torn from his foot, swollen from the leg wound, and placed on his naked skull.

With the sheet wrapped around him he was placed in Hornsby's saddle, the light-weighted Hornsby riding behind and holding the wounded man in his arms. Very slowly the horsemen filed towards the cabin in the river bend, six miles away.

There they found all in readiness for the rescued man: a bed, warm water to cleanse the wounds, poultices of wheat bread — a bread too scarce to eat — and bear's oil to dress the scalpless head. "I knew you would bring him," Sarah Hornsby said.

Wilbarger's own story made Sarah Hornsby's dreams seem even more remarkable. The shot that knocked him to the ground had gone into his neck from the rear and come out at his chin. It only creased — temporarily paralyzed — him, he said. He did not feel pain; he could not move a muscle; yet he was conscious. He knew when a savage cut his scalp around with a knife and jerked it off. He did not flinch — because there was no pain to flinch from and he could not flinch. The only sensation he experienced was a sound as of distant thunder. He knew when the Indians were stripping off his clothes. They had cut the throats of the other two men; the sight of the bullet hole under his chin perhaps made them think that act unnecessary with him.

There was a lapse of time during which Wilbarger knew nothing. The sun was halfway down the western sky when he recovered consciousness and felt pain and knew that he was alone and could move. Dried blood was all over him, and he was still bleeding. He felt a thirst that was agony. He tried to stand up and walk but could not. The directions of the compass were perfectly clear to him. He knew where the camp water-hole was. He dragged himself to it. He drank and lay down in the water. He lay there until he was almost numb with cold. Then he crawled out on dry ground, to be warmed by the sloping rays of the August sun. At last he fell into a deep sleep.

When he awoke green blowflies were buzzing around his head. It does not take the eggs they lay long to hatch into flesh-eating worms. His wounds had ceased to bleed. He was again consumed with thirst. When he had drunk again, sharp hunger came upon him. His wonderful constitution was crying for nourishment to rebuild what his body had lost. He crawled to some bushes and ate a few snails that he found. He drank more water. He felt the maggots in the naked flesh of his head.

About nightfall he determined to crawl to the Hornsby house. But he had gone only about a quarter of a mile before, utterly exhausted, he halted under a large post oak tree. There in semiconsciousness he rested until extreme cold roused him. The only sounds that came to his ears were the pulsing of the crickets, the hoot of an owl, and the long, long wail of a wolf. The dying moon came up.

Then, as he lay under the tree, he saw suddenly, distinctly, without warning, the figure of his sister Margaret Clifton. He saw her; yet she, he well knew, was living in Missouri, near St. Louis, more than seven hundred miles away. It was not until many weeks had passed that he learned she had died the day before he was wounded and even at the hour of his vision was spending her first night in the grave.

Standing near him, the sister said, her voice calm and restful, "Brother Josiah, you are too weak to go any farther by yourself. Remain here under this tree and friends will come to take care of you before the setting of another sun."

When she had spoken thus, she began to move away in the direction of Hornsby's house. Such was Wilbarger's state of mind, and so vivid was the visitant's form and so clear were her words that he did not question her reality. As the vision vanished, he raised himself and with an imploring gesture called after her, "Margaret, my sister Margaret, stay with me until they come! Margaret!"

But the air was empty of answering sound and of sisterly form alike.

Josiah Wilbarger recovered, though the skin never grew entirely over his skull bone. He lived for eleven years, leading an active life, until an accidental blow on the exposed skull hastened death. No one who knew him or Mrs. Hornsby ever doubted the veracity of either in their accounts of the dream — or spirit — visitations. Wilbarger told his story long before he heard of his sister Margaret's death. He was very definite in saying that the vision faded from sight while moving in the direction of the Hornsby home. As near as could be figured out, Mrs. Hornsby's first vision of the wounded man occurred shortly after Wilbarger heard his sister's voice and called out after her vanishing form.

Bigfoot Wallace and the Hickory Nuts

BIGFOOT WALLACE had big feet, certainly — and thereby hangs more than one tale — but they were not out of proportion to his frame. He stood six feet, two inches in his stocking feet and had the trunk of a Hercules. He could go for days, like an Indian, without food; then he had a vast space to fill. Once while he was driving the mail from San Antonio to El Paso, Apaches left him afoot and foodless three days' walk from the nearest Mexican *jacal*. When he came to it, he bolted twenty-seven eggs, and then walked on to a square meal. Captain Dan Smith used to tell how Bigfoot rode up on him out on the range one evening just after they had killed a maverick yearling. Captain Dan Smith was cow hunting with two other men, and Bigfoot had a man with him. They had been scouting after Indians and hadn't eaten anything to speak of for two days. They hadn't shot because they did not want to make a noise.

They got down and built a fire. Bigfoot pulled out Old Butch, as he called his knife, came over to where the other men were skinning the yearling, hewed off a forequarter with a side of ribs, and then began roasting the meat on a mesquite fork. "The other fellows," Captain Dan Smith said, "didn't eat more than three or four pounds of beef apiece, but Bigfoot gnawed away until midnight, besides putting away a good part of a sack of bread we were carrying."

Anyhow, Bigfoot Wallace was an enormous man. You'll have to understand that in order to appreciate this story. His brother had been killed by Mexicans in the Goliad Massacre in March, 1836. Not long after that he himself came to Texas to "get even with the Mexicans"; yet he was too easygoing and openhearted to be vindictive. He was descended from the great Scottish chief of his name, belonged to a Virginia family of education and stability, and used good English. He had been in the fantastic Mier Expedition and drawn a white bean — life — while every tenth man among his comrades drew a black bean of death. As ranger captain,

> He kept the Comanches from off the ranches
> And fought them far o'er the Texas frontiers.

He could trail like a bloodhound and read sign like an Apache. A bachelor, he lived alone for many years in his cabin west of the Medina River, but he loved genial company and was as convivial a soul as ever sat by the blazing ingle with Tam o'Shanter or sang:

> If the ocean was whisky and I was a duck,
> I'd dive to the bottom and suck it all up.

He was as honest as daylight, even if he did stretch the blanket when it was blanket-stretching time.

Bigfoot Wallace was a character wherever he went. People were always after him for stories and wanting to know about his "most remarkable experience with Indians." When he knew they were expecting something extra, he did his best to give it to them. Captain Dan Smith said he had heard Bigfoot tell one story many times, and I imagine it did not lose much in the captain's retelling.

Captain Dan Smith, when I came to know him and heard him tell this Bigfoot story, was an old man, trembly all over.

His hand shook even when, sitting, he rested it on his cane; and his voice quavered, but his eyes were as bright as mesquite coals with the ashes blown off and his laugh was a tonic. A long, sharp-pointed beard seemed to sharpen his tall, spare frame. When a story possessed him, agility came back to him and he would flourish his cane with Hotspur fire. He drew the small pension granted to Confederate veterans, and added to it by selling a patent medicine. I never saw him offer it for sale, but he always had with him a little oblong tan satchel labeled BROWN'S HERB TABLETS. He would sit in the lobby of the cowman-dominated Gunter Hotel in San Antonio, the tan satchel on the floor beside his chair, while men stood around delighting in his reminiscences and yarns. He read books as well as newspapers and was conscious of the art of story-telling. He was a story-teller belonging to campfire life on the open range who had brought his stories to a city of the machine age.

When the moon was full — the "Comanche moon," as people called it — Indians were expected, and then Bigfoot Wallace kept his horses shut up in a picket pen back of his cabin, except one in the cabin leanto or else staked in a little natural clearing amid brush two or three hundred yards away. He had some mongrel dogs that could be depended upon to warn him when Indians came within smelling distance. What with horses penned, dogs watching, and himself sleeping lightly, plus the reputation he had among Indians, he never lost an animal — until one November night not long after the Civil War ended.

In the early, foggy morning he looked out and saw that his horses were gone. The dogs had not whined or barked once during the night. Some people claimed that Indians could mesmerize dogs. Bigfoot figured the Comanches had mesmerized his. Going around to the back side of the corral, he saw where the thieves had cut the rawhide strips holding the upright pickets together and pulled the pickets out of the ground. Moccasin tracks were as thick as pig tracks around a corncrib. It was against Bigfoot's religion to let Indians get away with his horses.

He walked down to the clearing in the brush where he had staked a gray mare named White Bean. She was still there. He led her up to the corncrib, threw his hull on her, crawled up into it, and took out on the trail. He was armed with Old Butch, Sweet Lips — as he called his long-barreled, muzzle-loading rifle — a powder horn, some molded bullets and cloth patches to hold them snug in the gun barrel. He used to say, "Varmints don't seem to like the kind of kisses Sweet Lips gives."

The ground was moist, and as he followed the trail of the stolen horses, moccasin tracks seemed to get thicker, even though some of the Indians were undoubtedly riding. Bigfoot said he began to wonder just what he was going to do when he caught up with all those Comanches. Still, he kept on going, trailing as fast as White Bean could gallop.

After a while, as he topped a hill, he saw smoke rising from a flat maybe a mile and a half ahead. He knew then the Indians had stopped, close to a lake, and were cooking their favorite breakfast food, colt meat — one of his colts. The deed riled him and made him as hot as a bush red all over with ripe chilipiquines. Yet, now that he was catching up with the Indians, he wondered more than ever what he was going to do when he struck them on that prairie. He kept on going.

Before long he came into a heavily wooded swag in which grew many hickory trees. It was hickory-nut time. The nuts were thick on the ground and thick on the low-hanging branches. There wasn't much to them but the hard, thick shells, but they gave Bigfoot an idea. One time when he was going out to fight Indians he had hung two window shutters on himself as protection against arrows. That's what he told. He didn't have any window shutters along today. He didn't have one of those shields made out of buffalo bull hide that Indians parried against arrows and bullets. He didn't have a Spanish coat of mail. He decided to armor himself with hickory nuts.

He wore buckskin breeches and a buckskin shirt, and he always, in Carlyle's phrase, wore his clothes "cynically loose." Until the day he died, he liked roomy clothes as well as a roomy range. Gloves "choked" his hands; a collar choked his neck. Now he got down, pulled some buckskin strings out of a pocket, and began tying his clothes so they would hold the hickory nuts. He tied the cuffs of his shirt about his strong wrists, and he tied the bottoms of his breeches legs at the ankles above his big feet. Then he began gathering the hickory nuts and stuffing them in. He picked hickory nuts until he thought he'd go blind, he said. He stuffed them into his shirt and breeches until he was padded out bigger than Santa Claus. Finally there wasn't a cubic inch of space between his own skin and the buckskin not fortified with hickory nuts, and they were so evenly distributed that not a finger space of his body was unprotected. He took off his hat and filled it half full of hickory nuts so the top of his head would be protected.

Thus armored, he started to get on White Bean and ride for the attack. But he could hardly walk, much less pull up into the saddle. The mare went to snorting at him and cavorting around as if a bear were trying to mount. At last, though, Bigfoot led her up to a fallen log and gingerly stepped from it into the saddle. He got himself balanced, and with the hickory nuts working against his tough hide rode on towards the Indians.

Just before he got to the edge of the big prairie, he rolled off the horse — for he could not dismount in the usual way. He peeped through the brush fringe and saw smoke still rising and Indians lolling around after their big bait of colt meat. In those times the waters were all clear and the grass was stirrup-high. Through this tall grass Bigfoot began crawling, Old Butch in his belt and Sweet Lips by his side.

He crawled until he was within maybe a hundred yards of the Indians. He took time to count them, and there were forty-two, including three staying with the horses. Then slowly, still keeping well hid in the grass, he squinted one eye and lined up the sights on Sweet Lips. She spoke, and a Comanche buck answered with his last yell. The shot was such a surprise that the Indians did not even locate the smoke made by the black powder, the only kind used in those days.

Bigfoot poured a charge of powder from his horn into the barrel, put in a bullet, rammed down the wadding, and again aimed. Sweet Lips sent a kiss as fatal as Cleopatra ever gave, and another Indian was converted.

This time the Indians were wildly alert. They saw the gun-smoke, and now, all on foot, they took out for it lickety-brindle, hellety-split, a-yelling and a-drawing their bows. Bigfoot had prepared another charge of powder and lead. As quick as you could say "scat" he rammed it home. But this shot, if he had to use it, would, he knew, be his last. He was saving it for hard times.

Meantime, Sweet Lips in position, Bigfoot raised up in all his majesty and all his stature and all his hickory nuts. He said those Indians halted "like they had been paralyzed by Davy Crockett's grin." (Davy Crockett could grin a knot on a log into splinters.) Those Comanches didn't seem to know whether they were facing some sort of supernatural giant swelled out worse than a dead mule, or "just Old Big." They knew whose horses they had stolen. They knew he was "pizen" unadulterated to Comanche depredators everywhere between the Pecos and the San Antonio rivers. Now, they seemed to debate with each other and within themselves for a minute or two. Then they must have decided that it wasn't a giant but the Patas Grandes (Big Feet) they had so often had on their trail.

This time they came not only a-yelling but a-shooting. It was a mighty lucky thing for him, Bigfoot said, that not a buck had a gun. But they were the most unerring marksmen with bow and arrow a man could imagine. Every time a bowstring twanged, an arrow hit a hickory nut, split it, and then fell to the ground. Bigfoot said the arrows got stacked up so high in front of him that he stepped up on the pile and stood three inches taller. Then the Indians made a right flank movement and bombarded him from that side, then a left flank movement and poured in the arrows from that direction. The hickory nuts were getting shelled faster than a Missouri mule could bite the grains off an ear of corn. Every once in a while an arrow aimed high would hit his hat and split a hickory nut there.

Finally, all the Indians concentrated on a rear assault. By gravy, he said, those arrows kept jamming the hickory nuts in under his knee joints until he got so tickled he had to bust out laughing. Then he whirled around, and just as he did the last Indian shot the last arrow in the last quiver of the whole band.

Well, sir, when they saw that their ammunition was all gone and that, though not an arrow had missed, the enormous target was still unharmed, they acted as if a bolt of lightning had struck the ground in front of them. For about a minute they stood with their eyes rolling and their tongues hanging out. Then all at once they stampeded like a herd of longhorn steers jumping up off the bedground. They made a bee-line for

the Rio Grande, seventy miles away. They didn't even give the horses a look.

"I stood there in my tracks," Bigfoot said, "as still and solemn as a cigar Indian, until the devils were clean out of sight. Then I untied the strings around my wrists and ankles, and the hickory nuts just rolled out. If there was a peck of them there were two bushels, and you can kick me to death with grasshopper legs if a single, solitary hickory nut in the whole passel hadn't been split open.

"I thought what a pity it was to lose all those hickory nuts when they were so good at fattening hogs. I walked back to White Bean hid there in the brush and got on her and rode up to the battleground. Then I tied up the coltskin the Indians had peeled off and filled it with hickory nuts until it looked like a Mexican's goatskin full of pulque. I loaded it on White Bean and got home before dark with all my horses, except the et colt.

"I guess this was the most remarkable experience I ever had with Indians."

Jim Bowie's Knife

T HE Bowie knife is the weapon most in vogue," wrote Francis C. Sheridan of the British Foreign Office, July 12, 1840, in an official report on the Republic of Texas. "During my stay on the coast, many murders were committed in the Island of Galveston and in the country, and I could never learn that one offender was brought to justice." Most of the Bowie knives in use, the reporter added, "are manufactured in Sheffield and Birmingham and brought over in British ships. I have seen one from Sheffield with a blade 18 inches long ornamented in beautiful tracery on the steel as 'The Genuine Arkansas Tooth Pick.' I have been offered another, also of British make, the vendor hinting that I ought to pay him a dollar more than he demanded, as it had tasted blood."

It was the Knife Age. The publisher of the first newspaper (1839) at Grenada, Mississippi, named it *The Bowie Knife*. After looking at the vast assemblage of ancient weapons in Warwick Castle, Nathaniel Hawthorne, who was as far removed temperamentally as he was geographically from the Land of Knifing, wrote in his journal, October 30, 1857: "The short Roman sword was probably more murderous than any other weapon of the same species except the Bowie knife."

In the Knife Age it was the rule to "use a knife and save powder and lead." It also saved time. At the battle of San

Jacinto perhaps three fourths of the Texans carried Bowie knives in addition to rifles. If they surprised Santa Anna's forces by attacking at the siesta hour, they surprised them more by not halting to reload but plunging on with guns for clubs and with knives more difficult to parry than swords.

When Bigfoot Wallace presented himself at a quadroon ball in New Orleans and was told that he must disarm before entering, he said, checking his accouterments, "I don't care much about the derringers, but take good care of Old Butch. I have a sort of affection for him on account of the many scrapes he has helped me out of and the amount of hair he has lifted." Bigfoot liked to divert people. Use of the knife by the thug element, as exemplified by a steamboat gambler who boasted that Bowie steel was his looking glass and pistol fire his favorite tune, classified it for some people as thuggish. Just the same, probably as many respectable men carried a knife as carried a pistol. Violence and honor were necked together in the South. Daredevil Jack Smith of Missouri, whose favorite oath was "Jesus Christ and General Jackson" and whose rifle was christened "Hark from the Tombs," belonged to the culture of high violence as well as to that of low violence.

There were saddle knives, butcher knives, machetes, dirks, Green River knives — favored by the Mountain Men and so called because of a trademark — and other styles of the instrument to cut and stick, but the knife of all knives came to be the Bowie. It was a particular kind of knife, but in common parlance the name became generic, just as the name of the rubberized raincoat devised by Charles Macintosh came to include all waterproof coats.

In woods and mountains and all along the frontiers the Bowie knife was as essential as a steady eye. For work in close quarters, some backwoodsmen regarded firearms as "fit only for the weak." Any dude could shoot a bear; it took a real man to meet his hug with a knife. For dozens of purposes, the Bowie was as handy as a shirt pocket. The name "Arkansas toothpick" suggests one use. It was the main eating implement not only in camps but in many a cabin. The blade, especially of the longer knives, hacked limbs from trees and cut up the carcasses of beef, deer and buffalo. It served to skin and dress all kinds of game. It was the tool for mending saddles and harness, and for cutting thongs from cowhides to be plaited into reatas and whips. On occasion it was used to dig a grave on the lone prairie for a fallen comrade. A Texan lassoed by a Mexican horseman might cut the reata with his Bowie knife. The horn handle was a pestle to crack parched coffee beans. At San Jacinto it cracked heads.

The knife was a fact. James Bowie was a fact. Both were of a character to seize human imagination, and human imagination welded them together and forged them into an extraordinary legend.

Born in Logan County, Kentucky, in 1796, of strong-bodied, strong-minded upper-class stock, James Bowie was the eighth of ten children. The family settled down in Louisiana about 1802, and here young Jim became noted for roping wild horses, riding them and alligators, hunting bear and wild cattle, and for other feats in the wilderness. He was with Long's filibustering expedition into Texas. About the same time he and his brothers Rezin P. and John J. were buying captive Africans at a dollar a pound from the pirate Lafitte on Galveston Island and smuggling them into Louisiana to sell as slaves.

If — a very iffy if — Jim Bowie excelled in knife throwing and juggling as well as in knife wielding, he must have reached his climax at this period of operations. Knife juggling was mainly a tent-show stunt. J. O. Dyer, who sometimes made slight distinction between romance and history, said that "Big Jim" Bowie in convoying smuggled slaves armed himself with three or four knives so that he could transfix any who tried to break away. Jerking a knife out was quicker than reloading a horse pistol at the muzzle. Both Jim and Rezin P., Dyer said, could keep several knives moving in the air at the same time without allowing one to touch the ground. "At twenty paces either could send a knife clean through a small wooden target."

After clearing sixty-five thousand dollars on slave smuggling, the Bowies turned to speculating in land. James joined Rezin P. in developing a fine plantation named Arcadia and joined John J. in selling fraudulent titles to land in Arkansas. Land operations kept him in New Orleans a great deal, and he became as much at home with sophisticated city people as he was with bellowing alligators, mustang horses and cattle, and knife-wielding backwoodsmen of the wilderness. He was a magnificent specimen of masculinity, six feet tall, well proportioned, agreeable in manner and speech. At maturity he spoke French and Spanish in addition to English.

One of the turning points in his life was stabbing a man to death with his specially made knife. That episode will be detailed in the proper place. The next year, 1828, he rode through Texas looking over the land business and on to San Antonio, where he became interested in the legend of the Lost San Saba Mine, which he considered a fact and which still lures men on.

In the years of life remaining to him he was constantly riding — back into Louisiana, up into Mississippi, down into Mexico, over wide parts of Texas. He married Ursula de Veramendi, daughter of the vice-governor of Texas. He organized an expedition to look for the Lost San Saba Mine and had perhaps the most desperate fight with Indians recorded in Texas history. He tried to get rich quick on big deals in Texas lands — and failed. He belonged to the war party before Texas made revolution against Mexico and was a leader when the revolution came. He was dying on a cot in a remote room of the Alamo when at daybreak on March 6, 1836, five thousand Mexicans under Santa Anna made the final attack against a hundred and eighty-odd Texans, leaving not one as a messenger of defeat. Nobody knows exactly how Bowie died, but it is popularly believed that at sight of Mexican soldiers coming into his room he rallied and littered the dirt floor with knifed bodies before he was overwhelmed.

Bowie was a legend — a gaudy legend of gaudy violence — before he died. The Alamo blotted out all but the heroic from popular memory and imagination. The Knife Age in the Land of Violence was at its crest, and the forgers of the Bowie knife legend were as active as the dwarf smiths who forged for the Norse gods. Bowie did not institute the knife as a fighting weapon, but his use of it at the right hour came to epitomize knife fighting in the South. Its fame spread as far as the bragging of Texans has gone in a later time. When Theodore Parker, Boston preacher and reformer, visited Carlyle, always fiercely hungry for biographical detail, he told him tales about Bowie's prowess with the Bowie knife. "By Hercules!" — Carlyle is supposed to have exclaimed — "The man was greater than Caesar or Cromwell — nay, nearly equal to Odin or Thor! The Texans ought to build him an altar."

The Bowie knife was the New World's counterpart to the battle-axe with which Beowulf slew Grendel in the den deep under dark waters; to Siegfried's great sword Gram; and to King Arthur's bright Excalibur of mystic powers.

Who devised the Bowie knife? Who made it? What circumstances brought it into use? How did Bowie use it? The answers are conflicting, some valid — even the most valid subject to the gross fallibilities of memory — some sheer inventions. All belong to the legend.

The two witnesses nearest to Bowie contradict each other on the knife's origin but agree on the event that gave it fame. In 1838, only two years after the fall of the Alamo, Rezin P. Bowie wrote, from Iberville, Louisiana, a flaming letter to the editor of *The Planters' Advocate* to refute a "dastardly scribbler's" story about the Bowie brothers and the knife. "The first Bowie-Knife," he said, "was made by myself in the parish of Avoyelles, in this state, as a hunting knife, for which purpose, exclusively, it was used for many years" before James drove it "as a weapon of defense into an individual with whom he was at variance." The phrase, "made by myself," was an abbreviated way of saying that Rezin P. Bowie had his blacksmith make the knife.

In 1858, *De Bow's Review* published a remarkably frank sketch by John J. Bowie on the Bowies of Louisiana. According to John J., his brother James, while living mostly in the woods, had a blacksmith named Lovel Snowden make him the "hunting knife" that he used years later in the so-called Sandbar

Duel to kill an opponent. He had "a neat scabbard" made for the knife, "affirming that he would wear it as long as he lived, which he did."

The weight of testimony is on the side of Rezin P. Bowie's account. The circumstances that led to the making of the knife seem to have been as follows. In Louisiana, as in Texas, many unbranded, ownerless cattle — later called mavericks — of the Spanish longhorn breed ran wild. Sporting planters hunted them in two ways. One way was to shoot them from horseback, as sportsmen on the plains shot buffaloes; the other was to ride against them and stab or lance them with a long hunting knife. Sometimes they were lassoed and then stabbed. The chase with knife was more daring, dangerous and exciting than shooting; therefore, the Bowie men preferred it.

One day while Rezin P. was thrusting his knife into a fleet heifer she lunged her head in a way to drive the blade up through his hand, cutting three fingers severely. After having his hand dressed, he called the plantation blacksmith, Jesse Cliffe, and told him to make a knife that would not slip in a man's grasp. Using pencil in his left hand, he roughly traced on paper a blade with a strong guard between it and the handle. Then he gave the smith a large file of the best quality of steel. With fire and hammer, Jesse Cliffe wrought the weapon. It proved so serviceable in hunting and Rezin P. came to prize it so highly that for a long time he kept it, when not wearing it, locked in his desk. Meantime he had Jesse Cliffe make replicas of the blade to give friends, who called them Bowie knives.

The size of the original knife will always be in question. Rezin P. Bowie wrote that "the length [of the blade] was nine and one quarter inches, its width one and a half inches, single edge, and not curved." Other specifiers go on up to eighteen, even twenty-four, inches. The knife probably had a buckhorn handle. Proportion, balance and temper of steel went into its superiority. A curved point became a feature of the Bowie knife. "The improvement of its fabrication and the state of perfection which it has since acquired from cutlers, was not brought about through my agency," Rezin P. Bowie added. If Jim Bowie ever defined what he considered the final and proper Bowie knife, his definition has not survived. Handmade Bowie knives were never standardized like the .44 Winchester rifle manufactured by one firm.

For years Bowie made Alexandria, in Rapides Parish on Red River, business headquarters. One of the times while he was pressed for money, he learned that Norris Wright, sheriff of the parish and director in the bank from which he borrowed, had thwarted a loan of money to him. There was already bad blood between the two over political differences. Many prominent citizens (comparatively few of the not-prominent citizens of the Old South voted) were in constant ferment over politics. One day when Wright and Bowie met on the street, Wright fired a pistol at him, but the bullet was checked by a silver dollar in Bowie's vest pocket. Bowie's pistol snapped and he would have killed Wright with his hands if men had not withheld him. The two parted expecting to meet another day.

That day was September 19, 1827. The place was a sandbar, a kind of peninsula noted as a dueling place, on the west bank of Mississippi River across from Natchez. Bowie was one of four seconds, plus a surgeon, on the side of a principal in a duel. There were six men, likewise including a surgeon, on the other side.

Bowie had told his brother Rezin of the trouble with Norris Wright and of his pistol's snapping, whereupon Rezin had given him the knife made by Jesse Cliffe, saying, "Here, Jim, take old Bowie. She never misses fire."

The Sandbar Duel turned into a general fight in which two men were killed and two badly wounded. Bowie had emptied his pistol and was down, shot in four places and cut in five. Norris Wright had emptied two dueling pistols. Without taking time to reload, he rushed against Bowie with a cane sword. Bowie, a ball in one hip, rose to standing position and stabbed the knife into his enemy, "twisting it to cut his heart strings."

The fame of the Bowie knife was made. For years, claims

for this and that originator of it multiplied. It took James Bowie, lying at Natchez, two or three months to recover from his wounds. He was an ingenious whittler, and according to a story of diverse forms, he during this time whittled from soft pine an improved model for a knife and sent it to a Spanish cutler in New Orleans known as Pedro who had learned his trade in Toledo, where the finest swords in all Spain were forged, and told him he needed a blade "fit to fight for a man's life with." Pedro wrought the masterpiece of his career.

Or maybe Bowie turned over the model to two brothers named Blackman, skilled smiths in Natchez, directing them to spare no expense in time or skill to make the master of all knives. Again, it is claimed that, after recovering, Bowie made a trip to Philadelphia, taking his pine pattern with him, and had a cutler there make the ideal knife. More likely, as another account goes, a hardware merchant of Natchez sent a model of Bowie's knife to Philadelphia for replicas, which he sold in large numbers.

A persistent story has it that a half-breed Negro smith named Manuel, who worked for Rezin P. Bowie and specialized in the wrought-iron balcony railings that adorn old houses of New Orleans, came upon a piece of steel one day while he was at his forge and made a knife as graceful as any clipper ship that ever sailed. The point was long and sharp and could be jabbed upwards with as deadly effect as when plunged in and down.

Twenty-five years after Bowie died in the Alamo, the Natchez *Free Trader* published an article about a "weapon artist" of the town named Captain Reese Fitzpatrick, who was then making knives and swords for Quality Street gentlemen. Captain Fitzpatrick asserted that his knives were designed on a model given him by Jim Bowie while both lived in Louisiana. The original blade, he said, weighed only one pound, was elastic enough to quiver at the touch, and bore an edge as keen as the lightning's flash. Comparing it with the so-called "Bowie knives" manufactured in Sheffield and Birmingham and sold by the thousands in America, Captain Reese Fitzpatrick said that the blade he wrought for Bowie had "the spring and rebound of a Damascus blade," whereas the English-manufactured knives were made hard, to take a fine polish, but lacked elasticity and would gap like pot metal.

When in doubt go to the encyclopedia. This is what the *Encyclopedia Americana* (1928) sets forth: "Colonel James Bowie is said to have had his sword broken down to within about twenty inches of the hilt in a fight with some Mexicans, but he found that he did such good execution with his broken blade that he equipped all his followers with a similar weapon" — the Bowie knife.

But let us not be too rash in drawing conclusions. Arkansas has yet to be heard from, and Arkansas has a better right to speak on the subject than any encyclopedia. In honor of the "Arkansas toothpick," Arkansas is yet sometimes referred to as "the toothpick state." The very spring that Bowie died in the Alamo, Arkansas became a state, and members of the first legislature in Little Rock used, after adjournment in the cool of the evening, to take their knives and pistols and repair to a grove hard by, there to practice throwing and shooting at the trees.

Some members of the legislature were in fine practice. The Speaker of the House was John Wilson, sometimes known as "Horse Ears," from the fact that when he was excited, whether by love, humor, or anger, his ears worked up and down like those of an aroused horse. One of his political enemies in the house was Major J. J. Anthony. When a bill relating to bounties on wolf scalps came up, Anthony arose and in the course of his remarks made a cutting allusion to Speaker Wilson.

With ears working and quivering "in a horrific manner," Wilson leaped from his chair, at the same time drawing a Bowie knife, and started towards his antagonist. Alfred W. Arrington, author of a lurid item entitled *The Lives and Adventures of the Desperadoes of the Southwest*, describes the blade of this particular Arkansas toothpick as being engraved on one side with a coiled rattlesnake about to strike and on the other with a bear hugging a man who gouges at its heart with a Bowie knife.

Anthony was waiting for Horse Ears with his own knife drawn. A legislator thrust a chair between them. Each seized a rung in his left hand and went to slashing with his right. Anthony cut one of Wilson's hands severely and in the scuffle lost his knife. Wilson came on and literally disemboweled his enemy. He fell on the floor beside the dead man. However, he quickly recovered, was cleared of the charge of murder, and at a meeting of the legislature a few years later drew his Bowie on another member.

An Arkansas judge, William F. Pope, maintains in his *Early Days in Arkansas* that Rezin P. Bowie once came to Washington, Arkansas, and engaged an expert smith named Black to make a hunting knife after a pattern whittled from the top of a cigar box. "He told the smith that he wanted a knife that would disjoint the bones of a bear or deer without gapping or turning the edge of the blade. Black wrought the implement afterwards known as the Bowie knife. The hilt was elaborately ornamented with silver designs. Black's charge for the work was ten dollars, but Bowie was so pleased with it that he gave the maker twenty.

"I do not hesitate to make the statement," concludes Judge Pope, "that no *genuine* Bowie knives have ever been made outside the state of Arkansas. . . . Many imitations have been attempted, but they are not Bowie knives."

Despite Judge Pope's cocksureness, he seems to have had the wrong Bowie in mind. The classic Arkansas story comes from Dan W. Jones, governor of Arkansas from 1897 to 1901. According to Governor Jones, the James Black who made the only "genuine" Bowie knife also designed it. Black was born in New Jersey, May 1, 1800, and, after having served as apprentice to a manufacturer of silver plate in Philadelphia, came south in 1818, settling at Washington, Hempstead County, Arkansas.

Here he found employment with a blacksmith named Shaw. Shaw was an important man and he had ambitions for his daughters. Consequently, when Anne fell in love with the young smith, only a hired hand, Shaw objected. The young people married nevertheless, and James Black set up a smithy of his own.

He specialized in making knives, and very soon they had won a reputation. "It was his rule," to quote the Governor Jones narrative, "after shaping and tempering a knife, and before polishing it, to cut very hard wood with it, generally an old hickory axe-handle which had been used for a long time and had become quite tough and hard. This he would do for half an hour, and then if the knife would not easily shave the hair from his arm, he would throw it away. . . .

"About 1831 James Bowie came to Washington and gave Black an order for a knife, furnishing a pattern and desiring it to be made within the next sixty or ninety days, at the end of which time he would call for it. Black made the knife according to Bowie's pattern. He knew Bowie well and had a high regard for him as a man of good taste as well as of unflinching courage.

He had never made a knife that suited his own taste in point of shape, and he concluded that this would be a good opportunity to make one. Consequently, after completing the knife ordered by Bowie, he made another. When Bowie returned, he showed both knives to him, giving him his choice at the same price. Bowie promptly selected Black's pattern.

"Shortly after this Bowie became involved in a difficulty with three desperadoes, who assaulted him with knives. He killed them all with the knife Black had made. After this whenever anyone ordered a knife from Black, he ordered it made 'like Bowie's,' which was shortened into 'Bowie knife.' Thus this famous weapon acquired its name."

The blade was so superbly tempered and Bowie was so superbly dextrous in using it that one day, in order to give a store-keeper change for some article, he laid a silver dollar on a plank and with a single blow of his knife cut it in exact halves. Occasionally a dollar was quartered or halved to make two-bit or four-bit pieces, but knives were not the usual cleavers.

"Other men," to resume the Arkansas governor's narrative, "made knives in those days, and they are still being made, but no one has ever made 'the Bowie knife' except James Black. Its chiefest value was in its temper. Black undoubtedly possessed the Damascus secret. It came to him mysteriously and it died with him in the same way. . . . He often told me that no one had taught him the secret and that it was impossible for him to tell how he acquired it. Large offers were made him for the secret, but he refused them all. He was stealthily watched, in order that his process might be discovered, but his reputation for courage was such that no one approached him too closely after having been warned to desist."

The death of the secret is a part of the story. About 1838 Black's wife died. Not long thereafter Black himself was confined to his bed by a fever. While he was down, his father-in-law, who had all along been jealous of Black's growing reputation, came unto him and beat him over the head with a stick. Probably he would have killed him had not Black's dog seized Shaw by the throat. As it was, inflammation set up in Black's eyes and he was threatened with blindness. As soon as he had strength enough to travel, he set out for expert treatment. A quack doctor in Cincinnati made him stone blind. He returned to Arkansas to find his little property gone and himself an object of charity. Doctor Jones, father of the future Governor Jones, gave him a home. When Doctor Jones died, the blind man went to live with the son.

"Time and again," recalls Governor Jones, "when I was a boy, he said to me that notwithstanding his great misfortune, God had blessed him in a rare manner by giving him a good home and that he would repay it all by disclosing to me his secret of tempering steel when I should arrive at an age to utilize it.

"On the first day of May, 1870, his seventieth birthday, he said to me that he was getting old; that I was now thirty years old, with a wife and growing family, and sufficiently acquainted with the affairs of the world to utilize properly the secret so often promised; and that, if I would get pen, ink, and paper, he would communicate it to me and I could write it down.

"I brought the writing material and told him I was ready. He said, 'In the first place —' and then stopped suddenly and commenced rubbing his brow with the fingers of his right hand. He continued this for some minutes, and then said, 'Go away and come back again in an hour.'

"I went out of the room, but remained where I could see him, and not for one moment did he take his fingers from his brow or change his position. At the expiration of the hour I went into the room and spoke to him. Without changing his position or movement, he said, 'Go out again and come back in another hour.' I went out and watched for another hour. He remained seated immobile except for the constant rubbing of his brow.

"Upon my speaking to him at the expiration of the second hour, he again said, 'Go out once more and come back in another hour.' Again I went out and watched. The old man sat there, his frame sunken, immobile, his only movement the constant rubbing of his brow with the fingers of his right hand.

"When I came in and spoke to him at the expiration of the third hour, he burst into a flood of tears and said:

" 'My God, my God, it has all gone from me! All these years I have accepted the kindness of these good people in the belief that I could repay it with this legacy, and now when I attempt to do it, I cannot. Daniel, there were ten or twelve processes through which I put the knives, but I cannot remember one of them. When I told you to get pen, ink, and paper, they were all fresh in my mind, but they are all gone now. My God, my God, I have put it off too long!'

"I looked at him in awe and wonder. The skin from his forehead had been completely rubbed away by his fingers. His sightless eyes were filled with tears, and his whole face was the very picture of grief and despair. . . .

"For a little more than two years he lived on, but he was ever after an imbecile. He lies buried in the old graveyard at Washington, and with him lies buried the wonderful secret of the genuine Bowie knife steel."

Noted wherever he went, especially after the Sandbar fight, and generous by nature in a society accustomed to exchanging gifts, Bowie might have had various knives made to give away.

if for no other reason. Touching the hem of a garment worn by a great man gives some individuals the honest conviction that they have cast it upon him.

In 1829 John Sowell, gunsmith and blacksmith by trade, moved to Texas from Tennessee and opened a shop in Gonzales. According to his grandson, A. J. Sowell — who in chronicling pioneer life was as honest as daylight but not infallible as to memory — James Bowie, "the noted Indian fighter and gold hunter, often came through Gonzales on his way east after a prospecting tour." One time he stopped at Sowell's blacksmith shop and asked him to make a knife according to a model that he had whittled out of soft wood. He said that in a body-to-body tussle with an Indian his hand had slipped down on the blade of his butcher knife, and now he wanted a guard between it and the handle. He was well pleased with Sowell's handiwork. Sowell then asked permission to name it.

"Certainly, certainly," Bowie responded. "Give it a name."

"I will name it in honor of you," the blacksmith said — "the Bowie knife."

Sowell "made a great many" knives on the same model after this. "A Texan did not think he was fully armed unless he had one of them."

Noah Smithwick added wit and perspective to honesty, and his *Evolution of a State* is the meatiest and readablest of all Texian autobiographies. At the battle of Concepción he saw Bowie command by virtue of natural leadership. He had known him since 1828, the year Bowie rode through the settlements on his first trip to San Antonio. Smithwick, skilled by an apprenticeship in "the gun and blacksmith trades," had at that time a shop in San Felipe de Austin. Bowie brought his "blood-christened weapon" to him to have a duplicate made. He did not want to "degrade" the original by ordinary use. He had had the blade, "about ten inches long and two broad at the widest part," polished and set into an ivory handle mounted with silver, and he carried it in a silver-mounted scabbard. "When it became known," says Smithwick, "that I was making a genuine Bowie knife, there was a great demand for them; so I cut a pattern and started a factory, my knives bringing all the way from $5 to $20, according to finish."

How many men Bowie killed with the blade that saved his life on the Mississippi sandbar will never be known. So far as documentary evidence goes, that was the only deadly deed with a knife he ever did. Rezin P. Bowie flatly affirmed that his brother used the knife to kill only the one time and never fought a duel "with any person soever." All men of honor in the South recognized, of course, the distinction between a duel and a difficulty, also between a killing and a murder.

John J. Bowie, who was pronouncedly franker on family history than his brother Rezin, said that when "aroused by some insult" James was "terrible in an anger that frequently terminated in a tragical scene," and that his knife became famous "owing to some very tragical occurrences." Put in another way by an acquaintance, "It was generally said that Bowie had been in several violent transactions, but not on his own account."

About 1895 a young man of the Bowie tribe told Judge William F. Pope of Arkansas, already quoted on the origin of the Bowie knife, that his great-uncle James once fought a knife duel with a "Mexican," the combatants sitting face to face within striking distance of each other, astride a log to which their leather breeches had been "securely nailed." A duel under these conditions could end only with the ending of one of the knife wielders.

Walter Worthington Bowie, historian of the Bowie family, relates that James and a neighboring Spanish planter in Louisiana, having become "involved in a difficulty, decided to fight it out with knife and dagger." The left hands of the two men were lashed together. The Spaniard, of course, held the dagger. "As he drew his arm back to strike, Bowie thrust forward and drove his awful knife through his antagonist's body." Then he wiped his knife on the Spaniard's shirt and, cutting the cords that bound their left hands together, freed himself of the corpse.

This Spaniard story takes with every teller a different turn, blending with other stories, as a popular ballad often incorporates parts of other ballads. One time, a wild story went, one of the Bowies challenged an offensive Spaniard in Cuba, tauntingly requesting that each stand up to the other with feet shackled. The Spaniard was game, but no opponent to a Bowie with a Bowie knife ever survived. In another version, Bowie and the Spaniard took positions fifty yards apart, back to back, rifles held perpendicular. At the command "Wheel," the Spaniard, a military precisionist, made the about-face in three movements. Bowie whirled about in one movement and put a bullet through his opponent's brain before the latter could even aim.

These stories may all branch from one related by the actor Edwin Forrest, who met Bowie at New Orleans during the 1820's and admired him and certain members of his coterie immensely — a race-horse man, a gambler-duelist and a half-horse, half-alligator steamboat captain. Ten years younger than Bowie, Forrest was himself a magnificent animal; he excelled in stage-bellowing. Bowie entertained him on his plantation and gave him, along with its history, "his favorite knife," the handle "corrugated with braids of steel, that it might not slip when the hand got bloody." Forrest used it in playing *Metamora*, a melodrama he made very popular of an overpowered but un-yielding Indian chief who at the end holds up to his white conquerors — and to the audience — "this knife which has drunk the foul blood of your nation."

As Forrest transmitted the story, joining Bowie's plantation was one owned by a quarrelsome Spaniard who had killed several men and who threatened to kill Bowie. Bowie chal-lenged him. He accepted and named knives for weapons, each man to choose his own. He stipulated that "an oak bench six feet long, two feet high and one foot wide should be firmly planted in the earth and then the combatants, stark naked, securely strapped to the bench, face to face, their knees touch-ing." "The Spaniard stabbed at me," Bowie is quoted as saying. "I took his blade right through my left arm, and, at the same time, by an upward stroke reaching to his spine, ripped him open from abdomen to chin. He gave a hoarse grunt, the whole of his insides gushed out, and he tumbled into my lap, dead."

In response to another challenger, another multi-versioned story goes, Bowie stipulated that the fight take place at night in a locked room, the combatants naked, except for socks— to soften the sound of footsteps. At midnight he and his oppo-nent, each accompanied by a second, went to a deserted house, stripped, and entered with Bowie knives, one going to the left, the other to the right of the entrance. The seconds listening outside the locked door could not for a long while hear any movement. Then they heard a scuffle, the click of steel and a dying moan. When they opened the door and held up a lighted lantern, there lay Bowie in a pool of blood. He was considerably cut up but got all right. The other man didn't.

Another time, Bowie fought his opponent across a log, each with one arm tied to his own back. Bowie's knife won.

Bowie was no less gallant than gory. One day, so a yarn goes, he met in Natchez-under-the-Hill the youthful son of an esteemed friend named Lattimore. The young man had just sold a large amount of cotton, and now "Bloody" Sturdivant, a notorious gambler and hard case, was cheating him right and left in a faro game.

"Young man," Bowie interposed, "you don't know me but your father does. Let me play your hand for a while."

The young man got up, Bowie sat down and before long exposed the cheater. He won back all the money young Lattimore had lost and gave it to him with the advice never to gamble again. "Bloody" Sturdivant, ignorant of who the rescuer was, challenged him to a duel, proposing that they lash their left hands together and fight with knives. Bowie accepted, at the first stroke disabled the right arm of his antagonist, and then let him go.

The hand-lashed-to-hand duel was not confined to fiction. In Texas it was called the "Helena duel," from the fact that a village by the name of Helena in Karnes County fostered it. Sometimes it was known as a "Mexican fight." The gauchos of the pampas varied the procedure by tying their left knees together, kneeling on the right and using their ponchos, held in the left hand, as shields against knife thrusts.

A person might suppose that Bowie lay awake nights planning fantastic arrangements for knife duels; somehow he — or his literary creators — missed the grave duel. The gunmen of the saddle generally looked upon knifing as beneath their status, but Clay Allison of the Washita, a six-shooter ace, once — and only once — made an exception. According to the tale, he and a neighboring ranchman agreed to settle a dispute with Bowie knives down in a six-by-three grave dug eight feet deep. Here, according to agreement, they stripped to the waist and sat flat on the ground, backs against the end walls, and then at a given signal stood up and began cutting. It was understood that the survivor would bury the other where and as he lay. Clay Allison of the Washita shoveled in the dirt.

In various "transactions" ascribed to him, Bowie did not make use of the knife; all he had to do was show it, or himself. "High-toned and chivalrous," as fiery John J. Linn characterized him — expressing the estimate of many patriotic partisans — Bowie took up for the weak, the wronged, the pure and innocent, wherever he encountered them on his incessant travels.

One day in 1832 he stopped at the Payton House in San Felipe de Austin while arrangements were going on for the signing of a marriage contract there. A marriage in Mexico could be legalized only by the offices of a priest, but as priests were not usually available in the colonies, the alcalde (justice) was empowered to make a civil contract that would hold until a priest came along — unless by that time one of the contracting parties skipped out. A girl had come in from Cole's settlement to "contract with" a man who claimed to be a parson and who was dressed in parson-black. Bowie, unseen by the parson-appearing man, recognized him as a horse thief who had run away from his wife and children in Arkansas. He intercepted the alcalde, informed him about the rascal, persuaded him to put on a black robe and pretend to be a Spanish priest who could not speak English and must use Bowie as interpreter during an examination preliminary to the marriage. When informed of the arrival of a priest, the pretended parson expressed himself as delighted with the prospect of being legally married. The examination, somewhat in the form of a confessional, was held in a room separated by thin planks from one in which the girl and other women were gathered. The disguised alcalde said something in Spanish and then Bowie boomed out questions about the candidate's wife and children and even called for details on horse-thieving. The man left town in a short while wearing tar and feathers; the girl from Cole's settlement was saved from ruin.

One time while Henry Clay, according to a story attributed to him, was riding in a stagecoach with doors tightly closed against cold, rainy weather, a man got in smoking a cigar. A frail-looking young woman, the only female passenger, presently whispered something to a frail-looking man who appeared to be her husband; he, in turn, timidly requested the man with the cigar to quit smoking.

"I've paid for my seat and have a right to smoke," the fellow said.

At this, a big man who had been sitting silent, wrapped in a great cloak, threw it open, passed his hand under his collar at the back of his neck, and pulled a long knife from its sheath.

"Stranger," he said, "my name is James Bowie. If you don't throw that cigar out the window in a quarter of a minute your vitals will be tasting this knife."

The cigar went out and James Bowie put his knife back into its sheath. He usually carried the sheath on his belt, but some knife men slung it from the neck, in front or to the back.

One time while Bowie was riding horseback on a road alongside a cotton plantation in Concordia Parish, Louisiana, he saw the owner lashing a slave out in the field. Acting on impulse, he dismounted, ran up to the planter, jerked the whip out of his hand, and laid it upon him. This led to a duel in which Bowie only wounded the brute. He sent a doctor to him, bought the slave and gave him his freedom.

As with other deeds — and some not-deeds — Bowie's rescue of a preacher from a gang of ruffians became a multi-formed folk tale. Sumner Bacon was a fact. During the Texas revolution he served as courier for General Houston, who would say to him, "Now, Brother Bacon, short prayers and long rides." He distributed Bibles and preached as a Presbyterian minister among the colonists while it was against the law for Protestants to hold services. It was not, however, the law or the church that interfered with him. Bowie came along while rowdies were threatening to break up a camp meeting.

"Go ahead," Bowie said to Bacon, speaking loud so that others could hear. "While you pray I will watch, and I will kill the first man who dares disturb the proceedings."

No man dared.

A story told more than once from the pulpit has Bowie riding along with a Methodist preacher, neither known to the other, until they arrived at a settlement, where services were promptly announced. The audience gathered in a log room was made up entirely of men. The preacher lined out a familiar hymn that all joined in singing, but when he announced his text, one bully went to braying like a jackass, another hooted like an owl, a third barked like a dog, and a fourth crowed like a rooster. The preacher stood hesitant.

Then he saw the man he had ridden with stand up and bellow out: "Men, this preacher has come here to preach to you, and I never saw people who needed preaching worse. He is going to preach. The next man that interrupts will have

Jim Bowie to fight." The preacher had no further interruption.

It is no detraction from Bowie's manhood to say that his knife and his reputation for using it stood with him wherever he stood up, like *In Hoc Signo Vinces* as a sign in the sky.

One must conclude that during the last decade of his two-score years Bowie carried several knives, not one of which is known to exist. The specimens labeled "Bowie knives" in the Alamo museum and in the Witte Museum at San Antonio are sickly-looking. John S. Moore, a descendant of Rezin P. Bowie, wrote that the original knife was in his possession until lost by a cousin about 1885. Edwin Forrest was sure that he had a specimen baptized in blood by Bowie's own hand. Cephas K. Hamm, who hunted for the lost Spanish mine on the San Saba with Bowie and killed Indians with him and was a comrade without an ax to grind, used to recollect that after having worn his precious knife for years, Bowie finally left it on the ground, near the Goliad road, where he had butchered a deer. He rode several miles before he missed it, and then rode back only to find it gone. He supposed a coyote had found it and packed it off into the grass somewhere "on account of the blood on it."

No matter what is fact and no matter what is fiction, during Bowie's lifetime and for a little while longer his knife came, in a phrase from Henry Adams, to represent "what society liked to see enacted on its theater of life."

Bowie was fortunate not only in an Alamo death but in the timing of it. He did not live to see his symbol outmoded. In 1836, the year the Alamo fell, Samuel Colt took out the first American patent for a revolving pistol — the six-shooter. A company at Paterson, New Jersey, began manufacturing "the great equalizer." Sixty years before, Jefferson had proclaimed that all men are born equal; on the frontiers it was soon to be said that "Colonel Colt made all men equal." The army and navy would have nothing to do with his "revolving pistol," but somehow — no known records tell how — some of the new-styled weapons reached the Republic of Texas and here became highly popular while they were still unknown elsewhere. The first model to win fame was called "the Texas." After a few Texas rangers on horseback overwhelmed a horde of Comanches, a model was named "the Walker" — for one of their captains, Samuel H. Walker.

Many Texans who were not rangers bought six-shooters as soon as they were available. One buyer was R. M. Williamson, better known as "Three-Legged Willie"; his right leg was drawn back at the knee and he wore a wooden leg from the knee down. He had edited a newspaper and fought at San Jacinto; he could speak six languages and was a lawyer. After the government of the new Republic got organized, he was elected judge of an immense district including Shelby County against the Louisiana line, where no court had ever been held and where various citizens were engaged in a feud called "the Regulator and Moderator War": nobody was moderate and nobody would be regulated.

Some of the citizens lived so far back in the piney woods that they had not yet heard about the birth of Christ, much less of a pistol that would shoot six times without having to be reloaded. They had heard, however, that court was going to be held. A number of men met and adopted a resolution against holding court, delegating a kind of lawyer to present it to the judge.

On the appointed day the log room designated as courthouse

was well filled with men, some for order and some not. Plenty of Bowie knives were visible. Judge Three-Legged Willie walked in, wearing a long, black alpaca coat. As he sat down in a rawhide-bottomed chair behind a plain pine table, the kind of lawyer came forward, saying that he wanted to present a resolution drawn up by a number of citizens. The judge took the proffered paper, glanced at it, laid it on the table and asked, "What law or authority can you cite for such a proposal as this?"

The kind of lawyer carefully, not at all threateningly, drew his Bowie knife from its scabbard at his waist and placed it on the paper, saying, "Your honor, this is the law in this country."

At this, Judge Three-Legged Willie reached under the long tail of his black alpaca coat and drew out the first six-shooter that some knife men in front of him had ever seen. He laid it across the Bowie knife on the table and said, "This is the Constitution that overrides the law. Sheriff, call the court to order."

He had announced the verdict of evolution in the case of Colt versus Bowie.

The Robinhooding of Sam Bass

In July, 1978, it will be a hundred years since Sam Bass, at the age of twenty-seven, met his fate at Round Rock, where he and his gang were preparing to rob a bank. He remains the best-known of all Texas bad men, and the best-liked. While he was dying he said to inquisitors of the law, "It's agin my profession to blow on my pals. If a man knows anything he ought to die with it in him." So far as the records go, he never killed anybody until the end.

A deputy sheriff named Caige Grimes walked up to Sam Bass in a store at Round Rock and asked him for his pistol.

"I'll let you have both of them," Sam Bass said.

Before the deputy could draw he was dead. He left three little children. They and their descendants have never regarded Sam Bass as a knight of goodness and generosity. The people in stagecoaches and trains that he robbed did not knight him either. It has never been the victims who made sympathetic songs about outlaws. Stories about Sam Bass by people of adverse feelings seem not to persist. What people like to believe does.

As the ballad goes, "A kinder-hearted fellow you seldom ever see." What follows here is mostly anecdotes by people who liked Sam Bass. They, more than biographies, have kept Sam's name

green; they and that ballad — swifter and vivider in detail than
any ballad about any other frontier notable.

Sam Bass had been in Texas only six years when rangers
killed him. He had been an outlaw on the dodge only ten
months. He had spent most of the time around Denton, spe-
cializing in horse racing. He never was much of a cowboy.

> Sam used to coin the money, he spent it just as free;
> He always drank good whisky wherever he might be.

In the spring of 1877 he rode down to San Antonio and threw
in with Joel Collins. They bought a small herd of cattle on
credit, drove them up the trail, and somewhere north of
Dodge City sold out for cash. They soon spent all the money
in riotous living and then got their names on the map by
robbing, in Nebraska, a Union Pacific express train carrying
California gold. Each of six robbers took $10,000 in freshly
minted twenty-dollar gold pieces. They split up and

> Sam made it back to Texas, all right side up with care,
> Rode into the town of Denton with all his friends to share.

In the months following, his reputation for lighthearted
generosity began to grow into legend. Now he had something
to be generous with — something that did not belong to him.
He and his followers made a few poor-paying train holdups
in north Texas. He tipped the porters and brakemen — so
people said. The rangers were after him; the people were for
him. He had not been robbing people — unless they happened
to be on board a train he stopped. He had been robbing
corporations. Going into a town to buy supplies became increasingly risky. He was on the dodge, covering lots of country;
he had to take, and when he took he put those twenty-dollar
gold pieces into circulation.

Sometimes Sam was sorely pressed for grain for his horses

and food for his men. One morning a farmer named Hoffman missed some shelled corn out of his crib. It had been carried off in a sack with a little hole in it. Hoffman trailed the grains until he saw he was approaching a camp known to be occupied by the Bass gang. He turned back home. A few days later Bass saw him, and, handing him a twenty-dollar gold piece, explained, "I had to have some corn in a hurry the other night."

One morning a woman on a farm on Elm Creek was alone in the house when Bass and his men rode up.

"Do you have anything cooked?" Sam asked.

"No."

"Well, we are terribly hungry. We haven't eaten anything for some time. Would you cook us a snack?"

"Nobody ever left this place hungry yet," the woman said.

She flew in and cooked a big bait of biscuits, eggs, bacon, and coffee, to which were added butter and molasses. After eating heartily, Sam Bass, hat off, asked, "How much do we owe you?"

"Nothing."

"Many thanks. Let's ride, boys." But as Sam passed out, he placed two twenty-dollar gold pieces in the farm woman's hand.

In 1927, the proprietor of an ancient-looking plank hotel at Van Horn was an old-time Texan named Jackson from Denton County. He was a great admirer of Sam Bass, and one winter night while he and I and Asa Jones sat by the wood stove that warmed the hotel lobby he regaled us with stories of the daring good outlaw. Sam, he said, was sandy-haired, kept a sandy mustache well-trained, and habitually wore a grin that showed sandy-hued teeth. He was good nature itself.

One time Jackson, then just a kid, and his small brother were carrying a bucket of water apiece from the well to their house when they were overtaken by Sam Bass and his crowd. "Give us a drink, kids," Sam said. The boys had a gourd, and they proudly ladled out water. Bass noticed that Jackson's brother was crippled with rheumatism, and as he started to ride away he pitched the cripple four silver dollars. He was headed toward a neck of woods.

He had hardly got out of sight when a posse of law-bringers led by Riley Wetsel came fogging up. "Clear out, kids," Riley yelled. "There's going to be a battle." Of course the kids did not clear out. A battle was what they wanted above all else. They climbed up on a stake-and-rider fence to watch half the law-bringers go on one side of the neck of woods and half on the other, both parties shooting into the woods. One of the crossfire bullets hit Riley in the leg. He thought Sam Bass had killed him, but by that time Sam was far away.

Sam Bass was a fool about good horses. One time rangers raided a little pasture where the fine horses belonging to the outlaw gang were kept. For several days the rangers paraded those horses around, keeping them in a livery stable at night. The stable was across the road from where the Jacksons lived.

"I woke up one morning hearing voices," Jackson said. "I thought I recognized Kid McCoy's. He was one of the Bass men and rode the best-looking horse in the outfit. I ran to the window and peeped out. The livery stable doors were wide open and there Sam Bass, Kid McCoy, and other men were, pulling saddles off some little, sorry ponies and saddling up their own horses. It did not take them long to change. Then they came out of the stable yard hellety-split, yelling like Comanches and emptying their six-shooters into the air. Shirt tails were dodging behind every door in town. My father was a very quiet religious man — never even said *doggone*. 'My, those boys are making a great disturbance,' he said."

If Sam Bass wasn't a killer, it wasn't because he could not shoot. While galloping by a live oak tree near Belton, they say, he six-shootered his initials into it. A vendor of mounted horns from old-time Texas steers named Bertillion used to sell at fancy prices pairs of longhorns purported to be from steers that Sam Bass had shot down in night stampedes.

"One day," Shelton Story of Denton County used to remember, "a neighbor who had butchered a fat cow said he'd give me a dollar to carry a hind quarter to a certain spot in the Denton Creek bottom, deliver it to men camped there, and ask no questions. The meat was wrapped in an old slicker and I tied it behind my saddle. That saddle was the first new saddle I ever owned. The skirts were fancy stamped; it had long strings of tanned elk hide, and its creaking sounded sweeter to me than waltz music.

"Along in the middle of the afternoon I found the camp. Four men were there, all wearing six-shooters. I said I'd come to bring some meat. One asked me if Pete Lenoir had sent it. I said he had. 'Well, get down, kid, and stay a while,' this man said. I didn't want to stay but got down to untie the old slicker.

"After I had delivered the beef, the man said, 'That's sure a fine saddle you're riding.'

"I agreed with him and was prouder than ever. Then he said, 'Kid, how about trading your saddle for mine?'

"I looked over at the old hull he pointed to. I looked at the six-shooters he and the other men were loaded down with and the saddle guns laying around in easy reach. I didn't have any say coming, and I didn't say anything.

"After the saddles were changed, this man asked, 'Do you know who I am?'

" 'No.'

" 'Well, I'm Sam Bass.'

"I left with a heavy heart. I wasn't scared so much as I was just down at having lost my fine new saddle. If it had been left up to me, I'd not have put the old hull on my horse. I'da left bareback. Sam Bass put his old saddle on my horse and girted it up himself. The leather on it was fair and it had good saddle pockets, but it was coming apart. I felt I had been taken advantage of by the meanest, low-downest man in Texas.

"I rode on home. When I got down, I yanked that saddle off and threw it on the ground like I was trying to split the tree. When I did, I heard metal chink. I looked in a saddle pocket to see what it was. It was three twenty-dollar gold pieces; in the other pocket were three other pieces. Well, I bought a rig sure enough with all that money — new saddle, silver-plated bit and spurs, Navajo blanket, fancy boots, leggins, everything."

In the spring of 1878 a youth named Chunk Porter was clerking in a dry-goods store owned by a Mr. Cates in the little town of Kaufman. Early one morning, as he told hundreds of times in later years and as his descendants and others still tell, he had just opened the store and was sweeping the plank sidewalk in front of it when three strangers rode up on good horses. Two got down and walked into the store; the other remained mounted, looking up and down the roads. Chunk was alone at the store that day, his employer being sick in bed at home.

One of the strangers, pleasant-featured and pleasant-voiced, said he wanted to buy a suit of clothes. Chunk was able to fit him with the best grade of wool in stock. The purchaser handed over two twenty-dollar gold pieces and said he would put the new suit on now. Chunk went to the safe, which he had not yet opened, for change. After he had worked the combination, opened the door and pulled out a tray full of money, he became aware of the man in the new suit standing at his side.

"Son," the man said, "that is a good deal of money."

Chunk explained that the town had no bank, that their cash had to be sent by stage or taken in person to Terrell for banking, and that the illness of his employer had prevented his attending to that matter. The stranger advised him not to let everybody who came along see how much money the safe held, and then rode away. After Sam Bass was killed in Round Rock the clothes he wore were identified as having come from the Cates dry-goods store in Kaufman.

Railroads, express companies, and the governor of Texas all offered rewards for the capture of Sam Bass, and these offers induced some citizens to join sheriff posses, out to get the money. They were all fiascoes. While the Sam Bass gang was dodging about the breaks on the Clear Fork of the Brazos in Stephens County, the sheriff set about organizing a posse. A settler named Hide, who was proving up a section of land, decided he'd join the posse and rode to the Caddo store to enlist another brave or two to go with him.

As he was dismounting with his artillery, a man carrying a sack of provisions from the store asked him where he was going.

"I'm going to hunt down Sam Bass," the settler replied.

"Then you don't need to go any farther. You've found him," the stranger said. "What are you going to do with him?"

"Nothing, I guess," Hide answered. There didn't seem to be anything else to say.

"How many children you got?" Sam Bass asked.

Hide told him. He had a big litter.

Sam went back into the store and brought out a dozen apples, a lot of candy, and a package of Arbuckle's coffee. "Take the candy and apples home to your children," he said. "When you get there make yourself a big pot of coffee and never tell a soul you have seen Sam Bass."

Hide waited thirty years to tell this story, he said.

One night soon after a train robbery by the Bass gang in the vicinity of Dallas, a deputy sheriff named Boyd from Denton County and several citizens ambitious for reward money were in a saloon at Pilot Point. None of the posse knew Sam Bass by sight, but they were full of plans for capturing him. Presently a stranger in the usual garb of range men walked in, glanced over the crowd, moved to the bar, and invited everybody up for a drink. Everybody accepted. After the stranger downed his whiskey he took a seat at a long table at the rear end of the room, his back to the wall and to one side of an open window. He asked for coffee and bread. Several of the men sat down at the table also, ordering coffee, Boyd opposite him.

The talk naturally drifted to the recent train robbery. Not in the least reticent, the stranger revealed a marked familiarity with circumstances attending it. Boyd was growing suspicious, but the stranger remained drawlingly calm. When the coffee came, he stirred his slowly and then asked Boyd to pass the plate of bread. Boyd was by now flustered. He seemed to feel that some action was expected of him as a peace officer. He paid no attention to the request. Rising, the stranger pulled his six-shooter, fired a bullet into the plate, scattering its contents over Boyd's lap. Then he stepped through the window. By the time the deputy and his posse got outside, Sam Bass had disappeared into the night. The country had another joke at the expense of Sam Bass hunters.

Most people who met Sam — and some who didn't — told of their encounters with pride. In one town that Sam had entered to buy ammunition he saw a sheriff and dodged into a dressmaker's shop. She had a mountain of ruffles on the floor; in those days party dresses were trimmed with yards and yards of ruffles. The dressmaker, recognizing Sam Bass, told him to get under the ruffles. He did. The sheriff came in and saw nothing that interested him. When she was a grandmother, the dressmaker used to end her story by saying, "Lots of folks loved Sam."

A peddler and auctioneer named Samuels didn't, but even he harbored no hard feelings. One time he and his teamsters, driving three wagonloads of merchandise to be auctioned off in Denton, had made camp when Sam Bass's company rode up. Bass introduced himself by name and asked if the merchant had any whisky.

"We only have five gallons," Samuels told him.

"Well," Sam said, "we don't want to swim in it. All we want is a little to drink. Five gallons will satisfy us."

The Bass men made camp, put out a guard, helped themselves to food as well as whisky, played poker a while, slept, and next morning breakfasted with their hosts. At parting Sam Bass was more than gracious in expressing appreciation for hospitality. "You'll probably see some rangers this morning," he said. "When you do, tell 'em which way I went."

A few weeks before Sam's betrayal and death, a well-armed rider dismounted in front of Dr. Isaac Mayfield's little office in the village of Deanville, away east of the Bass gang's usual range. Young Doctor Mayfield was fresh out of medical school and eager for practice. His horse, saddled and bearing saddle-bags loaded with a country doctor's full equipment, stood at the hitching post. The stranger said the doctor would have to make a considerable ride to get to a sick man. What kind of sickness, the doctor wanted to know.

"You'll see when you get there."

The stranger led over what passed for a road for about ten miles west and south to Yegua Creek, and then along a dim trail into the Yegua Thicket, still noted for the dense growth of yaupon and other shrubs and trees. Then they came to a camp that had apparently been occupied for several days. Eight men were visible. Their leader did not give his name. He told the doctor that one of the men had a wounded leg. He lay on a pallet of blanket-covered moss.

The doctor uncovered him and saw that he had been shot through the fleshy part of the thigh and that gangrene was setting in. He called for a pot of boiling water. It was soon brought. He washed the bullet hole at entrance and exit and applied an antiseptic. Then he told the leader that he must probe in order to remove pus and needed some clean cloth. The leader went to his pack and brought several plain silk handkerchiefs, new and clean. The doctor had no narcotics to give the wounded man; anaesthetics were then unknown.

"This is going to hurt," he said. "You all will have to hold him."

The men were standing around, back out of the way. The leader said, "Boys, those new silk handkerchiefs are going to be pulled through that bullet hole, hurt or no hurt. Now let a man get to each leg and arm and one to his head and hold him steady. No matter how much he hollers, hold him till the doctor says quit."

Five men stretched out the wounded man while the doctor ran the silk handkerchiefs through the bullet hole. The sun was low when he finished. He said that he would stay through the night if there were anything more he could do but there wasn't. He would return if called. Now he had better ride in order to get through the Yegua bottom before dark. The leader asked how much he owed.

"I guess ten dollars will cover the bill," the doctor said.

The leader handed him a twenty-dollar gold piece, adding, "Doctor, I would be obliged if you'll not mention this day's work, where you have been, or what you have seen."

The doctor replied, "My patients and practice are private, and I make it a point to keep my mouth shut on personal matters."

He rode away, and as there was no further word he presumed that the wounded man got well. He had concluded that the leader was Sam Bass; descriptions in the papers following the killing at Round Rock confirmed the opinion. He believed in law and order and was against robbers, but had a sympathy for hunted Sam Bass.

Almost immediately after news raced over the country that Sam Bass had been betrayed to the rangers by one of his own men named Jim Murphy, and killed, the ballad of Sam Bass came into existence. Nobody knows who composed it. In years that followed, millions of longhorns were soothed on their bed-grounds and steadied on their long, slow trailing by the strains of the song. One line in particular expressed the sympathies of the singers:

> Oh, what a scorching Jim will get
> When Gabriel blows his horn! . . .

Relic pirates went to chipping away the headstone that a sister put up at Sam's grave in the Round Rock graveyard. Meanwhile, according to a minor legend, Sam Bass, like Billy the Kid, Jesse James, Bill Longley and many another outlaw, was not in his proper grave at all. There is no boundary to human credulity. Shelton Story, who as a boy found six twenty-dollar gold pieces in the pockets of Sam Bass's discarded saddle, so developed his power of memory that he got to recollecting this end to his hero!

"Not many days after the Round Rock trouble, I took the T. and P. train at Eagle Ford to go to Fort Worth. The minute I stepped inside the coach I noticed a man hunkered over in a seat by himself like he was sick. I took a close look and recognized Sam Bass. He was sick all right. In fact, he was dying from his wounds. I didn't say nothing. He didn't say nothing neither — not there on the train. When we got to Fort Worth I put him in a hack and drove him to a house out towards Grapevine — a house where we both knew he'd be safe. Blood poison had set in. He lived only two days. We buried him decently, and nobody will ever rob that grave. The man buried at Round Rock was just one of the gang. While he was dying he pretended to be Sam Bass in order to protect his leader."

No tales are more persistent than those about treasure Sam Bass is supposed to have hidden. If he did not bury his loot, what did he do with all of it? The records, I believe, don't show that he ever went to Llano County. Just the same, a big jag of Sam Bass gold wrapped in a canvas mailsack branded US was buried out there, they say.

Many years ago, a ranchman hired three Mexicans to cut cedar pickets on one side of Packsaddle Mountain. He camped them and left. It rained, and it was two or three days before he came back. Camp was deserted. He could not understand why the Mexicans would leave without getting their wages. He began looking around. The rain made sign easy to read. He found where six pickets — exactly six — had been cut and leaned up against a cliff. Two of them, as he read the sign, had pushed their way through a very thin wall into a small cave. Just inside the cave he found a piece of an old mail sack, the US brand still visible on it, prints of coins showing on it too. The Mexicans had taken the gold and lit a shuck.

There are plenty of other caves, especially in the Round Rock country, where Sam Bass's loot has not yet been found. There are still plenty of people who have a personal feeling for the character when they sing,

> Sam first came out to Texas, a cowboy for to be,
> A kinder-hearted feller you seldom ever see.

A millionaire can buy propaganda agents, a king can knight, a president can decorate, a pope can decree sainthood; but nobody but just folks can robinhood an outlaw. In order to get robinhooded, the outlaw must, like Jesse James in the song, be "a friend to the poor"; he must be daring and gay; he must be merciful of life.

Part Two

Northers, Drouths and Sandstorms

O NE Texas claim is that it does not have a climate — just weather. The weather was here before Columbus sailed, and it has had a far more powerful effect on the lives of the inhabitants than all the Spanish expeditions, flag flyings and gubernatorial administrations recorded in history books. Also, it has done more than any other one factor to make braggarts out of Texans. You can tell a Texan who is out of the old rock from the other kind by how and what he brags on. He does not brag on how many million miles of barbed wire stretch across Texas, how many million barrels of brains operate in the oil business, or anything like that. He brags on the weather, and for his purposes the worst is the best. He brags in reverse.

He wishes for rain but is fortified in spirit and inspired in imagination by drouths. He sings about a home on the range where "the skies are not cloudy all day," spends — if he is a country man — a large part of his life looking for clouds, and brags of living in a country where six months are dry and six months without rain. He quotes a jingle about "the silvery Rio Grande," and blows about having the dustiest rivers in the world. He goes somewhere else in the summer and regales the company with General Sherman's remark that if he owned Texas and Hell, he'd rent out Texas and live in the other place — and with the Texan retort, "That's right. Every man stand up for his own country." If this gets a laugh he will recite "Paradise in Texas":

> The devil was given permission one day
> To make him a land for his own special sway.
> He put thorns on all the bushes and trees
> And mixed up the sand with millions of fleas.
> He scattered tarantulas along all the roads,
> Put spines on the cactus and horns on the toads.
> He lengthened the horn of the Texas steer
> And added a foot to the jack rabbit's ear.
> He put three devils in every bronco steed
> And poisoned the feet of the centipede.
> The rattlesnake bites you, the scorpion stings,
> The mosquito torments you buzzing his wings.
> The heat in the summer is a hundred and ten,
> Too hot for the devil and too hot for men.
> And all who remained in that climate soon bore
> Cuts, bites, stings, scratches and blisters galore.

The authentic Texan is proud that government scientists still can't predict the weather accurately. The only people who know are coyotes, but their haunting cries are unreliable, and they are vanishing anyway. The official prognosticators never say "norther"; they predict cool fronts and cold fronts. But the norther, which "comes sudden and soon, in the dead of night or the blaze of noon," was the pride of the earliest English-speaking settlers on the Texas coast, and now it is the pride of all Texans from the Gulf of Mexico to the Staked Plains, where the only protection standing between a cow camp and the North Pole is a barbed-wire fence. Sweet are the uses of adversity.

Two picturesque aspects of northers stand out: their suddenness, and the extreme cold they bring to an atmosphere extremely hot, thereby fulfilling Romeo's definition of love — "cold fire."

The Texas northers, especially the blue ones, don't blow as they used to. That is what the old-timers say. The weather bureau didn't keep records when the northers were at their best. They used to blow the world inside out and freeze the lining. They were cold enough to freeze the horns off a brass billy goat.

Towards the end of December of 1839, or maybe it was early in January of 1840, Josiah Bean was fishing in the Brazos River in Brazoria County. The day was hot enough for August. He was in his shirt sleeves and had a long pole so that he could sit or lie in the shade and hold his line out in the channel. About three o'clock he was disturbed from his rest by a nibble. He stood up, put a fresh worm on his hook, dropped it out in the water just beyond a dead tree, stuck the end of the pole in the muddy bank, and was about to resume his comfortable position, when he happened to glance to the north.

"Holy smoke!" he yelled out to himself. "Look at that blue norther a-coming!"

It wasn't more than half a mile to his cabin, but if he got to a coat and shelter before he froze, he knew it would be exercise that saved him. He made a grab for the pole, and just as he yanked it out of the mud he felt a tug on the line that indicated a good catfish. He gave the pole a mighty jerk, straight back. At the same time he heard the norther roar into the trees. He saw the catfish fly into the air, maybe thirty feet high, still over the water, and in the same moment, drop free of the hook.

"Well, of all the luck," he moaned to himself.

It was luck sure enough. He had become so excited over the

fish that he had not noticed how exceedingly far the temperature had fallen in such an exceedingly short time. Automatically he wiped his hand across his brow to clear the sweat from it and felt ice. Then he noticed the catfish flopping about where it had fallen — not into but on the river. He skated out and caught it barehanded. He nearly froze to death before he got home, but he brought in the fish.

In early days a man plowing with a pair of oxen on the prairie discovered that one of them had become overheated. He thought he had as well save its hide, but he had not more than skinned it when a regular old-time blue norther hit. It froze the other ox to death standing up. The only way the man saved himself was by wrapping up in the freshly skinned ox-hide.

One fall a squatter on the Canadian River, in the Panhandle, bought a thermometer. Thermometers were rare things then. The squatter wanted to give his and the weather both a fair test. It was a big thermometer, as long as the pendulum of a grandfather's clock. He drove a twenty-penny nail in the corner post of the yard fence he had just built and hung the thermometer on it, facing north. A few weeks later he happened to be looking out the window at this corner post when a norther struck. He said he couldn't believe his eyes. He saw the post push down into the earth as if driven by a pile driver. But there wasn't any pile driver. The mercury tube was so strong at the bottom of the thermometer, the nail in the post was so strong at the top, and the drop in temperature was so sudden, that the mercury simply took the post down with it. It drove that post into the clay foundation right at two feet, the squatter said.

An old Baptist preacher named Fuller used to tell that the first winter he spent in Texas, a cold spell froze Caddo Lake solid. Then the cold let up and within a few hours a steady rain put maybe two inches of water on top of the ice. Toward sundown a fresh norther hit with a bang, and Brother Fuller said he never saw so many geese in his life as came in. The whole sky was strung across with comet-tails of geese and thousands and thousands settled down on the lake, in the shallow water over the ice. He knew that water would be frozen mighty quick, he said, but darkness cut off further observation.

Next morning, as soon as it was light, Brother Fuller looked. There the geese were, countless thousands of them, stuck fast by their feet, flapping and squawking, trying in vain to get loose. One patch of about twenty acres of lake looked to be solid with wild geese. He spread the news. The weather had cleared off, though it was still bitter cold, and before noon people were coming in wagons from all directions to load up. At that, hardly a dent was made in the numbers. On the second day the ice loosened up enough for most of the geese to fly away.

One of the most noted characters of deep Texas — the Texas of piny woods and sorghum molasses — was Mr. Fishback of the Sulphurs. Fishback Lake in Titus County preserves his name, as does many a story of his race horses and coon dogs. On a certain delightfully mild, sun-blessed winter morning of a year that I have not been able to determine, though it was away back yonder, Mr. Fishback of the Sulphurs set out on the fastest of his race mares to ride from Clarksville to his cabin on Fishback Lake, twenty miles south.

He had traveled about half the distance when he happened to look back and see a gen-u-wine blue norther swooping down. It wasn't blue; it was black. In a second or two he felt the light breath that always runs ahead of the mighty blizzard. This was

before the days of slickers, but Mr. Fishback of the Sulphurs had a good long-tailed overcoat tied behind his saddle. Without stopping, he jerked the saddle strings loose and put on the coat but left it unbuttoned. His mare needed no urging. She was the fastest thing known in Texas before Sam Bass's "Denton mare" arrived long afterwards. But no race animal can run at top speed for ten miles. Mr. Fishback held his racer down, intending to save her best running for the final lap.

Before long, he looked back again and saw the norther twisting the mare's outstretched tail. He heard the roar of the great wind. He felt a fleck of sleet on his face. He slacked the reins a fraction, and the mare spurted ahead like a cry of joy. For six miles, Mr. Fishback of the Sulphurs used to swear, they kept exactly even with the howling, sleet-laden norther. That is, the front end of the norther was enveloping the mare's hind quarters, shoving her along at the same time. Meanwhile the mare's foreparts and his face kept ahead of the norther.

He had a stable for this fine mare. He rushed in, closed the door, got down and looked at the noble creature that had made such a race. Her forequarters were in a lather, but the muscles of her hind legs and all the rear parts of her body were frozen stiff. Within thirty minutes she was in the fever of pneumonia, and before daylight next morning was dead.

But not all the wind that blows in Texas is out of the north. One time a stranger who had been riding on the plains for three days asked a native he met, "Does the wind blow this way all the time?" "No," replied the native, "sometimes it blows the other way." Then he asked if those Kansas cyclones ever hit the Panhandle. "No," the native answered, "if one ever reaches the country, this here west wind tears the vitals out of it."

A traveler who came to Texas in the 1840's described the climate as "tropical between northers." Sandstorms may blow either during the tropical seasons or with the northers. "De rain he vas all vind, and de vind he vas all sand," a German farmer of the Dust Bowl said. The wind out of a cloud will blind the earth with sand, and then the cloud will catch up with the sandstorm and rain mud. "Never mind the weather, just so the wind don't blow," is an old saying out where the sandstorms are worst. West Texas chambers of commerce don't like having their dust advertised; ordinary citizens bolster their pluck with jokes on the subject.

They boast of the "west Texas wind gauge" — a log chain fastened to a post. If the wind lifts the chain and blows it straight out, it's a hard wind.

They tell of a newcomer who noticed a man hunkered down comfortably beside some house blocks without any house.

"You live here?" the newcomer asked.

"Yep."

"What happened to the house?"

"Blew away."

"Anybody hurt?"

"Can't say yet. Wife and four kids blew away too."

"Great Scott, man! It seems to me you'd be out looking for them."

"Now quiet yourself, stranger. If you had been in this country as long as I have, you wouldn't get so het up. The wind's already shifted around, and I figger I might jest as well wait fer it to blow the old woman and the kids back. If I took after 'em, I'd be liable to miss 'em. No, you don't understand about this here wind. Why, not long ago Jim Harper lost his hat in it. Jest five days later danged if the wind didn't change and lodge that hat right in Jim's own woodpile."

The newcomer was interested. "Say," he said after a minute's reflection, "how far do you suppose that hat traveled before it started back?"

"Well, it traveled jest as far coming back as it did going out. Mister, I guess you can figger distances as well as I can."

The newcomer was figuring when, glancing to the north, he saw a woman flying toward him with her skirts spread out and four urchins hanging on.

"Well, by gravy, old woman," the householder ejaculated as she lit, "you got back a little sooner than I was expecting." He unfolded his legs and got up.

The newcomer rode on. About noon he came to the town of Tahoka, close to Tahoka Lake. While he was eating dinner in a café he fell in with two old-timers named Jack Potter and Prairie Dog Dave. They saw he was eager to learn the country, and went to telling about the hardest winds they had ever experienced. In their time they had both drunk a good deal of alkali water.

"Speaking of shooting ducks," Jack Potter said, "minds me of the great blow of '79, when my outfit was camped on Tahoka Lake out here. Well, sir, the wind must have drove all the ducks out of the Panhandle into that water. They kept coming and lighting and coming and lighting until you couldn't see a drop of water in the lake. The cook had an old double-barreled shotgun in the wagon. I told him I was tired of eating other people's calves and we had as well have duck for a change. So I loaded both barrels of the gun and went down for a shot. The sand was so thick in the air that it made a kind of screen and the ducks couldn't see me. I jest aimed out over the water and turned both barrels loose. Then the queerest thing happened you ever see. The whole passel of ducks rose into the air. It looked to me like there were millions of them. And not a single one, dead or alive, was left on the lake."

"Cow-sucking jack rabbits!" Prairie Dog Dave put in here. "You don't mean to say that with the whole lake covered solid you missed killing a single duck! It don't stand to reason."

"I was coming to that," Jack Potter went on. "I was astonished myself at first. I watched them ducks rise maybe two hundred yards in the air, swooping off to one side of the lake. Then the flock begun to separate like, and dead ducks started raining down. It beat raining frogs or catfish all hollow. I started picking up the ducks. Then I saw I couldn't get nowhere by myself. I went back to the wagon and got the cook and four cowboys who were off herd. We must have picked up ducks for over an hour. We started to count 'em, but that was too slow. We had an empty water barrel and we measured 'em in that. We had twenty-nine barrels full exactly. I fed that outfit on ducks until they swore they were sprouting pin feathers.

"You see, the ducks were wedged against each other so solid on the lake that when I fired and scared them the live ones took the dead ones up in the air with them. The sand kind of glued them together. Then when they begun to spread out, the dead ones naturally dropped — twenty-nine barrels of 'em.''

"I remember that wind mighty well," Prairie Dog Dave agreed, "and I'm not surprised at its driving all the ducks between here and the North Pole into Tahoka Lake. That year I was trying to farm a little down towards Midland. I swore afterwards that if ever I tried farming again I'd boil all my seed in pine tar before planting them. Still, I raised a pretty good crop. I had a good corncrib and it chock full of corn — corn in the shuck. On the west side was a little window kept open for ventilation; the east wall had a knothole about the diameter of a good-sized corncob. The roof was raised about three inches above the top of the wall. I never did believe in shutting up corn too tight any more than I believe in shutting up people.

"You recollect that wind came up along late in the evening and blowed fierce all night. The next morning — about the time you were going out to shoot the ducks, I guess — I went down to the crib to look around. Over on the east side I noticed a line of fresh corncobs stringing out as far as I could see.

"I looked inside the crib. Well, sir, it was five feet deep with shelled corn and not a shuck or a cob in sight. You see, that wind blowing in through the window on the west side would twirl the ears of corn around and snatch off the shucks. Being light, the shucks flew away through the opening between the walls and the roof. I never did see any sign of them. After the ears were shucked the wind went to blowing them endwise into that knot-hole. It was better than a cornsheller. The cob couldn't get through until all the grains were shelled off. I trailed that line of cobs eleven miles east of the knothole in my crib. It was wonderful how straight the line was. I don't know how much farther the cobs would have been carried if they hadn't struck a line of telegraph poles. For a ways these telegraph poles were jobbed full of corncobs. Maybe woodpeckers had drilled the holes the cobs stuck into. I don't know."

All this time the newcomer had not said a word. "Gentlemen," he now remarked, "from the wind I myself have experienced in west Texas I can well believe you, and thank you for all the information you have been giving me. I want to thank you also for not telling about how postholes are sometimes left standing up out of ground that's gone with the wind. Also for saying nothing about the poor devil who drilled for oil, got a dry well, and then after a big storm found it sticking up a mile high in the air, and to cover expenses cut it into three-foot sections and sold them for postholes. Also, I want to thank you for not telling me about the cowboy who staked his horse to a twig one night and the next morning found him hanging from a cottonwood tree sixty feet high. You two have avoided such matters of common knowledge and given me fresh facts. So long."

After the stranger left, Jack Potter and Prairie Dog Dave went to speculating on how many pounds of sand a dogie yearling can carry in its craw without starving to death.

The stranger went on to El Paso, and got into a Shriner convention. It was March and the wind-driven sand was so dense that a driver couldn't see past the radiator of his own car. When the president of the Chamber of Commerce got up to make the welcoming speech, he apologized for the weather, said the oldest inhabitant of the city had never experienced such a sandstorm, and poured out a lot more hokum about "this point on God's fair footstool." He concluded by introducing Captain Jim Gillett, who had come to El Paso when it was just a camp-yard and who would now give the audience the real thing. Captain Gillett's *Six Years with the Texas Rangers* had just been published — the best ranger narrative there is.

He began, "I came to El Paso in 1879. They were having sandstorms then and they have been having sandstorms ever since, but here lately it seems like the wind has sorter lost its strength. I remember one time we were riding in with a pack mule off an Indian scout. The wind had been blowing for three days and nights and sand had covered up all the grass and most of the mesquite bushes. . . . Yes, the country had some grass then; it hadn't all been grazed off. . . . That pack mule was the only one of us that could follow the trail. She went ahead.

"As we rode along through the sandhills between Fort Hancock and El Paso, I noticed the mule shy, and then the lead ranger stopped. He was right over the crown of a man's hat sticking out of the sand. It looked like a new hat, and when the ranger got down to dig it out, the rest of us stopped to watch.

"Well, sir, when he uncovered the brim and went to lift the hat up, he discovered a man's head inside it. We got down and worked carefully with our fingers to scratch the sand out of the man's ears and eyes and mouth and nostrils. He gave a little cough and said, 'Get a shovel. There's a good horse under me.'"

Down in the Nueces country one year, Dave Woodward was selling — or trying to sell — land to Minnesota farmers. An agent up there was shipping them down. One night he and his prospective purchasers arrived in the little town of Cotulla in the midst of a sleety norther. Dave spent an hour trying to convince the strangers that sleet was almost unprecedented in that part of Texas. A mild climate was what his prospects were after.

Early next morning when the party started out to view the land, Dave was still harping on such unprecedented weather. Presently he sighted a brush-popper jogging down the road.

"There comes a man who has lived in these parts all his life," Dave said. "I'm going to stop him, and one of you ask him if he's ever seen such weather as this."

Dave stopped the man, and one of the land buyers asked the question.

"Can't say that I ever did see it sleet like this before," the brush-popper answered; "but I'll tell you what's a fact. I've seen it rain."

It was in the same part of Texas that a certain rancher who was better at raising children than calves went out one September night soon after dark and began throwing handfuls of pebbles on the roof. His wife ran out and asked him what in the world he meant.

"Why," he said, "it's lightning in the west and might rain. This drouth has got to end sometime. That's certain. I thought it would be a good idear to kinder break the kids into hearing something fall on the roof. Then if it ever acturally rains, they won't stampede."

Out close to the New Mexico line a man filed on a section of state land, built a shack to live in and somehow stayed there until he got a deed. All this time he hauled water by wagon in barrels from a creek eleven miles away. Right after he got his deed he sold out to a stranger. He threw in the water barrels with the land; and the day he loaded up family, washpot, quilts, frying pans and other belongings, he left a barrel full of water beside the front door.

The new owner was leaning against the doorframe watching the homesteader drive away when he saw him halt not fifty yards off, give the lines to his wife, get down, come back with a bucket in his hand, dip it full of water from the barrel, and throw it on the roof. After he had thrown a second bucket of water on the roof and was dipping up a third, the purchaser asked, "What you wasting water that away fer?"

"Well, I'll tell you," the water thrower replied. "Three year ago this past summer when I built this house I put extra good shingles on it. I always have had a curiosity to know if the roof would leak, and, by grabs, I decided not to leave the country without finding out."

One time, during a terrible drouth, a mover heading east stopped his team at the water trough in front of the courthouse at Belton to water. The team consisted of a brindle-legged blue mule with long whiskers and a dun ox with a drooped horn.

While they drank and a speckled hound that followed the wagon lapped and a woman on the wagon seat took a fresh dip of snuff out of a brown Levi Garret bottle with a hackberry toothbrush, a man moved over to the wagon from the shady side of a store facing the courthouse square and remarked, "Sorter odd-mated team you got there."

"Maybe so," the driver said, looking by habit around the circle of sky to see if he could detect a cloud. "You see, it's this away. It had quit raining in that Aberlene country before I filed on a section of land, out there. I had a pair of mules, but one of them died. Then I traded off a quarter-section, for this ox, so I could pull out; but the damned fool I traded with couldn't read — and I got the whole section off on him."

Another squatter had his house on a seep-draw close to a cottonwood tree. It was dry, of course, and he had been cutting sotol for his milk cows. There was no grass in the country. All the tanks in the big pastures were dry. There wasn't wind enough to turn the windmills; water had to be pumped from deep wells with gasoline engines.

One night the squatter was lying on a pallet on the gallery worrying about the drouth and wondering if it was ever going to really rain again. While absorbed in his worry, he felt a fresh wind stir. Then he heard, he thought, the sweet sound of rain. He listened to it a long time — the sweetest music that ever comes to a man in the drouth country. After a while he got up to step out into the blessed rain and feel it upon his head and body.

There wasn't any rain! He realized that what he had heard was the cottonwood leaves talking in the breeze. Many times, like many other people, he had been comforted by that leaf talk, but now his disappointment turned into anger against the tree. It seemed to have been mocking him. He grabbed an ax and cut the tree down. Before long he was saying he wished he had the tree back, not only for shade but for the sound it makes like rain.

Jack Helms did not live within fifty miles of a cottonwood or any other kind of wood except the roots of switch mesquite. His ranch was in a country where it takes fifty acres to run a barren cow. The Spanish daggers grow there big enough to shade a jack rabbit, but nothing larger.

One summer, though, it rained several times, and cattle were a good price. It certainly looked as if Jack Helms's ship was coming in. He bought himself a new pair of boots and his wife and children a phonograph, and had no trouble getting his note extended at the bank.

After the papers were signed the banker asked, "What are you going to do, Mr. Helms, when you sell this fall and have all your money?"

"I tell you what I'm a-going to do," Mr. Helms replied. "I'm a-going to get a new waggin, and I'm a-going to drive it up in front of my house, and I'm jest a-going to leave it there until it rots. Everybody in this country knows the only real shade a man ever finds to take a nap in is under a waggin. Half the time mine is in use. When I sell my yearlings I'm a-going to buy a new waggin that won't have a derned thing to do but supply shade for my nap every day."

Along with drouths there have always been prayers for rain, politicians especially advocating both rain and prayer; and, along with drouth stories, other stories about prayers to break the drouths grew up.

In 1888 people in the East were collecting money to buy food for drouth-sufferers out West. The drouth was as bad in Jack County as it was anywhere, and a camp meeting on Keechi Creek dedicated one service to prayers for rain. It was election year, and, of course, all the politicians in the country were on hand to impress the great Weather-Maker. Among them was the district judge, a pillar in the church, who was running for re-election. The ramrod of the "Rain Dance" — as the Hopi Indians call their ceremonials to make it rain — was Grandpa Brummet, a strong partisan of the judge's. He invited the judge to lead in prayer, kneeling at his side.

After praying for "copious showers" to moisten the earth and cause it to produce crops for the farmer and grass for the rancher, the judge turned to the subject of internal revenue.

"And, O God," he continued, "in the meantime soften the hearts of the people in the East and cause them to send us drouth-sufferers barrels of meal, barrels of flour, barrels of bacon, barrels of coffee, barrels of sugar, barrels of lard, barrels of molasses, barrels of rice, barrels of Irish potatoes and sweet potatoes too, barrels of onions, barrels of beans, barrels of pepper, bar —"

Here Grandpa Brummet nudged the Judge in the ribs and said in a very loud whisper, "Oh, hell, judge, that is too much pepper."

During another drouth in another part of the country, several farmers and ranchmen who happened to be together began discussing a meeting to pray for rain. Two or three thought it would be a good idea to consult an aged preacher who had lived through many drouths. They were delegated to consult him. He listened to them sympathetically, and then said, "As long as this wind keeps steady out of the west, it won't do any good to pray."

Frozen Inside a Buffalo Hide

I T was late in January, after repeated northers had frozen the ground; yet this particular day was mild and fair — too warm and still for the season. The inactivity of the prairie dogs indicated that they had little trust in the mildness and fairness. John Rotman and two other hunters out on the plains to bring in a load of buffalo meat did not trust the weather, either. The night before and on after sunrise they had heard the long, deep howls of lobo wolves on every side of their camp.

As the hunters rode away from their big wagon and the thin blue smoke of burning buffalo chips, they had no fear of not getting back ahead of the blizzard. Their only concern was locating a bunch of buffaloes. Their plan was to kill a number, as close together as possible, and then, after gutting them, to bring up the wagon and butcher out the carcasses, taking only the choicest meat and the tallow. There were no signs of Indians. At this time of year the Comanches and Kiowas generally kept within reach of their camps in Palo Duro Canyon and other sheltered places.

Circling so as not to get too far from camp, the hunters remarked that buffaloes seemed as scarce as Indians. It was mid-afternoon before they sighted an animal. Then they saw the tail-end of a vast herd walking steadily south, several miles away. After galloping behind the animals a distance, Rotman told his companions that he would ride ahead to one side and try to push some of the buffaloes into a rolling, uneven country where the other two men would have a better chance to shoot.

"Dark is going to come early tonight," one of the other men remarked, and all glanced north, where an atmosphere rather than a cloud, a grayness more than a blackness, thickened the horizon. The sun had a yellow glaze over it. Hardly had the men separated before there was a stir in the sea of grass. Again, all was still, and the angle between the one lone rider galloping southwestward and the two going southeastward broadened. And then with incredible swiftness, even though its forerunners had given warning, the blizzard struck. Before he knew it, Rotman could no longer see the buffaloes. He untied his old Confederate overcoat from behind his saddle and buttoned it on. Camp was north of east. His horse, as well as he, knew that; but only with the greatest difficulty could he make him quarter into the wind. The air was filled now with driving sleet and snow. There was no longer any sun, just a dimness soon to turn into blackness.

A man could not stay out in a night like this and live, unless he kept moving. Rotman decided that the only thing to do was to turn his back square to the storm and keep moving until he got to a break or until daylight came. And where on those illimitable plains was any break? Rotman got down to warm himself with walking. His feet were already blocks of wood. He had no saddle scabbard, but, like other men of that day, carried his long rifle across the front of his saddle in a sling. When he got down, he took the rifle with him, in gloved hand.

With back to the storm and eyes protected by a wide-brimmed hat of rawhide that had been waterproofed with smoked tallow, Rotman could still see perhaps two horse-lengths ahead. Suddenly he found himself almost against a giant buffalo bull, facing him, standing still. Because of the very heavy hair on head and shoulders, buffaloes, unlike cattle, stand facing a storm. Before the animal could move, Rotman sent a ball into his heart.

Now he had something that has kept many a man from freezing to death on the plains. He had the warmest robe afforded by nature. In that temperature it would have been impossible to skin a cold animal, but he slit the buffalo's belly and warmed his hands in the vitals. He was an expert skinner and soon had the hide laid out on the ground, hair side up. His horse stood humped to one side. He staked him to the buffalo bull's horns. He and that horse seemed to be the only living creatures in an Arctic blizzard over a blind world of blotted-out plains.

He lay down on the hide and, rolling over and over, wrapped himself in it. Who can describe the sensation of warmth driving out cold that makes a man's back ache, numbs his feet and hands and stings his nose and ears raw? Rotman gradually grew warm. He thought of his horse with a pang. He wondered about his two comrades. He drifted into a drowsiness comforting like raw eggs in hot sweetened milk spiked with whisky to a cold man just come to fireplace warmth, like the feel on a frosty morning to a boy's bare feet standing where a cow has lain warming the earth all night.

When John Rotman awoke he felt, rather than saw, that it was daylight. He had been aroused by sounds he could not at first identify. He started to raise up but could not budge. Then he heard gnawing mixed with wolf snarls. Attempting to unwind himself from the buffalo hide, he comprehended that it was frozen as stiff as boards. No mummy swathed in the tombs of Egypt could be more effectively bound from head to foot. He had enclosed his head well, leaving only a small opening for air. He attempted to yell, but his muffled voice must have sounded very dimly to the wolves. Soon their gnawing and snarling were louder than ever. He guessed they were chewing on the fresh buffalo hide. In the hasty skinning some slabs of meat had been left on it.

It might be debated whether lobos would attack a man in motion, but a hungry pack coming to human flesh wrapped around by buffalo hide would hardly hesitate. Rotman made all sorts of efforts to scare the beasts away. They kept on gnawing and clawing. No doubt they had already eaten the buffalo carcass. Cold will make wolves, just as it will make man and other animals, savagely hungry. Finally, losing some of his own skin in the effort — for even the hairy side of the buffalo hide now had iron-hard wrinkles — Rotman worked his right hand up to the air opening in front of his forehead. His hand was utterly futile at increasing the size of the opening. His knife was at his belt, but he could not get to it.

Now the wolves were tugging their bundle this way and that. After a while Rotman's cramped hand felt itself full of hairs. Involuntarily it clenched shut. There was a jerk, and Rotman deduced that he had a strong hold on the tail of a lobo. The lobo, in twisting around, fighting for a place among other lobos, had somehow put its tail into the opening. The jerk made Rotman and the lobo both stronger. Instantly Rotman felt himself moving and soon he was moving fast, his hand holding tight.

Primitive people make fire by friction. Friction that will ignite wood will thaw ice. Within a short time Rotman was conscious of a loosening of his bindings. Presently he was jerked out of the unrolling buffalo skin. He turned the tail loose. The lobo never looked back. Taking a survey of the world around him, Rotman saw that it was covered with white,

that snow had ceased to fall, that the wind was laid, and that he had been dragged down a slope into one of those depressions common to the plains country.

As he walked up the drag-trail, he saw his horse, standing still. Too still, he thought. The horse, in fact, was stone dead, frozen upright in his tracks. No doubt the lobos would have devoured the horse had they not been diverted by the buffalo hide episode. Picking up his rifle, Rotman started toward camp. About noon he was sighted by his two partners. They had made it to camp the night before and left at daylight to hunt him.

There are stories of various men being bound up in a frozen buffalo hide, but this is the one I like best. It seems much more reasonable and credible to me than some of the others.

The Cold-Nosed Hounds

Mr. Jim Ballard can talk without whittling. I've heard him. But he won't settle down to bringing characters of the past to life and telling stories without a piece of red cedar in one hand and a pocketknife in the other. He keeps one whetstone at home and another in the back office of the bank at Beeville, where he has as much time as on his own front gallery. At both places he specializes in whittling miniature cowboy boots. He's wiry and satiric, composed and kindly, soaked in folk wisdom and sayings, and sophisticated to the degree that all first-rate intellects are sophisticated. He can believe one thing with his mind and the opposite with his imagination. He remembers what his grandmother Hallett, who belonged to the Republic of Texas, remembered and whatever else he has heard and lived interesting to him, during his eighty-odd years.

He never was "a fool about a dog," but has had plenty of experiences with them and with dog men, ranging from his father to modern coyote hunters in automobiles.

His father, Pal Ballard — Pal being short for Palestine — had sixty long-eared hounds to run deer out of the Devil's Pocket on the Navidad River, out of Tiger's Bend and other bottom thickets. When the first settlers came to that part of Texas, deer ran like antelopes on Goldenrod Prairie, between the Navidad and Lavaca rivers, but after they had been hunted a while they took to the thickets. Pal Ballard was sheriff of Lavaca County and the finest piece of furniture in his house was a gun case. He had a hunting horn that he could make sound for miles. He kept only twenty hounds around his home at Hallettsville, and these he fed mostly on cornbread. The other forty hounds he left in good hands over the country. He had many friends, and sometimes on an organized deer hunt he would place twenty-five or thirty of them at different stands.

Jim Ballard considers Jeff Porter's pair of cold-nosed hounds as probably the most remarkable dogs that ever ran in southern Texas. Jeff Porter imported them to his ranch on the San Antonio River years ago. A cold-nosed dog is a dog that can follow a cold trail. These two that Jeff Porter brought in and trained got so that hardly any trail was too old and cold for them to follow. They would snuff the cobwebs out of some coon's trail, warm it up with their breath and follow it. Jeff Porter was mighty proud of them, understood their voices as if they were talking to him in Mexican or English, and had absolute confidence in their abilities.

Late one fall he invited his friend Jim Borroum to come over for a coon hunt. The dew had fallen, and maybe it was ten o'clock that night when the two ranchers stopped and made a fire. Bowie and Bonham — those were the names of the two cold-nosed hounds — didn't seem very anxious to hunt. They had not scented a thing so far. Now, for a brief time they tarried with the men. Directly Bowie sat on his haunches and let out one of those long, long lonesome howls that seem to go up to the remotest nebulae of the Milky Way and back through the ages to the night when sorrow became a companion of man. Bowie howled and Bonham howled after him, and their howls awakened memories in Jeff Porter and Jim Borroum that actually brought tears. If you have never heard that longest and lonesomest of all l-o-n-g, l-o-n-e-s-o-m-e hound-howls, you cannot conceive its effects. This night the howls of Jeff Porter's cold-nosed hounds made the leaves on a knockaway tree close to them flutter and fall; actually they nearly covered Bowie up.

Then the dogs set out to hunt. After they took off, Jeff Porter boiled a can of coffee. He and Jim Borroum smoked, listened to geese honking southward, talked about the way wild turkeys hold a strutting party, and felt better.

Then a sound that comes to a hunter like the break of dawn of the Promised Day galloped over the air.

"Listen," Jeff Porter said, raising his hand. "That's Bowie, and he's struck a trail sure as shooting. . . . He's working it. . . . Listen, now he's on the royal highway and headed fer the throne. Amazing grace! Jest listen!"

It did sound as if Bowie were going home. And then, away over to the right, the other hound opened up.

"That's Bonham, and he's hit another trail," Jeff Porter announced. "It's cold, but wait and he'll warm it up. . . . Listen. . . . Listen. Now that coon ain't got no more chance of hiding himself than the North Star has on a clear night."

For an hour or so the hunters listened to the bayings of the hounds coming over the almost frosty air. "By ganny, the trails are going to cross," Jeff Porter said. "By ganny, they have crossed. Now Bonham's on the right of Bowie."

The men put some more dry mesquite limbs on the fire and waited, always listening. "Derned if the trails ain't coming back together," Jeff Porter said. "Yes, sir, they're nearly side by side now and still going. Let's ride."

They rode, not too fast to prevent their continuing to enjoy the hound music. After a long gallop Jeff Porter pulled up. "By ganny," he said, "they're barking 'Treed.' "

"Sounds that way," Jim Borroum agreed.

"Yes, sir, treed, and two coons from two different directions climbing into the same tree at the same time. That is peculiar."

A full moon was overhead and the Morning Star was about to dim when the hunters came up to the dogs, now only intermittently barking. They were under a dead live-oak tree, dead so long that its bark had fallen away, leaving the trunk and a few stubby limbs bleached and bare. It stood apart, in clear ground, not far from a motte of timber.

"Now listen, Jeff," Jim Borroum said, "you don't mean to tell me that those fine dogs you been talking about are barking up that old dead tree. Why, who in the nation ever heard of a coon going up a dead tree?"

"Yes, a coon wants cover and I've never seen one take to anything but a tree with leaves and moss on it," Jeff Porter admitted. "But when Bowie and Bonham tell me something, I know it's true, and all your laws about coons can just be blowed."

About this time Bowie reached his forepaws up on the trunk of the dead oak and gave a few scratches. Then Bonham did the same thing.

"Coons in that tree, shore," Jeff Porter yelled.

"Jest as well talk about razorback hogs smelling honeysuckle when they could be picking up acorns," Jim Borroum answered. "Look. You can see for yourself all the coons there are in this tree."

By now Porter was off his horse. "Help me pull off my boots," he said. "I'm going to skin up and show you something."

He climbed to a fork. "Here's the hollow they went into," he yelled.

He lit a match and held it in the opening. "Pitch me up some old dry moss," he called. After he got it and made a good light, he reported. "Hollow ain't deep at all. I can reach to the bottom of it. Look out, the coons are coming down."

He hauled out the bleached skeletons of two grown coons and dropped them at the feet of his friend. After he had descended and put his boots back on, he said, "I'll still admit that coons won't take up a dead tree, but this tree was not dead and them coons weren't dead neither when they clumb it. I told you Bowie and Bonham were the best cold-nosed hounds that ever worked a cold trail."

They were smart dogs in other ways. When one got too full of fleas he would take a wad of Spanish moss in his mouth, jump into the San Antonio River and swim against the current, gradually sinking lower and lower into the water until nothing but the tip of his nose and the moss remained above it. The fleas would retreat from the water and when most of them had taken refuge in the moss, the dog would let it go.

Bowie and Bonham probably had just a little the edge on Lindy, as trailers; but that dog's reasoning powers sometimes seemed beyond this world. Lindy was a Walker hound, straight from Mr. Walker's kennels in Tennessee. Jim Laudermilk brought him to Beeville back in the days before government trappers caught out most of the coyotes, ruined hunting, increased jack rabbits and rats and did nobody any good except themselves. Laudermilk used to take Lindy out alone and chase down many a coyote. He wouldn't let Lindy work with other dogs. He said that in the first place Lindy would not work with them, he'd simply work ahead of them; in the second place, his superiority would make the owners of the other dogs feel bad.

About the time Lindy reached the zenith of his fame, a certain coyote in Bee County reached his. His reputation spread far beyond his range, though that was pretty wide. He was known as the "Graveyard Wolf," from his habit of always passing, before the chase was over, near the old graveyard east of Beeville. His home seemed to be along Medio Creek, but no matter where dogs started him up, he would work around to the graveyard before the night was over. All the dogs in the country had chased the Graveyard Wolf, and always he got away. Packs were brought in from other places; the Graveyard Wolf made fools of them all.

Finally, Jim Laudermilk agreed to let Lindy run this coyote, provided no other dog was turned loose in the field. No hound had to have a keen sense of smell to pick up the trail of the Graveyard Wolf; he was so sure of himself that he never bothered to conceal his tracks.

Out close to the Medio, Lindy struck his plain trail. Jim Laudermilk had permitted several hound men to come along to watch Lindy work. After they heard Lindy open up, they went back close to the graveyard to await developments. It wasn't an hour before they heard Lindy coming. Then he did a remarkable thing. When he got up close to the ground from which the wolf habitually made his getaway, he stopped, howled a lone howl or two, and started back the way he had come.

Jim Laudermilk at first seemed sort of embarrassed. Then he caught on to the hound's sagacity. "Just be patient," he said. "Just give Lindy time."

The other hunters, tired of what appeared to them nothing

but nonsense on the part of both dog and man, were going in when Laudermilk explained.

Lindy had realized that he was not cunning enough to catch up with the Graveyard Wolf. Now he was backtracking to catch him as a pup coming up. And — he actually caught the pup, though it took him thirty-six hours to do it.

Honey in the Rock

"See yonder!" said Tom Owen, stretching out his long arm. "There's a bee."

We looked in the direction he pointed, but that was the extent of our observation.

"It was a fine bee," continued Tom Owen, "black body, yellow legs, and went into that tree," pointing to a distant oak. "In a clear day I can see a bee over a mile, easy."

Thus T. B. Thorpe, in *The Hive of the Bee-Hunter*, published in 1854, proceeds to delineate a type common on the frontiers. On his way to the Alamo, David Crockett fell in with an unnamed bee hunter bound for the same destiny — and the Bee Hunter of the Alamo has his place in history.

Andrew Sowell, living at Seguin on the Guadalupe River, was so noted as a bee hunter that settlers said if you put him in a barrel and rolled it through the woods he would locate a bee tree by an occasional glimpse through the bunghole. In one day he located twenty-seven bee trees and chopped an X, the discoverer's sign of pre-emption, on each. Men with eyesight less keen than his used to chop down trees he had marked and rob the honey. He turned the tables on them by marking big trees without a hollow, and then later finding those trees cut down.

Once while he was running a bear he saw bees going into the

hollow of a bent-over limb he was dodging. He killed the bear, dressed it, and then brought the carcass back to the tree and took out the honey. Another time, while he was on his stomach drinking from the Guadalupe, he noticed shadows of bees in the water. He looked up and saw bees going in and out of a knothole in an overhanging cypress.

Bees do not usually enter a hollow tree through a hole big enough to admit a bear, or even a possum. They seek a hollow protected from weather and varmints. The opening into it is often no bigger than a two-bit piece. One woodsman told me that for three years he watched bees working in a big tree in his own yard before he discovered their hole. Still, a good eye searching the trunk and limbs of a tree can usually detect the hole by movement of the bees and by discoloration of the wood or bark around it.

If the professional couldn't see a bee "over a mile off," he knew how to course one to its tree. After a bee has gathered a load of honey, she flies directly in a straight line—a "bee line" — to her colony's comb, in order to deposit the honey. The bee hunter would select a clear space and put out a dab of honey in a saucer or pan; the bait would soon attract any bees in the neighborhood. As soon as one had a load of honey, she would line for home. The direction of the tree, but not the distance, could thus be determined. Moving his bait some distance, to one side or the other, the hunter would course other bees. The intersection of the two bee lines would mark the deposit of honey. Of course, it might take numerous trials to locate a tree two or three miles away in a forest. The hunter, instead of coursing by triangulation, might walk forward with his saucer, often stopping, until he came to the tree. But bees from more than one swarm were likely to come to the bait, especially if he moved it; so sometimes he would sprinkle a few baited bees with sulphur, so as to recognize these when they came back for more honey and thus avoid being deflected by bees from other colonies.

During the days of the Texas Republic, the ford across Onion Creek on the road between Austin and San Antonio was known as "Sasser Crossing" — from the fact that a bee hunter had placed his saucer of bait on a stump at that place. In those times a "bee gum" was still a hollow tree — gum tree, or some other kind — and not a manufactured hive.

The professional bee hunter traded off his honey as he did pelts and game taken on the side. Almost every settler robbed bee trees now and then. Bands of frontiersmen, strong enough to resist an Indian attack, would sometimes go out in the fall to haul in wagon loads of honey, along with game meat. One such band in Iowa in 1839 found sixteen hollow white oaks in one vicinity from which they strained eight barrels of honey and tried out a great quantity of beeswax. Captain Flack, who wrote two books about wildlife in Texas and the South, gave "Bee Hunting" a place amid chapters on the hunting of buffaloes, wild turkeys, and other game.

The bee hunter flourished at a time when a traveler in Texas often sat down to a meal "composed of dried venison sopped in honey." Out on long scouts, Texas rangers supplemented their diet of game meat with honey kept in rawhide or deerskin sacks. Occasionally, Comanche Indians in friendly mood would bring deerskins of honey on pack horses to trade to settlers at Fredericksburg. "We kept our honey in a deerskin," wrote Captain Jesse Burnam, "for we had no jars, jugs, nor cans. I would take the skin off a deer whole, except having to cut around the neck and legs, and tie the holes up tight. Then I would hang it up by the forelegs, and we had quite a nice can, which we always kept pretty well filled."

Bread or no bread, the excellence of anything was summed up in the current phrase, "As good as venison and honey." Nobody ever appreciated this particular goodness more than Gideon Lincecum, unflagging in his passion for liberty and knowledge of nature, his genius flavored with a tang as sharp as the juice of the mustang grape. Of his wanderings through the Texas wilderness in 1835, he wrote: "I lived plentifully all the while. Three or four times I found honey. Once I tried fish. I did not relish them — had no bread nor salt. But every time I found honey I would have a feast of the first order. I could kill venison any time, and to broil the back-straps of a deer on the coals, dip the point of the done meat into the honey, and then seize it in your teeth and saw it off with your knife, is the best and most pleasant way to eat it. I have often thought that there could be no other preparation of food for man that is so suitable, so natural, so agreeable, and so exactly suited to his constitutional requirements."

In a land where money was so scarce that "many men of property do not handle five dollars a year," as one of his leading settlers wrote Stephen F. Austin, people depended on honey for sweetening just as they depended on corn for bread and bear grease for lard. Soon after arriving in Texas, January, 1836, David Crockett wrote a letter to his children back in Tennessee describing the league of land on which he expected to settle. It had, he said, "bees and honey a plenty."

The ways of the American bee hunter, along with much pleasant bee lore from many lands, have been put into two essays by John Burroughs, but tales of honey mines — sometimes lost, and always as rich in sweets as lost mines are in gold — seem to belong peculiarly to the limestone-cave country of the

Edwards Plateau in Texas, where Bee Cave, Bee Creek, and
Bee Hollow are repeated place names.

H. B. Parks, for years director of the State Apicultural Labo-
ratory near San Antonio, sucks in knowledge and lore as
eagerly as a bee sucks honey. Most of the tales that follow are
his.

The best place to hear them used to be some bee yard in the
chaparral, after the day's work was over and the extracting crew
were lounging in camp. Then some fellow would tell how a land
surveyor, while running a line out of the Frio Canyon back in
the eighties, saw something like a funnel of smoke hanging over
a cliff, discovered that the smoke was bees going in and out of
a cave, and entered the cave to behold vast chambers filled
with honey in pure white comb. Another would tell how a well
driller somewhere on the Edwards Plateau struck a layer of
honey and wax and bored thirty feet through it before hitting
rock.

One of the famous lodes has long been Bee Mountain, on
the Bosque River. A man named Hornbeak, who was born in
1852, in a log cabin only three miles from the "mountain," said
that during his childhood Indians came after every wet spring
to get honey from the caves and crevices in the bluff. The openings were about seventy feet up; the Indians would splice poles
into ladders and then one of light weight would mount and
send down the honey by means of a rawhide rope and a grass
bucket. When Hornbeak was ten years old, a band of the Indians, after having secured all the honey they wanted, killed several settlers. That was their last trip into that section of the
country. . . . The Hornbeaks moved away. Distance and time
naturally made the honey increase in Hornbeak's recollections.
When H. B. Parks heard Hornbeak expand on the subject, he
resolved to investigate. He counted some three hundred colo-

nies of bees attached to the overhanging rocks. None, however, appeared to be prosperous.

Being beyond investigation is a great conducer to anything's enlargement. There is a tradition that in early days a cave in a bluff fronting the San Antonio River, within what is now a crowded part of the city, was unbelievably rich in honey. Americans who came not long after the Texas Revolution tried to get to this honey, but were unsuccessful. The earth over the cave was covered with trees and brush. Finally a man bought the land and cleared it off for building. Then something remarkable happened.

The removal of the brush allowed the sun to beat down with full summer force on the white chalk of the cave. The heat naturally melted both honey and comb, and a stream of the molten mixture began running down into the river. There the honey dissolved into the water, and was carried away; but the wax solidified. There was so much of it and it flowed down so rapidly that, before anybody discovered what was happening, it dammed the water back and forced the river to cut a new channel. Then somebody took possession of the dam, cut it out, and sold the wax to a candlemaker in Mexico. The river went back into its old channel, but the great honey mine was ruined forever.

That wasn't the only place where honey literally flowed. "As a sixteen-year-old boy back in 1882," a Texan wrote me, "I was sitting on a baggage truck at the railroad station in Weatherford one day while a section foreman entertained several of us with his reminiscences. He was helping build the Texas and Pacific Railroad west, he said, when construction reached the Brazos River. They built the bridge and then began working up a gorge, laying the track as they went. While blasting out the rocks in this gorge, they uncovered a bee cave that looked to have been used a thousand years. It was summer time, and the great mutilated mass of exposed honey began melting and running down to the river. It flowed like lava between the rails and over them. Before the work train coming up from the river could get over the rails, they had to be sanded.

About the time of the Civil War and for years afterwards, as tradition has come down, a person standing on one of the hills near Round Rock and looking toward the southwest could, during certain times in the spring and fall, see something like a column of smoke standing out against the sky. It appeared to issue from wooded hills along the Colorado River. The column varied with the wind. It seems not to have been investigated until Gustaf Wilhelm Belfrage, who from his hut in Bosque County sent specimens of insects to the chief museums of the world, came into the vicinity of Round Rock on a collecting expedition. Gigantic in frame, gargantuan in thirst for corn whisky, as isolated in his scientific pursuits as Robinson Crusoe on his island, Belfrage was always inquiring.

When people told him about the strange smokelike column, he explained that blackbirds, gnats, bats, bees, all sometimes move in such numbers that at a distance they look like streams of smoke. There was certainly nothing supernatural about the sight, he said. At his urging, a beekeeper set out to investigate.

After coursing and hunting all day, for the smoke effect was not constant, this man found millions of bees coming and going from a sinkhole on the crest of a limestone ridge. He reported that the orifice was small and that the bees had worn the edges of it slick all around. He thought, however, that with help he could get through the hole and explore the honey chamber below.

The next day he and several other men returned. Provided with a veil, smoker, and lantern, he tied a rope under his arms

nd was let down. But he had not descended far before the in-
initude of bees going in and coming out began to smother
him. He jerked the rope and was pulled out.

After this experience, Round Rock became bee-cave mad.
Expeditions scoured the ground for a long distance all around
he sinkhole on the ridge. Some of the searchers found an open-
ng in a ravine that might connect with the honey chamber.
Here they built a fire of cedar brush. In time they saw a wreath
of smoke coming with bees out of the main opening. For two
lays the fire was kept burning, and bees continued to pour out
with the smoke. Unable to re-enter, they hung in huge clusters
from trees and rocks about the ledge.

On the morning of the third day came a change. Bees no longer issued forth. The smoke no longer smelled like burning cedar, but like burning sugar. Its color changed from gray to bluish. Then the sinkhole turned into a belching furnace. The wax and honey had ignited. For four days and nights the fire raged. The heat calcined the whole hill. The edges of the opening fell in until it was many yards across. Today the place, which is still pointed out, resembles a long-deserted lime kiln.

But not all honey deposits have been destroyed. An old-time hunter said that one time while he and another man were going up the Blanco River they noticed a vast number of bees flying in and out of a hole high up the canyon wall. He managed to climb up to this opening, but there the bees covered him by the thousands. He wore clothes and gloves made of buckskin and so his hands and body were protected. He managed to avoid the bees long enough to glimpse a solid wall of white honey — not dark like that found in trees — back in the cave.

He returned to his fellow hunter. They arranged their clothing so that they would be better protected, and prepared cedar torches with which to smoke the bees. Considering the number of bees and the size of the cave, the smoke was remarkably effective. They were approaching the beautiful wall of honey when they heard a warning note, one that no man who has ever heard it disregards. They halted and looked cautiously ahead. The floor of the cave was a wriggling, twisting mass of rattlesnakes. The honey prospectors got out.

There was another rattlesnake-guarded cave in the same county. A Yankee who came to San Marcos in 1885, after hearing about the deposits of honey and wax, went to Austin and ormed a company. He sent back East for a patented smoke gun. With it, and with lanterns, ropes, and other paraphernalia, he company reached the opening of the cave.

It proved too small to enter. They sent to San Marcos for ledge hammers and crowbars and then assaulted the rock. The vibrations immediately set astir all the rattlesnakes denned up in the bluff. They began to crawl out from every crevice. There were so many and they came from such unexpected places in such a stealthy way that the honey miners retreated, never to return.

The story lived on, and about ten years after World War I ended, a chemical division from Fort Sam Houston, at San Antonio, made an expedition to this cave to try out the effect of poison gas on rattlesnakes. After having gassed the cave for twelve hours and allowed time for the air to purify, the gas warriors entered. They found one stupefied rattlesnake and no honey at all.

A beautiful Negro spiritual has as its burden, "You'll find honey in the rock." The imagery goes back to Biblical hopes and promises sweeter than honey and the honeycomb. Some connoisseurs consider no other honey so tasty or so beautiful in hue as that made from huajillo. Huajillo is an acacia bush growing on ranch land south and west of San Antonio. Its profuse flowers, creamy-soft to the eyes, are wonderfully fragrant. Its leaves afford the best of browses. Beekeepers from the north truck thousands of hives to the huajillo for an early spring gathering of honey, and then take them back to clover fields.

Back in the days while General John R. Baylor was making the Uvalde country an unsafe place for cow thieves, at the same time keeping a lookout for the lost Spanish mine in the Nueces Canyon, bears were plentiful. One day an old bear hunter told him that if he would go to a certain bluff during springtime while the huajillo was in bloom, he could hear bee wings roaring like a canyon flood, or like the sound made by a thousand sandhill cranes startled from the prairie. The cave that these roaring millions of bees carried huajillo honey into was, the old bear hunter said, exceedingly inaccessible; but he believed the honey could be reached somehow.

General Baylor wasn't much interested in anything as tame as honey. In 1894, a land surveyor to whom he had passed the bear hunter's account heard, while looking for a bench mark of a Spanish grant, the roar of bee wings and then saw the cloud of bees going into and out of the cave. He could not get to the entrance without ropes and a helper, but discovered a second entrance.

He was so eager that he set his own coat on fire to make a protective smoke while he explored with a torch. What he saw was worth a store full of coats, so he reported. Room after room was almost filled with long white curtains of the purest brush-blossom honey, some of them fifty feet high from top to bottom. Although not a bee-man, he estimated that there were at least two thousand barrels of comb honey.

That night in camp, while he was telling plans for getting the honey and selling it, the surveyor became so ill that one of his chain carriers went to Uvalde for a doctor. The doctor saw that the surveyor was beyond help and told him so. Before breathing his last he made, with the aid of the doctor, a chart showing the location of the honey mine. At one time this map was offered for sale in San Antonio for five hundred dollars.

Whether Jim Jones ever saw the map is hardly material. He did see the bees; he heard the roaring of their wings in huajillo-blossom time, and he located the entrance they streamed through. He was used to rough country; he had an ingenious mind. He took in a partner who had some money and knew how to extract honey. They bought a pair of blacksmith bellows and rigged it up with two hundred feet of hose to blow sulphur fumes into the cave. They mounted this contraption on one mesquite "lizard," a sled made out of a forked limb, and a honey extractor on another. Next, they bought a string of pack burros and were ready about the time the spring crop of honey had been gathered. The day before they were to start, they robbed six hives of domesticated bees, leaving the empty comb in the frames and imprisoning the bees.

Then Jim Jones led the caravan forth, followed by three burros, each with two beehives on his back, one on either side. Behind these burros came a dozen others loaded with empty five-gallon cans. Behind the can carriers another burro pulled the smoke-making machine; behind that came the extractor. Then came a pair of burros loaded with provisions. Jim Jones's partner was at the rear of the column; three hired Mexicans hissed and punched the burros along.

They made camp near the base of the cliff into which the bee cave opened. After firing up the smoke machine next morning, Jim Jones got himself and one end of the hose hoisted by ropes to the orifice of the cave. All day the bellows pumped sulphur fumes into the cave. By sundown it appeared that all the bees had been killed. At sunrise the six colonies of domesticated bees were released. In no time they began filling their hives with undefended honey from the cave. The way they worked was a sin to Mussett. Bees will steal from each other if they can. There were no bees left in the cave to fight off the newcomers. They did not quit carrying honey till dusk.

Jim Jones and his partner now opened the hives and extracted the honey, leaving the comb in the frames so that the bee could fill them again the next day. Three hundred pounds o extracted honey — pure huajillo honey — was the net amount o one day's work. By means of scaffolding and ladders men migh have gotten directly to the wild honey, but it was a fixed policy with Jim Jones not to work his back when his brain might accomplish the results. He sent for more hives of bees.

The bees worked so hard taking free honey that a colony would not last over two weeks. Jim Jones and his partner had a stream of burros packing honey to Uvalde and bringing empty cans and fresh bees out. Their plan worked so well that they decided to leave the old comb in the cave for wild bees to fill again with honey the next spring. That winter, however, the bottom dropped out of the honey market, and Jim Jones drifted on west.

He followed the Southern Pacific Railroad to the Pecos River before he saw anything of interest. Bees often deposit honey in the protecting timbers of railroad bridges. A bucket set on the ground directly under a comb may catch a good deal of honey jarred loose by passing freight trains on a hot summer day. Jim Jones set buckets under the Pecos bridge, the highest and one of the longest in the West, and caught lots of honey.

He discovered some richly stored combs about a hundred feet beneath the sleepers — too remote from the rails and sleepers for the honey to be jarred out, but still over a hundred feet from the ground. He rigged up a rope ladder for letting himself down from the top of the bridge to this honey. He owned a perpetually hungry hound that had learned to be as fond of honey as a bear. He tied his rope to the top of the bridge at a time when he would not be disturbed by a passing train, and, leaving the hungry hound whining at the rope knot, let himself down to the honey. The weather was exceedingly hot and at the least displacement the honey flowed. It went to dripping, but instead of dripping down, it dripped up. This can be understood only by remembering that the rope went up from the honey instead of down.

As fast as the honey dripped up the rope to the knot, the hound lapped it. In his eagerness for more, he chewed the rope in two. Jim Jones dropped more than a hundred feet to the rocky floor of the Pecos Canyon. Like the Chinaman that Roy Bean once held an inquest over at this place, Jim Jones lay dead. A Greek poem some three thousand years old tells how the dog of a honey hunter caused the death of his master in almost exactly the same way.

Part Three

The Texas Bluebonnet

B ECAUSE the flower has a white tip, Mexicans call it *conejo* —
"cottontail rabbit." Some old-timers called it "wolf-flower,"
the belief being that the plant was predatory, like a wolf, taking
nourishment from the soil. This erroneous belief gave the plant
its generic name, Lupinus (lupine, or wolf). The Texas bluebonnet sometimes thrives where other plants are sparse and
weak; but, instead of impoverishing the soil, it, through the
curious nodules on its roots called "nitrogen fixers," actually
nourishes it.

Another name, common early in the present century, is "buffalo clover"— not that buffaloes ate it. Although not poisonous
like the loco weed — which also belongs to the pea family and
which ruins any horse or cow that eats it — the bluebonnet seems
to be palatable to only goats and sheep among domestic animals.
They have killed it out in many places.

Like seeds of other native plants, including grasses, those of
the bluebonnet may lie dormant for a long time. They come up
in the fall; through the winter the little plants grow only
slightly; then in the spring, if it rains, they burgeon. If the
ground has no moisture in the fall, not many seeds sprout; they
reserve themselves. If the following fall is seasonable, they will,
in a bluebonnet area, come up "as thick as blossoms in para-

dise." S. S. Bundy, an observant rancher in the hill country, told me that when, about the time of World War I, he began raising goats and sheep on his ranch — which had been stocked mostly with cattle — bluebonnets were plentiful. Before long they became scarce, and then disappeared entirely. For eight or ten years he had not seen a flower on the ranch — until he fenced off about sixty acres for a deer park. The spring after he fenced sheep and goats out of this plot, several bluebonnet plants bloomed there, and then propagated themselves. Some seeds had probably come up each year, the plants always eaten down before they could bloom. But over all those years a few seeds had kept themselves in reserve.

The name bluebonnet goes back to the days when women folk wore sunbonnets. Each single flower on a spike of many flowers resembles that style of headdress. In 1901 the bluebonnet was by legislative action adopted as the state flower of Texas. The cotton bloom was a close contender, and John Garner, later known as Cactus Jack, a member of the legislature at that time, urged the claim of the prickly pear.

A few years later Julian Onderdonk, of San Antonio, took the breath of the sensitive with his painting of a bluebonnet field. "Nature follows art." Texans have become increasingly conscious of the beauty, the fragrance, and, when seen in mass, the power of their bluebonnets. Seizing upon the flower's popularity, every dauber in the country tries his hand at painting it, and bluebonnet chromos are as plentiful as cowboy figures on pulp magazine covers. Yet no amount of commercialism, no fad running into insipidity, no betrayal in the name of art, can detract from the essential loveliness of the flower springing on the hills and in the valleys of Texas, yielding

A passion of blossom, a splendor of spread.

No other flower — for me at least — brings such upsurging of the spirit and at the same time such restfulness.

Like the artists, poets without number have tried their hands on the bluebonnet. Margaret Bell Houston's "Song from the Traffic" alone makes my heart go "gallivanting."

> (*Manhattan — Manhattan — I walk your streets today*
> *But I see the Texas prairies bloom a thousand miles away!*)
>> Primroses burn their yellow fires
>> Where grass and roadway meet.
>> Feathered and tasseled like a queen,
>> Is every old mesquite.
> (*It's raining in the barren park, but on the prairie-side*
> *The road is shining in the sun for him who cares to ride!*)
>> The plum tree's arms are burdened white,
>> And where the shrubs are few
>> Bluebonnets fold the windy ways —
>> Is any blue so blue?
> (*Clouds of them, crowds of them, shining through the grey,*
> *Bluebonnets blossoming a thousand miles away!*)
>> How could I live my life so far
>> From where March plains are green,
>> But that my gallivanting heart
>> Knows all the road between?
> (*Manhattan — Manhattan — when you jostled me today,*
> *You jostled one a-galloping a thousand miles away!*

Of the lupines there are scores of varieties over the Americas, some large, some small, but none so winsome in its intense, yet soft, color as the bluebonnet, and no other so "takes the winds of March with beauty." It alone, too, has the bluebonnet fragrance, the evanescences of petal and leaf mingling into an aroma that is at once delicate and as tonic as a heifer's breath. What else in the world can be like passing a field of bluebonnets in a spring night and sensing them only by smell!

Despite sentimentality, one legend about the bluebonnet is worthy of survival. A great drouth was on the country. There had been a spring of dust, a summer of parching heat, a fall with no color in the leaves and grass turned to dust, and then a winter of cold and starvation for man and beast. Now spring was coming again and still the drouth persisted. Many and many a buffalo would not shed his hair this spring; bones dotting the raw prairie told why. The people had only roots left for food. They had drifted, like the deer and the buffaloes, to the southern coast-line, where the weather is usually mild; but even here they found nothing but famine. The jack rabbits seemed to have disappeared, and the coyotes were gaunt.

It was clear to the people that the Chief of All Spirits had turned away his face. Day and night medicine men chanted their incantations, danced to the beat of tom-toms, and strewed dust upon their bended heads. Warriors with knives of flint and bone cut their own flesh and sent up wild cries of supplication. Women and children cowered in silence, as noiseless in their movements as shadows. A great fear was upon all the people. They had, they knew, done some deed that must be forgiven before rain would bring back life.

At last the Chief of All Spirits heard them. He spoke his message through the medicine men. The tribe must make a burnt offering of their most valued possession, and the ashes of this offering must be scattered to the four cardinal points of the earth, to the north and the east, the south and the west. Until such a sacrifice was made, drought and famine would continue.

Darkness was upon the world when the people heard this message. On the outer rim of the assemblage was a little girl. She had said not a word. She said not a word now as the crowd dissolved, but within herself she knew that she possessed and held tightly clasped to her body the "most valued possession" among her people.

It was a doll. Fashioned of bleached buckskin, it simulated the figure of a warrior. Eyes, nose, mouth, and ears were painted on it with the juice of berries. Its leggings were beaded with bits of polished bone and brilliantly colored seeds. It wore a belt of wildcat teeth, strung on twisted hair from a buffalo tail. Its war-bonnet was made from the blue feathers of the crested bird that cries "Jay, jay, jay." No mother could have loved the child of her own flesh more fiercely than this little Indian girl loved her blue-bonneted doll warrior. No price within her knowledge would have tempted her to part with it. Heavy indeed was her heart now as she realized that this most precious thing of hers must be also the "most valued possession" among her people.

The council fires went out. The families were gone to their tepees, and the gleam of coals that came through the cracks faded into darkness. The little girl lay near the flap of her home tepee. She lay there wondering if other people were awake, and she hugged closer her precious doll. Once when she started to get up, she heard the footfall of a dog and felt the sniff of his nose. She hugged the doll closer. The last lone wail of a coyote beyond the edge of the encampment died away. The cries of geese winging their way northward made the silence more silent.

The listening doe lays back her ears not more noiselessly than now this child of the camp turned her head and saw that a stick of wood in the tepee fire kept its light under the ashes. It was almost within arm's reach. By their breathing she knew that her father and mother and her brothers and sisters were asleep.

Then, moving as softly, yet swiftly, as the killdeer runs on the sandy edge of a lake, she arose, took the chunk of fire and passed out of the tepee. She stopped behind some bushes to listen. All she heard was the twit of a redbird, disturbed but for a moment. The stars shone, but there was no moon.

Then she prayed to the Chief of All Spirits that her offering might be acceptable, and she asked for a sign of acceptance. As she arose in resolution, the tears dried from her eyes. She gathered twigs and kindled a little fire. Then she thrust the prize of her life headfirst into the flame. The smell of scorching feathers and buckskin was strong, but there was no wind and she trusted the smell would not wake any person. She stood, her eyes fixed on the burning sacrifice, until not a fragment of the doll was left. Then she scooped up the ashes, and, in the manner she had seen her father and other men offer the peace pipe, she scattered the ashes to the north and the east, the south and the west. She heaped some dirt on the big coal, the only fire left, and then she lay down where she had scattered the ashes.

She had brought her blanket with her. She had no thought of sleep, but she wanted to be near all that was left of her doll. She did fall asleep, but not for long. Awaking, she reached her hands out on the ground to feel.

Against her palms she felt something as fine and soft as the softest feathers in the bonnet of the warrior doll. Yet what she felt was not feathers — or fine ashes. And in her nostrils was a new fragrance. Then she found that the delicious-feeling and delicious-smelling thing was rooted to the earth. She would not tear it loose.

She saw the Guide Star far up the heavens in the east and the Morning Star following it. A little later she saw one of the medicine men step into the open, his hands lifted. It would soon be day.

Lightly she ran into her own tepee. "Oh, Mother, come!" she whispered. Without words, the mother arose. As hand in hand they stepped out, they met the dawn. The little one led her mother to the opening beyond the bushes where she had scattered the ashes. She was afraid to look, yet a-tremble to see.

There where the ashes had been scattered was, as it were, a little lake, in the early light almost a blue-black; then as the dawn rushed on, a blue as intense as indigo; then a blue as soft yet shining as ever flashed from the spring-fresh feathers of the bold bird crying "Jay, jay, jay" in the trees. These blue flowers were so rich and thick that they almost hid the ash-green leaves of the plants.

The little girl told her mother about the sacrifice. The mother told the father. The father told the men of the council. And all the people came to behold the miracle. There could be no doubt that it was a sign.

That very day soft, warm rain soaked the ground. Trees and bushes began to put out. The prairies greened and grew gay with flowers. Birds sang and built their nests. Game animals came back and fattened. While the men hunted, the women planted corn and pumpkins, and everything that was planted grew in a magical way.

Up until this time the little girl had no real name. Now she was named One-Who-Dearly-Loves-Her-People. Every day, often for many hours, she watched the blue flowers that had come in exchange for the wonderful doll of the blue warbonnet. She saw the flowers develop into podded seeds and the green of the stalks turn brown. In time she saw the dried seed pods twist and, with a little crack, open and shoot their seeds out.

The next spring the lake of blue was far wider. Winds, rain, water and birds carried the seeds to places far beyond where the pods could pop them. Year by year the range of the bluebonnet extended, its blueness mixing with the red and pink of wild phloxes and the orange and rose of Indian paintbrushes. In time nature planted the seeds over hills and valleys, beyond rivers and across canyons, away and away from the tepee of One-Who-Dearly-Loves-Her-People. So today, at the time of year when the mockingbird sings in the moonlight and the mesquite, sure that winter is gone, has put out its lacy leaves, then along laned roads and on pasture slopes the bluebonnet makes the Texas landscape lovely.

The Headless Horseman of the Mustangs

About the middle of the last century, not long after the Mexican War ended, a rider without any head was reported to be ranging in the great mustang country along the Nueces River in southwest Texas. Several borderers who saw him said that he carried his head, under a Mexican sombrero, tied to the horn of his saddle. Some added a "band of gold bullion" to the sombrero. About his shoulders fluttered a brush-torn serape over a buckskin jacket, and his legs were encased in rawhide leggings, such as were then made and worn by most vaqueros, the light-colored flesh side turned out. His horse was a heavy black mustang stallion as wild as anything that ever raced over prairie or plunged through chaparral thicket.

There was no particular time or place at which mustang and rider were to be seen. In the bright sunshine of morning some hunter might glimpse them climbing the rough breaks far up the Nueces Canyon, and then in the dusk of evening a lone rancher on the Leona forty miles away might see the bleached buckskin and rawhide of the strange rider on the black stallion tearing across prickly pear flats. Neither horse nor horseman seemed ever to tire, and it was observed that the rider never bent or turned in the saddle but sat as rigid as if he were made of wood and had been spiked to the animal's back.

The creature carrying the awful thing was shunned by all

other mustangs. Sometimes he could be located by a stampede of wild horses away from his presence. He never stayed long in one locality, as horses usually range, but roved far and wide. Indeed, he seemed a thing possessed. At sight of a man he would tear away at a speed that even the unconquerable Pacing White Stallion — fleetest of all mustangs that grazed on the mesquite grasses of Texas — could not have exceeded.

Indians, ever superstitious and ever horse-hunting, saw the mustang with the headless rider on his back and tried to keep clear of his range. Mexican vaqueros and *pastores* (sheep or goat herders) were just as scared. A glimpse that some of the troops stationed at Fort Inge on the Leona River got of the rider resulted in a much-expanded tale. According to tradition, the adventurer and romancer Mayne Reid, who had certainly been with the American army at Mexico City, was for a time right after the Mexican War stationed at Fort Inge. He was an eager listener to camp tales about mustangers, buffalo hunters, scalp hunters, and other frontier types. In *The Headless Horseman, A Strange Tale of Texas* (London, 1886), a romance immensely popular for a generation, he added to the legend that he heard growing up.

"No one," he wrote, "denied that the thing had been seen. The only question was how to account for a spectacle so peculiar as to give the lie to all known laws of creation. At least half a dozen theories were started. . . . Some called it an 'Indian dodge'; others, a 'lay figure.' Still others said that it was a real rider so disguised as to have his head under the serape that enshrouded his shoulders, with perhaps a pair of eye-holes through which he could see to guide his horse. Not a few swore that the headless horseman was Lucifer himself."

Perhaps the "lay figure" Mayne Reid had in mind is explained by the following. Patrick Burke, who was born in 1834 on the Texas coast about an hour after his mother landed with other settlers from Ireland, became a noted rancher east of the Nueces River. He said that in early days mustangers he ranged with would, if they could, catch a strong stallion and tie a scarecrow, a kind of imitation man, on him and then let him loose. He would tear away, and after a while make for his own *manada* — band of mares — trailing it like a bloodhound. As soon as any mustangs saw the scarecrow, they would stampede. Their frightened running would set other mustangs running. Sometimes thousands would be running over the prairies at the same time, all going in the same direction, band after band joining together. Their hoofs pounding on the earth sounded like the terrific roar of a cyclone. After the mustangs had run themselves down, the mustangers could guide them into pens with long wings that had been built to hold them.

One theory not mentioned by Mayne Reid was that the phantom horseman of his tale was the *patrón* — the ghostly guard — of the lost mine of the long-abandoned Candelaria Mission on the Nueces, to protect it against profane prospectors.

No one ever got very close to the black mustang, but a few frontiersmen who took long shots at the headless rider declared that their bullets passed through him as easily as through a paper target. They were less superstitious than Indians, Mexicans, or soldiers, but even some of them developed a feeling of awe. Finally, a half-dozen or so united to capture the mustang and put an end to the mystery.

They ambushed him at Bull Head watering on the Nueces and shot him down. On his back they found a dried-up Mexican carcass perforated with bullets. It was lashed to horse and saddle so tightly that the rope had to be cut to unfasten it, and a skull with a frayed sombrero bound around it was tied to the horn of the saddle.

But the mystery was only half solved. How had a vaquero's body come to be fastened on a mustang and his head lashed to the saddle? In time Bigfoot Wallace and Creed Taylor answered the questions, but a full explanation carries us back years before the mystery began.

On the night of December 4, 1835, a little while before the besieging Texans heard that deathless cry, "Who will go with Old Ben Milam into San Antonio?" a deserter from the Mexican stronghold slipped into their ranks. He was a lieutenant named Vidal. He brought valuable information, and he convinced the Texans of his friendship. One who noted the Mexican's lithe body, deft movements, and alert eye was Creed Taylor.

After the battle of San Jacinto had temporarily settled the fight between Mexico and Texas, and the fighters had turned to occupations of peace, Vidal took up horse stealing. It was a risky business, for at that time a man could get away with a neighbor's life better than with his horses. At first Vidal's reputation as a patriot cloaked his operations. By the time his real character became known, he was commander in chief of a chain of horse thieves operating on both sides of the Rio Grande and sneaking stolen stock clear into Louisiana and Mississippi. They were cunning enough to throw suspicion for their own operations on the ever horse-raiding Comanches.

In the summer of 1850 Vidal and three picked confederates gathered up a considerable bunch of horses on the San Antonio River and headed southwest towards Mexico. The raid was well timed, for most of the sparse settlers were away to the north chasing a band of Comanches who had swooped down on the Guadalupe settlements a few days before.

But not all were away. Contrary to custom, Creed Taylor was not after the Indians — and some of his horses were among those stolen. Creed Taylor was a Texian among Texians. He had killed Mexicans with Bowie and Milam, fought the Indians as a ranger under Jack Hays, and scouted for old Rough-and-Ready in the Mexican War. He was yet to be a principal in the lethal Taylor-Sutton feud. He was not the kind of man to let any thief gallop off with his horses.

A Mexican rancher named Flores who chanced also to be at home had likewise lost horses. Both he and Taylor suspected Vidal as they struck out on the trail of the thieves. The farther they trailed, the surer they were that they were following Vidal. They found cattle carrying arrows that had been shot into them. "Vidal's trick to make greenhorns smell Indians," Taylor said, and went on.

At the Frio the trailers met Bigfoot Wallace — always ready to "up" any "copperbelly" who needed upping. With joy he joined in the hunt.

At the Nueces, the trail of the horses veered up the river. Two days later, close to dusk, about twelve miles from Fort Inge on the Leona, the trailers, unseen, sighted the stolen *caballada* and the camp of the thieves. The Mexicans, who had been pushing ahead hard, now seemed to consider themselves secure from pursuers. The smoke from their campfire was rising thick and high; only one man was on herd; no sentinel was out scouting for sign. The Texans lay low and waited.

Night came on. There was no moon but the stars were bright. When the Evening Star was well up, Creed Taylor crept forward to reconnoiter. He avoided passing too near the stolen horses and kept the wind on them. He was more afraid of their giving the alarm than he was of the man on herd, who occasionally moved around at a sleepy walk. The camp was on the edge of a mesquite and prickly pear thicket. Crawling up to it, Creed Taylor made out three sleeping forms. One of them, he was sure, was Vidal's. Then he stole back to his waiting confederates. Their work must be done before the man on herd awakened his relief.

Each of the three Texans had a six-shooter and a rifle. They made their plans. Flores was to give Creed Taylor and Bigfoot Wallace ample time to crawl to the sleeping Mexicans. In ambush, he was to wait until the horse thief on herd passed near him, and then to shoot. The sound of his shot would be the signal for the other two men.

They had reached the camp, each had picked his man, and, cocked six-shooters in hand, they were awaiting the signal shot when it rang out, followed by the yell of a struck man. In an instant the sleeping Mexicans were on their feet. Two revolvers flashed, and two horse thieves went back to sleep — forever. The third broke for the thicket, but two bullets stopped him. As it turned out, Flores's man was only wounded and got away in the brush, but he did not take any stolen horses with him.

At daylight the bodies of the dead men were inspected. There was no question as to the identity of Vidal's. He was a little man. Bigfoot Wallace, always daring and eccentric, now made one of his original proposals. In the recaptured *caballada* was a black mustang stallion that had been herd-broken but that had never felt a cinch under his belly. Bigfoot proposed that he be roped, saddled, and mounted with Vidal's body. Perhaps Bigfoot jested. He thought it a good joke, once, when in a brush with Indians he picked out the biggest one for his own, saying he "needed a pair of leggings," and, after killing him, actually pulled the leggings off and wore them. Perhaps Bigfoot wanted to give warning to other horse thieves. At any rate, his proposal was considered good.

The black mustang was roped, tied up, blindfolded with a red bandana, and saddled. Then the Texans cut off Vidal's head and, with chin-strap and thongs, fastened the horse thief's sombrero firmly to it. Next, making deft use of buckskin, they laced the sombreroed head to the horn of the saddle. It was a Mexican saddle, rawhide-rigged, with a wide, flat horn. They dressed Vidal's headless body in full regalia — leggings, spurs, serape — and with more care than an *arriero* in the Sierra Madre takes in packing a mule with silver bars, fixed it in the saddle. They tied the dead man's feet in the stirrups and double-fastened the stirrups to each other under the mustang's belly so that they could not fly up.

During all these operations the black mustang was shivering and snorting, for nothing terrifies a wild horse more than the smell of foreign blood. Finally the blind was removed from the stallion's eyes and, without bridle or halter, he was set loose. In after years Bigfoot used to declare that he had seen many pitching horses, but that he had never seen any other animal act like that black stallion with a dead Mexican on his back. After he had pitched in every direction, snorted, squealed, pawed the air, reared up and fallen backwards, rolled and then stood quivering, the thing was still on his back. For maybe five minutes he stood with feet spread out, sides heaving, nostrils dilating, his whole body quivering. Then, with a wild and terrified squeal, he broke away into a run that, as we have seen, scared up a legend not yet dead.

Creed Taylor, Bigfoot Wallace and Flores drove the captured horses back to the ranches on the San Antonio River. They agreed to keep still for a while.

A Ranch on the Nueces

MANY an old ranch house by its very looks calls up human destinies. Such is the Ray Ranch on the Nueces River down in the brush country of southwest Texas. It was established so long ago and the story has passed through so many people on the way down that it must be considered subject to the fallacies of memory. I heard it on a ranch gallery one night while the only sounds besides the voice of Rocky Reagan were the south wind in the trees, the hoot of an owl now and then down in the river bottom, and the occasional howl of a coyote out in the brush.

After the Civil War was over, Elijah Ray still had lands and a big store in Alabama, though no money. He preached on the side and ran the store in partnership with a man named Hess. Hess had a bull-like build and a red face that marked him among other men. He was capable and energetic, but about the time business began to pick up, Elijah Ray discovered signs of dishonesty in him. When two Yankees showed up with cash, he decided to sell out his interest in the store, along with a farm. The family lived on a better one. Hess sold his interest also.

Elijah Ray had made a prospecting trip into Texas in the late '40s and had never ceased to talk about the land there. This talk and fresh reports of the great cattle drives out of Texas and the free grass on which herds were raised filled the two Ray sons, Wallace and Jim, with ambition to go to Texas. They wanted a ranch of their own.

In 1868 Jim Ray was eighteen years old and Wallace was twenty. One day their father said: "Since you boys are bound to go to Texas, I want you to go prepared. I once thought I would go, but now it's getting late. Your mother and I have talked matters over. We have enough to live on and to take care of your sisters until they marry. We are going to give each of you five thousand dollars for a stake."

Banks at this time were very scarce and communications with Texas were scarcer. Elijah Ray remembered how in that sparsely populated land most business was transacted for cash. Indeed, for a few years after Wallace and Jim reached it, cattle buyers carried bags of gold and silver with them to "cow works," left the money lying in camp until a herd had been "shaped up," and then counted out the gold and silver on a blanket to the sellers. It was decided that the two brothers had better take their money in cash. Bank notes were at a discount and in the South, where paper money had sunk to nothing, were not wanted.

The father had a fine money belt made for each of the boys. When filled with five thousand dollars in gold pieces it was plenty heavy. It was worn under shirt and trousers, but any observant eye could have detected it. Each of the boys bought himself a six-shooter, a long rifle, and clothes of the best grade. Their mother saw that each had a Bible in his bag. They figured they could do better in Texas on saddles and other horse equipment.

The preparations went on for a good while. Outside of the family only Hess knew that they were taking five thousand dollars apiece in money belts. Having a hand in the business transactions, he had somehow found out. He knew also that they were going to the mesquite grass country on the Nueces River west of most settlements, where Elijah Ray had been in a seasonable year — when there was no sign of drought. Five or six weeks before they left, Hess of the bull build and red face disappeared. Wallace and Jim went down the Mississippi on a steamboat to New Orleans, and there caught a boat to Indianola on the Texas coast — a one-time important port, long since annihilated by a Gulf hurricane. They found Indianola booming with trade, freight wagons leaving every day for San Antonio and other inland places. The stores offered everything a frontiersman could want. The Ray brothers spent several days looking around, getting the lay of the land and completing their outfits.

They bought two extra good Spanish horses, well broken and in good flesh: a coyote dun — a dun with a stripe down his back — for Jim; and a grullo — slate-colored like a sandhill crane — for Wallace. Each had a cowboy saddle, leather leggings, boots, spurs, Saltillo blanket with a hole slit in the middle of it so that it could be worn to turn water — slickers not yet having arrived. It was late summer and these blankets, carried rolled up behind the saddle, would serve as pallets. Instead of burdening themselves with a pack horse, they rolled up extra clothing in the blankets. They each carried cartridges and some food, principally crackers, coffee, sugar, and bacon, with a small coffeepot and tin cups, in a *morral* — the fiber bag of Mexican make that swung from nearly every saddle horn in the country. They traded off the long, heavy Alabama rifles for light saddle guns carried in scabbards.

One night in a wagon yard at Indianola, Jim Ray overheard talk that led him to believe Hess had been at this place and had gone on west. This was surprising but neither Jim nor Wallace attached significance to the news.

The two set out with a wagon train bound for Beeville. Traveling was slow, but the coastal prairies afforded plenty to see. The earth was a carpet of grass, in many places belly-high to a horse. It was dotted with deer, cattle, and wild horses; prairie chickens and bobwhites flew out of it constantly along the road. September, the month of rains, had come and the grass was green and all the streams were running with clear water. Until the route crossed an arm of post oak country, the only brush and timber were along creeks.

At Beeville, the Rays bought a few extra provisions and cut loose from the freighters to prospect alone. They could kill meat any time they wanted it and expected to live largely upon it. They went west by north. They knew there were few ranches west of the Nueces. They expected to locate perfection — water and grass — somewhere out in that vast vacancy. Ten thousand dollars would buy two thousand heifers. Even if they did not buy that many to raise calves, but kept some money for improvements, more horses, and expenses, they could set up a good-sized ranch. They expected to file on a section of land each for headquarters, and build a house. The problem would be to control their stock on a range that belonged to nobody and so to everybody.

They crossed the Nueces at Puente Piedra, where a ferry was installed years later, and camped under live oak trees. They saw cattle, some not branded, but no people. They caught a few glimpses of mustang cattle, which ran separately from the semi-domesticated stock. Some were black, some yellowish, most of them line-backed, the thick, sharp-pointed horns on the bulls indicating the fighting strain of Spanish cattle from which they were descended. They were literally wilder than the deer and as unclaimed. Along the creeks and river wild turkeys were as common as jack rabbits out on the prairies. Now and then a band of startled mustang horses, always alert, ran against the sky line.

The second day, the Rays rode upcountry from the Puente Piedra without seeing a sign of a ranch. A big rain that had fallen during the night blotted out all tracks. A little before sundown, while they were nearing a heavy line of timber that indicated a creek, eighteen riders dashed towards them at a dead run, shooting and yelling. It would have been foolhardy to try to stand them off, and the brothers headed for a brushy draw to their left. Travel in heavy ground had jaded their horses; now, as they made the best time they could, they turned in their saddles and fired their six-shooters at the raiders. Neither, so far as they could tell, made a hit. Jim caught a glimpse of the red face of a hatless man with a red bandana tied around his head. He had a different look from the other riders, who were unmistakable Indians.

A short distance from the brush, Wallace went down under a dead horse. Jim stopped to try to get him loose and saw that he was dying. He seemed to have been shot through the lungs. He was plainly past being saved. Jim remounted and, with bullets hitting around him, made it to the brush. There h.. horse stumbled in a soggy gopher hole and as Jim cleared his back he decided that the best policy would be to run in the direction opposite to that the recovered horse was headed. He jumped into a hard-bottomed gully and ran down it to thick covering, where he stopped. All he had now was his six-shooter, and it had only one unfired cartridge. He realized how useless at the moment all his gold was.

He could hear the Indians above him and in other directions and knew they had caught his horse. Then dark came. Flying clouds, played on by lightning, banked to the west. After all was quiet, Jim half-crawled back to where his brother had fallen.

Occasionally he could hear a voice from the creek timber, where the Indians had evidently camped. Wallace's body was not mutilated, but some of his clothes had been removed — and his money belt was gone. Comanches were not out after money belts.

Daylight found Jim in tall grass partly protected by brush whence he could view the camp. The Indians were bringing in hobbled horses. He saw his coyote dun among them, and he saw plainly what he had waited to see. The red-faced man with a bandana tied around his forehead, blockier in build than the other men, was unmistakably Hess. Until the end of his life Jim Ray speculated on how Hess had got in with the Indians, but figured it must have been through one of those chains of horse thieves, some making use of Indians, that operated from the Rio Grande clear across Texas into the old Southern States.

The Indians instead of riding up the creek now prepared to cross it. It was up big swimming, indicating that heavy rains had fallen to the west. The south bank was a bluff; the north bank sloping. During the excitement of crossing the creek, Jim, hiding behind trees and brush, got closer. Circumstances seemed to be favoring the use of his one cartridge. Two or three of the riders managed to leap their horses into the stream, but the others had to blindfold theirs and back them off the bank. Some men swam free, some holding the tails of their horses.

When the last man reached the sloping bank on the other side, Jim steadied his six-shooter with both hands and aimed at Hess. The bullet, apparently, did not even graze him. It was part of Jim's plan to show himself. He stood up and yelled, and one of the bullets that replied flecked his left thigh, barely bringing blood. The whole pack, leaving their horses on the far side, plunged back to hunt down the man they had missed. The

stream carried them downward, and they had considerable difficulty clambering up the high bank.

Meanwhile, according to his plan, Jim ran upstream under cover, jumped in, swam across, and, still under cover, ran down to the horses. He had no difficulty catching his dun, which carried not only his saddle but the scabbarded rifle. It was loaded. He gave the other horses a scare and started down the creek, keeping close to cover. He realized, however, that within a short time the Indians would be back on their horses trailing him. After he had galloped maybe two miles he discovered that he was at a slough roughly paralleling the Nueces River. The Nueces makes a big bend in this region, and he was much nearer it than he had supposed. The slough was wide but deep only in the middle. He rode up it in knee-deep water for several hundred yards, leaving no tracks. Then he swam across it and followed a shallow arm of water into flat country. He stopped in a motte of trees and granjeno brush, satisfied that he and his trail were both well concealed. He stayed there all day without seeing a horseman. Once only he heard a yell away off across the slough.

He found that all his ammunition had been removed from the *morral*, but a few water-soaked soda crackers were still in it. They tasted good. During the day he had located an island of grass near the motte, and at night he and the coyote dun camped on it, the horse faring superbly. By now, all ideas of prospecting farther for a ranch had left him. He was restless to get back to what was left of Wallace, near the creek crossing. At daylight he rode. The world seemed so empty that when he came upon the tracks of his enemies they made a kind of human association. The creek had run down enough that it was no longer swimming.

He carried his brother's body to the head of a gully, wrapped

his own shirt around the head, and spent almost the whole day digging dirt with his pocketknife to cover the body. Then he carried drift-logs from the creek to hold the dirt down.

When he was through, he noticed three buzzards in a dead tree down the creek a short distance from where the Indians had swum it. The tree might be their regular roost, but curiosity took him to it. At its base was a mound of drift, in which a patch of red caught his eye. After he had yanked out a few sticks, the patch expanded into a bandana. It was still around Hess's head. The current, probably aided by a drifting log, had carried Hess under into the tangle of drift. The only care Jim gave Hess's body was to remove Wallace's money belt from it.

He had meant to kill meat that evening, but now the light was too dim for shooting. He got under a tree. It rained again, just enough to keep him wet through the night. He was really getting hungry now — and the coyote dun was feasting on mesquite grass. Clear, warm sunshine next morning seemed a special benediction from on high. As the sun came up, Jim heard gobbling. When he stepped out cautiously, he saw two big old gobblers making passes at each other while other gobblers circled around them. The sheen on their feathers was wonderful. He aimed his rifle, pulled the trigger and had meat. The fact that he did not have a dry match did not keep him from enjoying and assimilating while he swallowed several pounds of prime turkey.

His only course now was to get to fire and food. He rode to the river. It was on an immense rise. He knew that if he went down it far enough he would reach people. An idea came to him. Had he had more experience he would have rejected any idea that parted him from his horse, but he was still, in a way, a young greenhorn. He unsaddled, hobbled the horse, hid saddle and money belts, lashed some drift-logs together with his rope, tied his rifle to one of the logs, and with a pole to steer with, shoved off into the current. It carried the raft rapidly, but every once in a while eddies or treetops along the sides of the river slowed down the voyage.

After Jim had been on the river maybe two hours, the raft made a lunge against the inside bank of a sharp curve. Some of the crooked logs had already worked loose in the roping. As they hit the bank they twisted apart and, almost instantly, with his rifle gone on down the river, Jim was left holding to a root growing out of the bluff. He pulled himself up until he got his elbows on the ground and then swung free.

After his breathing became normal, he walked out for a view.

He thought he had never seen a more beautiful sweep of country than the land in and beyond that bend of the Nueces. While he watched some deer graze, they lifted their tails and bounded away and then he saw what had disturbed them — a man on horseback. He carried himself like a white man. Jim yelled and waved his hat. The man approached to within about two hundred yards and then, ready to shoot, waved for Jim to come to him.

He proved to be the owner of a ranch five or six miles away. He was looking for a horse that he suspected of having taken up with the mustangs. He would have impressed anybody as a man to be trusted. He carried Jim home with him, and there Jim ate and slept for two days. Lending him a horse and saddle, the rancher rode with him to recover his outfit and the ten thousand dollars in two money belts.

Jim Ray had no need to prospect farther. He had found the ideal location for a ranch. The rancher informed him that it was state land, subject to sale or homesteading. He bought horses, a wagon, lumber, provisions, tools and other necessities, hired Mexican help and built a house on the bluff. He bought landscript, then for sale cheap, and had several sections surveyed out from the riverbank. He had been gone from home nearly two years by the time he got stock branded and well located on the range.

Then he went back to Alabama to marry a girl supposed to be waiting for him. He had not written. She had not waited. He knew that a dun horse with a line down his back and two or three faithful Mexicans were waiting for him back on the Nueces. He returned to them and in time the Ray ranch, fenced in by barbed wire, became well known.

Desperate Rides

Long before Curtius the Roman jumped his horse into a deep chasm to appease the gods and save Rome — by sacrificing Rome's most precious possession, a brave citizen — tales of fearful leaps by desperate men were no doubt popular. They also belong to the Horse Age of America. According to an account that used to be repeated in talk and in print many times, in 1775 Major Samuel McCullough, hemmed in by four hundred Indian warriors near Fort Henry on the Ohio River, jumped his horse off a hundred-and-fifty-foot bluff overlooking Wheeler Creek. They say that his horse cleared the ground for seventy-five feet, hit a hump of loose rocks and dirt in the slightly inclined bank, slid, cleared the remaining seventy-five feet, struck deep water still upright, and swam with rider uninjured to safety.

Fifteen feet is a high dive for horse and rider. One day in 1832, Ad Lawrence and three other Texas frontiersmen rode out on the prairies west of the Trinity River to capture mustangs. Their method was to slip up on a bunch of wild horses and each man rope the best animal he could get in throwing distance of. The best mustangs usually got away, but many a good saddle horse in the settlements had been captured on the prairie.

On this particular day Ad Lawrence and his fellow mustangers rode picked mounts; Ad's was a black mare named Bess, a little ahead of anything else in the country for speed and bottom. About ten miles out they sighted a large bunch of horses afar off in grass up to their sides. The wind was in the mustangers' favor; the lay of the ground and the very tall grass enabled them to approach rather near without being discovered, so they thought. They estimated the number of horses to be a hundred, among them several fancy paints. As they rode closer, they were surprised that none of the horses took alarm and that they shifted about so little.

When a man looks intently for one thing he is often blind to other things. The mustangers were looking for loose horses. Suddenly a hundred painted Indians bounded out of the high grass, leaped onto their horses, and, coiling up their lariats on the run, came yelling for hair.

The surprised mustangers broke for the Trinity River, and for three miles held their distance. Then the Indian ponies began to show their mettle. "You've no idea," Ad Lawrence lived to tell, "how much an Indian can get out of a mustang pony. Instead of weighing their ponies down, those Indians after us seemed to push them along, and a body could have heard their yells clean to Red River."

Then the Indians split, half veering to the left and half to the right. They knew every deer trail and drainway in the country. The Texans learned something new in local geography when a deep and impassable ravine, unmarked by tree growth and hidden except from a near view, appeared in front of them. There was nothing to do but ride around the head of it — almost into one wing of the racing savages.

Ad Lawrence was in the lead. When he rounded the head of the gully, the Indians were so close that one whizzing arrow stuck in his buckskin jacket and another in his mare's neck. She did not run any slower.

"As soon as I got headed for the river again," Ad later told, "I looked around to see what had become of the others. One look showed me. They were all down. About half the Indians had stopped to finish them, and the balance were coming for me like red-hot lightning. I felt so dizzy for a minute that I dropped my rifle. Then I straightened up and told Bess I was still with her. I figured we could make it if we didn't run into another gulch. The Trinity timber looked about three miles off."

The mare had been running so hard that now she was panting for air. Ad jerked the arrow from her neck and worked out of his heavy buckskin coat, which was flopping about with the arrow in it, and threw it away. He ran a mile without gaining or losing on one Indian who had outdistanced all the others. Black Bess just had to have a little time to blow, though she would never quit until she was dead. Ad drew her to a stop, jumped down, loosened the cinch. The lead Indian was not more than a hundred yards away.

He was game all right. He didn't stop until he got within ten feet of the white man. Then he pulled his horse to its haunches, dropped his bow to the ground, and came on with a long knife. Ad was waiting for him with a Bowie knife in his right hand, the bridle reins in his left, for he was afraid the Indian might scare Bess into running off.

There was no time for a long fight. "The Indian seemed too sure," Ad said. "He ran just right for me to ram my knife into him and twist it around. He hardly made a movement after he fell. As I pulled off my heavy boots to lighten the load, I heard an awful howl. I tightened the girth, and we were flying for the timber. When we struck it the going slowed down.

"I knew that for miles up and down the river the banks were bluff, from fifteen to twenty feet high. Where I struck they were about fifteen. If Bess wouldn't take the jump, I was going without her. She stopped, snorted once, heard the yell close behind, and leaped straight out into air. She hit on her feet plump into deep water and we both went under. She came right up and went to swimming. I should have loosened the girth before we jumped in; maybe I did, automatically. I don't know. After she got about two-thirds across she gave a groan and sunk. I hated to leave her as bad as if she had been human."

While the Indians, unwilling to take the leap he had made, lined the bank behind him, Ad Lawrence reached the opposite one and crawled up a mustang grapevine to safety. It was too far across the river for arrows to make an effective hit. He had added another chapter to the riding tradition of mustang days.

About 1858 two men with their families, one named Booth and the other Gedrie, were neighboring on the Trinity River in east Texas. Each had a patch of corn fenced in with brush and pickets. One day some cattle belonging to Booth broke into Gedrie's corn and ate most of it up. In those days cattle were fenced out, not in. Gedrie saw the intruders and killed three. Booth protested, and Gedrie did with him as he had done with the cows.

Now, the dead settler had a boy, John, twelve years old. John shook his fist in the face of his father's slayer and said: "Gedrie, when I am big I will kill you for killing my pap."

Then the widow Booth moved three hundred miles west to

the Nueces River — "the deadline of sheriffs," as it used to be called. The Civil War came on and John enlisted. When the Confederates stopped fighting, he was nineteen years old and had been a man for four years.

He returned to the Nueces and made open boasts that he was now "big enough" to kill Gedrie. He made the boasts so that they would reach Gedrie and keep him uneasy with the vigilance of the hunted. When fall brought cool weather, he quietly arranged a string of horses so as to have one every thirty or forty miles between the Nueces and the Trinity. It was his private pony express. He had friends.

One evening he rode up to the house of a neighboring ranchman. After supper he asked the rancher the date of the month, the day of the week, and even the hour by the clock. In out-of-the-way places such questions were not unusual.

"Would you swear in court that I was at your ranch on the date and at the hour you have given me?" asked Booth.

"Of course I would," replied the rancher.

"Then write the time of my visit down in the Bible."

The great family Bible was brought out, and on one of those pages provided for vital statistics the facts were slowly written, the witnesses signing their names. It was the twentieth of October, seven o'clock (sun time), 1865.

John Booth said good night, mounted his horse, and was lost in the darkness.

According to evidence later brought out, when Gedrie on the morning of October 22 started to ride away from his cabin in the Trinity valley, his wife came running out with a shotgun in her hand.

"Here," she called, "you are getting too careless. You know that John Booth is going to try to kill you sooner or later."

"Oh," carelessly replied Gedrie, "I've had so many messages

from him that I'm getting to believe he's nothing but bluff. Besides," he added, slapping his hip, "this here old hogleg knows how to talk back."

Nevertheless, he took the shotgun and rode off. Twenty-four hours later a riderless horse hung his head against the gate opening into the Gedrie pens. As in the old Scottish ballad,

> Hame cam' the saddle, all bluidy to see,
> O hame cam' his guid horse, but never cam' he

It was about an hour by sun on the morning of October twenty-fifth when John Booth walked his horse up to the ranch where his last visit had been recorded in the family Bible. Right under the record was added, at his request, the hour of his return.

Some weeks passed, and then one day rangers appeared at the Booth ranch with a warrant of arrest for John. He peaceably submitted. In the session of district court that followed he was charged with having killed Gedrie. A jury was impaneled to try him; witnesses were summoned. The state proved that John Booth had threatened to kill Gedrie; it proved that Gedrie had been killed. The defense proved that John Booth had been on the Nueces three hundred miles away two days before Gedrie met his death, and that he had again been seen on the Nueces less than three days later.

The alibi was incontrovertible. The jury, to a man, said that no human being could have ridden three hundred miles, killed a man, and then have ridden back three hundred miles in the four days and five nights that Booth had not accounted for. Booth was freed, and many times afterward he told, not without pride, of the wonderful ride and the vengeance he had done. The law is that after a man has been tried in the courts and declared innocent he cannot be tried again for the same offense.

It may be added as a postscript that the feud was ended years afterward when Gedrie's two sons shot John Booth's son, Robert, from a horse. But Robert proved true to his blood when he raised himself up from the ground on which he was dying and killed both his opponents.

Childless and penniless, John Booth died long ago in the Home for Confederate Soldiers at Austin. The ride he made and not the killings have kept his story alive.

The Planter Who Gambled Away His Bride

LUDWIG Baron von Roeder of Prussia and his wife had nine sons, all over six feet tall — and all restless under military tyranny. In 1832 Sigismund, the wild one of the breed, fought a duel at the University of Breslau with the Prince of Prussia and killed him.

The fact that the duel was fair prevented the king from putting Sigismund to death but not from sentencing him to life imprisonment. After he had been in prison about a year, his father went to the king for audience.

"What do you want?" the king glared.

"You know what I want," the baron replied.

"No," the king bellowed, "I will not."

"Is there no condition at all?" the baron asked.

"Yes, one condition only. I will release your son if you and all your family will leave Germany forever."

"How much time will you give us to leave?"

"One year."

The baron began at once to sell off his lands and other properties, keeping a few of his best hogs, chickens, horses, and cattle to take to the new home. Mexico was at this time offering hospitality to foreigners, and the baron set his compass for Texas, then a part of Mexico. Several other Prussian families joined the von Roeders in preparation for emigrating. They chartered an English ship, and as the end of the year approached, loaded it with livestock, household gear, carts, buggies, tools, farm implements, clothing, food for a long voyage, plows and whisky stills. The day before they were to sail, a prison guard escorted Sigismund von Roeder to the ship.

It was headed for the mouth of the Brazos River, but a Gulf hurricane drove it to Galveston Island. There the first child of the colony was born. The Baroness von Roeder was troubled with insomnia, and she had her piano landed so that she could play it at night and keep others from sleeping. People danced to its music. In his capital at San Felipe de Austin on the Brazos, Stephen F. Austin heard of these Germans stranded on Galveston Island. He sent an agent offering them lands out of his wide grant. They investigated, saw the fertile soil and the great abundance of game, and brought their ship and its holdings to the mouth of the Brazos for unloading. They settled around Industry.

Frontier conditions were not conducive to making Sigismund von Roeder tamer. He learned to substitute Bowie knife for sword, but still wore his rapier. He rode and hunted with young men who slept with their guns and relied on them to enforce their democratic ideas. Some were hard gamblers, more were hard drinkers.

One morning about a dozen of the Sigismund von Roeder crowd assembled for a celebration at the plantation home of Benjamin Buckingham on the Brazos. It was not a mansion but was more ample than most of the log houses. The owner had just returned from Kentucky with a bride. She was beautiful and she was rare in that world of young men. They were making festival to honor her, but after the hard corn whisky began to flow free and she saw that an especial amount of it was flowing into her husband, she withdrew from the crowd. Soon the celebrants turned to cards. Benjamin Buckingham was foremost in turning a social game into one for stakes.

The stakes began low. As they rose, all players but Buckingham and von Roeder dropped out. Von Roeder was doing most of the winning. He proposed a limit to the bets, but Buckingham, growing more reckless with each deal, called for the sky. After he had lost all his money, he began betting his mules, horses, oxen, then his slaves. Every time he lost a unit of these chattels, he made out a bill of sale. His opponent stacked the bills of sale under a red brick made from valley earth.

At noon the onlookers ate beef and wild turkey, corn pones and greens, cooked by a slavewoman in the log kitchen out in the yard to the rear of the main house. The only pause made by the gamblers was for another drink. Paper slips representing buggy, wagon, plows, harness, race horses, saddles and other personal property piled up under the red brick. Buckingham's friends begged him to stop.

"I will not stop," he shouted in frenzy. "Luck will change directly. You will see."

"I'll quit when Buckingham says quit," von Roeder said. As winner, according to the code, he was honor-bound to keep on playing, giving the loser a chance to win back until the loser cried a halt.

The shadows outside were long when Buckingham began to put up the deeds to his lands. Against the tract on which the house stood, von Roeder staked everything under the red brick. He won.

There was a pause and a bitter oath from Buckingham. In the fading light a white-haired Negro brought in candles, set them on the table, went out, brought in a blazing pine knot and lit them. Every eye was on von Roeder, but nobody was saying a word.

As the old slave withdrew, the bride entered and placed her hand on her husband's arm.

"Come, Benjamin," she said. "It is time to quit. You are tired out."

"And that ain't all," said one brazen young man.

"You mean I am broke?" Buckingham yelled.

While his bride waited in a silence intensified by every man present, he strode to a cabinet. He took a paper out of a drawer, walked back to the table, and laid it down between the candles.

"That," he said, "will cover everything under your brick."

Von Roeder spread the paper out. It was Buckingham's marriage license.

"Only with the lady's consent," he said.

Maybe there was bitterness in her smile, but it was a smile of assent.

Once more the cards were shuffled, dealt, played. It was a quick game. As von Roeder reached for this last document to add to the papers under the red brick, Buckingham reached for one of the pistols he wore and fired. He missed. As he raised the second pistol in his brace, von Roeder's sword pierced his heart.

It happened that an alcalde lived near. All agreed that nothing would be touched, which is still the legal practice in Mexico, until his arrival. That was within a short time.

The alcalde ruled that the killing was in self-defense. As the body of the dead man was borne out on a plank, the alcalde's voice rang in question:

"Do you, Barbara Buckingham, take this man, Sigismund von Roeder?"

In those days marriages in Texas were often made by contract. Von Roeder sold the plantation he had won and took the woman he had won and moved west. Descendants of the two are numerous in southwest Texas today.

Part Four

The Panther's Scream

A HUNDRED years ago and more, a settler on the Trinity River cut down a bee tree. Its crash to the ground broke the silence of the forest. Immediately a high scream from a panther in the distance responded, and out of mockery the man screamed back. The panther replied, nearer now. The man quit mocking to listen, but a panther's movements, even on the forest's leafy floor, make no sound. The man had no idea that the panther was so near until he saw it spring upon the stump of the felled tree.

He raised his axe to strike, but the leaping panther was already upon him. It bit him through a shoulder and clawed into his body and legs. He jerked his Bowie knife from its sheath and stabbed until the attacker retreated. He himself received no deep cuts, but his clothes were in shreds and he did not linger to rob the bees. The next day he came back for the honey and found the panther dead not far away. He announced his resolution never to mock another panther unless he had a gun along.

When I was a boy, I heard stories of ghosts and phantom riders, but no tale of the spirit world ever shivered my timbers like accounts of the panther's scream and its readiness to leap upon a man carrying meat, upon a woman entering a shed room into which the big cat had stolen to devour a fresh deer ham, or upon a child in the dark to eat it up. Nobody then called the panther a "mountain lion," as it is now called.

The favorite story was of a neighboring ranchman who located a turkey roost in the Nueces River bottom and rode out one evening to kill the turkeys. It happened that he had only two loads for his shotgun. He tied his horse at a barbed-wire fence, through which there was no convenient gap, and walked on about half a mile and hid himself near the roost. About dusk he saw and heard the wild turkeys fly up into a clump of live-oak trees. They took their time and it was dark before they were all settled. He waited for the moon to come up so that he could skylight the big birds blended into the foliage. He maneuvered around until he had several lined up and then fired both barrels. Six turkeys fell to the ground.

He was carrying them back to his horse, making slow progress on account of the weight, when the scream of a panther right behind him in the brush curdled his blood — a scream always described as more terrifying than the scream of a woman in fright or pain. The man knew what the panther was after; he dropped a turkey. He had gone but a short distance farther before he heard the awful scream again. He dropped another turkey. The next time the squall came from brush to one side of him. Finally he had only one turkey left to drop. If the panther leaped out of the shadows, the man's gun, even as a club, would be of little avail. And now the scream came nearer, more terrifying. He dropped his last turkey. Just as he got to his horse, which was plunging against the rope, the man heard the panther again. But, thank God, he was mounted, "tearing a hole in the brush."

After hearing this story — and it seemed never to be told except at night — I used to lie awake in bed for hours wondering what would have happened to the man had he killed only four or five turkeys to dole out to the panther instead of six, or if he had had a whole mile to walk instead of just about half a

mile. But above any concern for human destiny the panther's scream dominated my childish imagination. Years later when I read Blake's verses —

> Tiger, tiger, burning bright
> In the forests of the night, . . .
> In what distant deeps or skies
> Burnt the fire of thine eyes?

— I wished that some poet of the panther world would intensify the panther's scream as Blake in "England's green and pleasant land" had intensified the tiger's eyes. To this day I never look at a panther mounted in a museum without thinking what a lack it is that the scream — the very essence of the creature — cannot be mounted also.

Perhaps it would be, if the processes of petrifaction could be extended. Telling of the wonderful Petrified Forest of Arizona, Jim Bridger used to say, "Yes, them putrified trees stand up natural like any other trees. They are simply monstrous. You can ride all day and not get acrost the forest. And all up in the limbs there's putrified birds, some of 'em blue and some of 'em red and all other kinds of colors. And them putrified birds is act'ally singing putrified songs."

At the time I heard and reheard the story of the man's dropping his turkeys to placate a screaming panther, I did not know that it was "just an old yarn" — a folk tale. I still don't know but what it started with an actual experience that was appropriated as their own by tellers, in the way that a ballad is carried far away in time and space from its originator. It has been told for generations in many localities, pieces of venison or other game sometimes substituted for the dropped turkeys. Many of the narrators have no doubt believed their own narrations, and I can't help believing some of them myself.

"Late one evening in 1888," a pioneer of Hall County related — after years of recollecting emotion in tranquillity — "I took my gun and walked down into the Salt Creek breaks to kill a turkey. It was after dark when I shot four nice fellows out of their roost and started home. They were about all I could carry. Pretty soon something was following me, and when it let out a scream I knew it was a panther. It kept getting a little closer. I dropped one of my turkeys and walked a little faster. Before long it was following me again and let out another scream that seemed closer by than the first one. I dropped another turkey and walked still faster. I think there were several panthers. It was intensely dark and they kept following and screaming until I gave them the last turkey. By that time I was out of the breaks on open ground and almost home. My brother and I went to hunting them and that winter killed nine panthers."

Jim Buckner lived in one of the lovely little valleys among the wooded hills of Hamilton County. One day, as he used to tell his grandchildren, he drove his wagon to a neighbor's to help butcher a beef. It was dark before he started home with half the carcass. The weather was cool and the horses stepped along briskly, eager for feed and freedom. About nine o'clock, while still two miles from home, Jim Buckner happened to look back. There, coming along behind him in the starlit road, was an animal that at first he took to be a dog but that, getting closer, was plainly a panther. It was, he judged, following the fresh meat, and in a minute he saw from its actions that unless he did something it would jump up into the wagon. He took his butcher knife and cut off a hunk of beef and threw it back. He saw the panther stop to eat it. Then he cracked his black-snake and the horses broke into a lope.

A wagon behind galloping horses makes nearly as much noise to its occupant as a passing freight train. Jim Buckner didn't hear anything else, but when he looked back, he saw the pan-ther in a springing run right behind him. He cut off another hunk of meat, a big one, and threw it out. The panther stopped. It must have been an awful swift eater, for it soon caught up — to be detained by a third chunk of beef. The meat held out, and when the wagon drew up at the Buckner house the panther was not in sight.

If a panther's scream could chill the blood, the deathly si-lent approach of one in the dark until it got close enough to touch would freeze the marrow. Jeff Ake's people were with Old

Hickory in Tennessee but moved to Arkansas before he was born. He came on to Texas and drove cattle up the Chisholm Trail and all the other trails and then went out into the Apache country. He could charm the heart out of a whippoorwill with his fiddle, and his grandchildren thought he was the greatest story-teller on earth. This was their favorite.

"I was up on the Flower de Lucy that time, staying at a ranch shanty alone. The Indians was pretty bad, and nobody knowed when they might jump us. One evening late when I come in from riding all day, I saw that Charley Merritt and Bob Burch had left me the backstrap out of a deer and some bear steaks. They kept bach, down the country a ways, and had been on a little hunt. The meat was hung up high. You had to hang up everything to eat in them days; coyotes would steal the spurs out from under your head to chew on the leathers.

"Well, when I unsaddled that evening I throwed my saddle down on the floor next to the door. There wasn't no yard fence to this place. Then I et about three pounds of fried venison and hit the hay. Like always, I had my six-shooter under the piller. In no time I was snoring hee-haw, like that.

"I don't know how long afterwards it was, but I woke up in the pitch-dark feeling like something was wrong. It wasn't near time to get up, but I was wide awake. Then something touched me down the leg, like a hand jest feeling, soft — that way. 'Indians,' I thinks, and lays as still as a log. D'reckly there was the same soft touch higher up my leg. I was inching my hands up to my chest so that if the Indian grabbed for my throat I could grab his. It seemed he didn't know my geography any better than I knew his. Next the touch was on my stomach, and it sorter pressed down like he was a-leaning over to get a look into my face.

" 'Well, by gravy,' I thinks to myself, 'I ain't going to the

Happy Hunting Grounds by myself.' Then I makes one big grab for his throat and collars him. I whips him over on the bed alongside me, twisting out of the covers and trying to get them wropped around him. He's half under me and I throws my legs so's to hold his down. About then I discover the Indian has turned into a panther.

"He's clawing like a mowing machine, but them bed quilts is a shield of mercy. What I'm afeared of is his teeth. I manage to clamp his muzzle shut with one hand and get a good holt on a foreleg with the other. I am shoving him up and back and purty soon have him over by the saddle. I kinder wrop my legs around his hips so he ain't got no room to claw in and tie his muzzle up with the horn string. Then I get a buckskin thong out of a saddle pocket and half-hitch his forelegs together. He is still scratching me with his hind paws, but it's easy now to tie them up with saddle strings. I light the lantern and drag saddle, panther and all into a shed room and chain him up, and then go back to sleep.

"The next morning the owner of the Flower de Lucy come along and when I told him about the panther he wanted to see it. I told him he'd better go easy, but he was the kind of man who had to have his way, and shore enough he got a little too close and that panther took a mouthful out of his thigh. He started to kill him, but I told him this was my panther and he had to let him be. 'I'll give you fifty dollars to let me drill daylight into his insides,' he says. 'All right,' I says, and he handed over the fifty. He pulled his six-shooter and shot the panther dead. I don't know what I would have done with him if he hadn't. He wasn't no pet size."

What really made a panther hungry was the smell of a baby. Some people claimed a panther could locate a baby by scenting

milk from its mother's breast. They claimed that whereas
panther would skulk away from the sound of a man's voice,
would be attracted closer by the voice of a girl or woman. On
woman said that when she was a little girl her father woul
take her riding through the woods behind him on a horse. H
had his gun loaded and ready and would keep her singing so a
to entice panthers into view for a shot.

In 1875 Sam Shaffer and his bride "Queenie" came fror
Mississippi and settled on the Leon River. When she was a
old woman, she delighted her grandchildren with stories c
early days. The ones they called for over and over were abou
her experiences with panthers, and this is the way she tol
them.

"When our first baby was five months old, Sam said we ha
to go to Fort Worth, about ninety miles away, for supplies
He had made sideboards for our ox wagon, and we planned t
bring back some furniture as well as cloth and food. Nothin
much happened on the way, and it was the best time I'd eve
had, seeing the people and stores and all. I never dreamed Sam
had so much money. He bought me everything I admired —
trunk, a spinning wheel, a sewing machine and many a yard o
pretty cloth. Then we started home.

"We were on the last lap of the journey and it was beginnin
to get dark. Sam happened to look back and saw what he too
to be a man with a white shirt on a-galloping towards us. Th
baby had the colic and started to cry. As the galloping thin
got closer, Sam said, 'That's no man. It's the biggest panther
ever saw.' The panther had heard the baby and smelled us, and
musta been awful hungry, for he loped right close up to the
wagon. Sam stood up and cracked his whip and let out a holle
that would curdle your blood, and the panther stopped and
trotted off a ways and sat on his haunches. Then he got out o

sight a little off to one side and let out a scream that froze my blood. D'reckly he was back in the road.

"Well, this went on till we could hardly stand the strain, and the baby kept crying, and it got darker and darker. Finally, Sam said, 'Queenie, you'd better put the baby in the trunk.' I knowed then that he expected the hungry panther to leap up on the wagon, and I reckon he thought we'd better smother the baby to death than see it torn apart by the panther. I did like he said, and stuffed my Sunday hat under a corner of the trunk lid so as to let in a little air, and sat there near dead from fright. Sam kept up his whip-cracking and yelling till our cabin came in sight. Never before or after did it look so good to me.

"A cousin of mine, a big strapping backwoodsman, had come to Texas and soon afterwards married the oldest Willerts girl, Sary. She was the best friend I had. They took up a section of land close to ours, and I could cut across the woods and not have to walk over three miles to their house. Sam often told me I mustn't do this, but I loved to take baby on pretty, sunshiny days and walk over to Sary's. One day Sary was preserving, and I stayed late helping her, and before I got well started home the sun was down nearly to the treetops. I was hurrying along when something made me look back, and why I didn't just drop dead, I don't know. A big yellow panther was walking right after me. I started to run, and the panther ran too. When I slowed down, he would slow down, but still gain on me. It was getting darker and darker, and I was getting scareder and scareder. I seemed numb all over, but somehow I kept on running. The panther gained on me and I knew any minute he'd grab baby away.

"I snatched off baby's cap and dropped it, and the panther stopped to smell it. I gained a little. Then one by one I snatched off more clothes, mine and baby's both, whatever was handiest, and dropped them as I ran. Well, I made the cabin door and fell inside and managed to push the door shut. Thank Heavens, Sam wasn't there, and I come to enough to dress ourselves and start supper before he got in. He didn't need to ever warn me again to take my saddle pony and go around by the open pasture when I wanted to visit Sary."

Another woman of the frontier was ironing clothes one afternoon, having washed that morning. She had the ironing board in the kitchen, the door of which was open and, of course, screenless. After nursing her two-months-old baby, she laid it down on a pallet near the door, to her back. Presently, the smoothing iron in her hand, she looked around at the baby. A panther, as noiseless as an owl in flight, had grabbed it. She hit the panther's head with the iron, knocked it flat, and then pounded it until it was dead. Not long after that she killed two Indians attacking her house and the neighbors presented her with two fine six-shooters.

A camp meeting, always held in the summer, with babies on pallets around the edges of a brush arbor in the dim lantern light of the evening services, might have attracted all the panthers in the country if so much noise hadn't been going on. Noise or no noise, at a camp meeting on Wild Cat Slough one summer, a "painter" climbed up a tree and hid out on a branch unbeknownst to anybody until the people all knelt down to pray. Then it snatched up a baby and ran off with it. Nobody ever caught it or found a sign of the baby.

One hot summer while Ben Coates and his wife and a two-year-old baby were sleeping in front of the open door to their one-room cabin, she was awakened by feeling her baby move "as if it were falling off the bed." It was gone before she could rescue it, but in the dim light she saw something run out into the yard. She and her husband heard the baby screaming as it was carried deeper into the woods. The whole neighborhood was alarmed. Dogs took the trail and the next morning had the panther bayed in a narrow hole running up under a great rock. A man could not enter without crawling; dogs could enter only one at a time, and any dog that reached the panther was sure to get killed. The men decided to besiege the hole day and night until starvation or thirst drove the panther out. They stood guard in relays. More than two hundred people gathered, some from fifty miles away. On the fourth day, the animal jumped out and was shot. Fragments of a baby's dress were found in the cave.

What happened between one person and a panther, if it was narrowing enough, was bound to be experienced by another person in another part of the panther-haunted country, which covered the South. The Ozarks probably mothered more panther stories than any other region. Some of the best are in Wayman Hogue's *Back Yonder*.

"Right after Jim was born," he relates, "my father left home one morning to be gone till the next day. Jim was only five days old and my mother was still in bed. Lelia was six and was doing whatever had to be done. Nora was two. I didn't yet exist. My father took the gun with him, but left Tige, a very large and strong dog.

"Along after midnight Tige began barking and growling as if somebody or something were approaching. In no time the sounds he made told my mother the thing was close. Then there was fighting. My mother thought it was a wolf, and she had confidence in Tige's ability to defend the premises. Before long the intruder seemed to have left, for Tige quieted down but soon he was again in desperate struggle with something. My mother grew alarmed and had Lelia latch the door and prop it

"After fighting for a while, the thing seemed to have retreated once more, but Tige was not quiet for long. Now th struggle was more desperate than ever. Just as it quieted, my mother heard something light on top of the house. It could get there, she knew, only by climbing a tree and leaping off Wolves can't climb.

"She lay listening to the thing as it walked over the roof seemingly in search of an opening. Suddenly, pieces of the clay chimney began falling into the fireplace. It had a little fire The creature was actually coming down the chimney. My mother leaped out of bed, grabbed a case knife, ripped open straw mattress, and began piling the straw into the fireplace The straw caught fire and the blaze shot up the chimney. The thing gave a fearful squall, and she heard it spring from the roof to the ground. They smelt scorched hair. When my father returned, he said it was a panther after the baby. He located Tige away back under the house, hardly able to move."

Grandma Adams used to tell the Texas version of this story About dark one winter day, she heard a scream "like a woman in distress makes." She had little more than barred window and door before she heard the panther walking on the roof. To prevent its coming down the chimney she kept the fireplace burning. She ran out of wood and burned up two chairs, a quilt, an old dress, and some other things. The panther kept padding around on the shakes all night, now and then letting out a long wail. Just before daylight it left.

One winter day the White family on Bear Creek in Sabine County killed a hog, cut it up, put the meat in a wooden tub

nd set it in a corner of the cabin, to be salted down and
moked on the morrow. Then the man went off with his dogs
ɔ join a neighbor on a hunt. That night while Mrs. White was
hunking up the fire in the fireplace, the children covered up in
ed and a quilt wrapped around herself to shut out the cold
orther blowing through the chinks in the log walls, she heard
 panther scream. She knew it had smelled the fresh meat. It
rowled under the puncheon floor and then leaped up on the
ɔof, every once in a while letting out a scream. Then it went
ɔ clawing on the logs and finally got a paw through a crack
ear the tub of meat and took out a piece. At this, Mrs. White
hrew her quilt over the tub, seized an axe standing just inside
he door and waited. In a little while the panther put its paw
ack through the crack for another piece of meat. She had the
xe raised and now she came down with it, cutting the paw
lean off. That panther did not bother around the cabin any
ore that night.

It is the habit of the panther to gnaw into the vitals of its
rey and, after eating what it wants, to cover the carcass with
aves, grass, twigs — any dry covering at hand. It will come
ack for a meal when hungry. It is not a carrion eater, but likes
ɔ kill its own meat and likes it fresh.

Mrs. Ada Payne's grandfather died in 1898 at the age of
inety. She was only twelve, but she'll never forget his tale of
wo panthers he met as a sixteen-year-old boy. He was clearing
nd for a field, chopping down trees. At noon after he had
aten his lunch he lay down for a nap in a pile of leaves along-
de a big fallen tree. He had been asleep a little while when
e was awakened by warm breath on his face and a queer smell.
Instinct told him not to move or make a sound. He cau-

tiously half opened his eyes and saw two full grown panthers standing over him. After sniffing at him a few times, the larger of the two partly pulled him over with a paw and let him roll back into his original position. Then they washed their faces, in the manner of house cats, and sniffed him over again. All this time he had not moved a muscle.

Now the panthers turned their backs to him and with their hind paws began raking leaves and twigs over him. They covered him up completely from head to foot. He could barely see through the leaves over his face. They stood and sniffed around awhile, seeming to inspect their job, he said. Finally they left.

He gave them plenty of time to get away before he raised up cautiously for a look all around. He was sure they would return and he took out for home to get his rifle. His idea was to hide in a tree nearby and shoot them when they came back. In order to make them less cautious, he brought back an old shirt and a pair of trousers similar to what he wore, fitted them on sticks arranged in the form of a man, and covered up this dummy with the same leaves that had covered him. Then he hid.

Before sundown the panthers returned and were pawing the leaves away when he shot. He killed the big panther, but only wounded the other, which got away.

I guess it was better to be covered up alive by a panther than to be covered up dead. Otherwise, the man covered up couldn't make a story out of what happened.

There are stories of friendly panthers, too, but they belong mainly to the Spanish-Americans. W. H. Hudson's richly storied chapter on "The Puma," in *The Naturalist in La Plata*, discovered them to me, and I put the most remarkable one I have heard in *Tongues of the Monte*.

Bears Are Intelligent People

THE black bear favors pork beyond all other meats. For this reason the ideal hog of the South used to be the razorback. It could "outfight a bear and outrun a nigger."

In the Big Thicket country of east Texas, where, despite high lines, deep oil wells and wide clearings, a few bears still sniff for razorback "nests," an old colored camp cook named Kinley McCullock is remembered for his bear steaks and bear stories.

He never ate bear meat himself — but once. Then "it didn't taste lak no meat a-tall." The flesh of an animal that walks and thinks like a man couldn't be expected to taste like regular meat, could it?

"It war a long time ago," old Kinley used to tell. "Mister Cockrum he wus my boss man. Hav war still a-sucking, I member. We named him William McKinley Havana, but every body called him Hav, lak they still does. Bud wus old ernough ter tote in wood fer the fireplace. One mawning airly I wus out a-milking when I heared some old mockingbirds jist a-cussing and a-stewing. I knowed right away an uppity squirrel wus aggervating 'em. I thinks a little fried squirrel would package up mighty neat inside me fer breakfast. So I calls to Bud to bring the gun. He brung it and comes along with me.

"But Mister Squirrel musta got word I wus coming. Anyhow, he warn't thar and the mockingbirds quit saying whar he

wus. I goes on, down the aige of Mister Cockrum's cawnfiel'
looking up inter the trees along the fence. I got squirrel meat
on my min'. The roas'en years is shore fine that summer, and
we been a-playing 'Green Cawn' for dinner every day without
any banjo.

"Well, here me and Bud wus way down the fence peering up
inter the trees to the righthand side and a-listening fer Mister
Squirrel ter scratch the bark, when I heard somebody over in
the tall cawn. I knowed 'twarn't Mister Cockrum out in the
wet dew, and I knowed he wouldn't be sending enybody over
ter this fiel' anyhow. I kin hear whoever 'tis breaking the roas'en
years off, and sounds ter me lak he's mighty careless tromping
over the stalks. I says ter Bud, 'Cawn thief shore brung erlong
plenty o' brass.'

"We steps back inter some bloodweeds growing aginst the
fence and waits, jist ez quiet ez a hoptoad waiting fer a fly. The
cawn is still a-popping. Then d'reckly I catches sigh uv the
thief. He's wearing black, but I don't have no idees 'bout our
preacher. He's got a cawn patch uv his own. Now this gentleman is coming right down 'tween two rows, kinder spraddling
in his walk. His arms is full uv roas'en years, and then the first
good light uv mawning hits him and I sees it's a b'ar. Jist as I
seed this, he stops and stacks all the cawn in one arm, lak it
wus stovewood. Then he reaches down with the other hand and
picks up a big yaller punkin fum a vine. He takes hit under his
arm. Now he's all loaded up and ready to make tracks. I thought
at first he wus going to walk right over us, but he sorter takes
out to one side, and Bud and me jist stands. I'se telling my
eyes not to click too loud. That thief he steps over the picket
fence lak it wus the golden stairs. Befo' the Good Lawd, I never
seen no plain woods b'ar toting off cawn and punkins lak that.

"After he shuffled inter the thicket, I says ter Bud, We'll

kinder track him. . . . So we snuck along behind, he being so keerless he never looks back oncet. Purty soon he come to a big holler stump 'bout six foot eround and high ez my shoulder. I seen he wus a-going ter stop and so got behin' a big gum tree with huckleberry bushes growing all eround it. Shore nuf, he stands still by the stump, listening and looking about in ev-ery direction, 'specially down the way he's come fum. He seems ter suspicion somebody's spying on his doin's. He's ez smart ez any cawncrib thief that ever tuk off his shoes. D'reckly he 'pears to be satisfied.

"Then he pitches that load er roas'en years over the aige of the holler stump inside. Then he th'ows the punkin down so it's boun' ter bust. He looks over inside the holler a good while, lak he's watching sumpin'. Fin'ly he leaves, going inter thick timber.

"When he's good and gone, Bud and me snuck up ter the holler stump and scramble round ter get a good look inside. What yer reckon we see? Jist an ole narrow-face hawg with a crop in one year and a swallerfork in the other! That's Mister Cockrum's mark. There's mighty little meat on the hawg, but he's goin' to have meat on him if Mister B'ar keeps providing fer him and he keeps on wrapping hisself roun' cawn and punkin lak he's doing now. His jaws is champing ez happy ez a banjo talking to 'Little Brown Jug.'

"B'ars don't fancy lean pork, you know. No, sah, they's choosy. This one's going ter have pork that'll make cracklin's. I guess he stole that shoat fum Mister Cockrum's pen in the dark and maybe couldn't pick very choosy. We go over and tell Mister Cockrum, and he jist laugh lak he thinks I'm tryin' to 'splain away some shoat in my pen. No, sah, he don't wanter come and see what kind uv a hawgpen a b'ar uses. But after a while he consent, and when he see that hawg in his own mark and the cawncobs and punkin stems and b'ar sign and all, he scratch his haid. Then he taken the hawg out and turn him loose to rustle fer hisself till the fall mast will fix him up fer bacon. But I made a mistake when I didn't go back next mawning to see how Mister B'ar look when he come with another load uv cawn and find his hawg ain't nowhar."

As my philosophic old friend on the border, Don Alberto Guajardo, used to say, "Bears are very intelligent people." There was the bear that burned his hand on a pot of meat boiling on a cabin fireplace; he took down a bottle of liniment from the mantelpiece and doctored himself. There was the bear that walked into a country schoolhouse at recess, removed the lids from all the lunch buckets, and ate nothing but the pie and other desserts. One night a woman sleeping with her baby in a cabin that had only a quilt for a door saw a bear pull it back and walk in. She needn't have been afraid. All the bear did was step over to the fireplace, where a fire was still making light, and sniff at a pot of beans on the hearth. He must have liked the smell. The beans were warm but not hot. The woman watched him paw off the lid and gobble down all the beans and bacon. Then he walked to the door, wiped his face on the quilt, and left without even saying thank you.

David Crockett had a pet bear that would sit over on the other side of the fireplace from him and smoke a pipe just like Crockett until bedtime. He finally got so civilized that he took whooping cough and died from it. Crockett never did forgive the preacher for refusing to give that bear a Christian funeral.

An elevation in Grayson County, south of Red River, known as Bear Mound, marks the place where a long time ago Billie Clemens shot a black bear standing up and showing a white spot on his breast. The bear had his arms stretched out, facing the man. The bullet went into the white spot, and the bear threw up his arms and moaned, "Oh, Lawdy, oh, Lawdy."

If a wound was not fatal, a bear might gather up grass and stuff it into the bullet hole to stop the bleeding. At least, that is what some hunters told.

Jim Ingram was born in the piney woods on Sulphur River, not far from where Mr. Fishback used to live. He was raised on bear-lard biscuits and bear bacon, and was twelve years old, they say, before he tasted his first hog-ham gravy. When he grew bald, he greased his scalp with bear oil to bring back the hair. He never would admit that rattlesnake oil is as good for rheumatism as bear oil. He hunted mostly in a great tangle of brush, vines, fallen trees and soaring timber known as Hurricane Rake. He always hunted alone and he had no use for a dog, because a dog couldn't get through the kind of places he crawled into. He would ride to the edge of Hurricane Rake, tie his horse, take his gun, a strong rope to string the bear carcass up with, and a gunny sack to put the fat into, and strike out looking for sign.

When Jim Ingram discovered the enormous cypress stump, fully twelve feet high, that came to be called "Ingram's Snag," he was in a tangle of sweet gum and other growth almost against it. A scratching he heard told him the stump was hollow. He looked up and saw a big bear emerging from it. Two cubs, apparently intent on following her, stuck their heads up, but the old bear turned and gave each a slap that sent them back down. Then while Jim Ingram was trying to find an opening for his gun and a shot, the old she made off upwind, disappearing in the jungle.

Ingram felt sure that she had gone on a hunt for food. His best chance for bear grease, he decided, was to wait for her return. While he waited and waited, he got to thinking how much fun his five small children, not to mention the older ones, would have with those two cubs as pets. He knew as well as anybody that the timidest kind of bear would fight like a circular saw for her cubs, but as he waited some more, he decided that the mother of these cubs had gone off on a long hunt and that he could capture them and get away before she returned. His plan was to rope one of the snags along the rim of the hollow stump, pull up to it, let himself down inside by the same rope, put the cubs in his gunny sack, climb out and get gone.

He leaned his gun against the cypress, roped a snag, and a few minutes later was down inside a hollow ample enough to camp in. Leaving the rope dangling, he located the cubs by their whining and snarling away back in the darkness of a hollow root. While he paused to figure how he might get hold of them without making a trip up for a stick to twist them out with, he heard an echoing scratching noise against the hollow wood. He looked up.

There old Susie was, all four feet bunched on the rim, balanced like a hen on a limb, peering earnestly down into the shadowed hollow. She did not appear to find fault with the musky smell of bear and damp decayed wood that emanated from her home.

"No," Jim Ingram later reported, "there wa'n't nary a twitch to her nose. I was jest hunkered there, my mouth opened about as wide as the gunny sack I had ready for the cubs. I guess my eyes were bugged out like a pair of purple grapes on a mustang vine. I don't remember ever staring so hard in my life at anything else as at that bear. I didn't have no right to be supprised, but I was. The bear was supprised too, but she was still madder. She was the maddest bear I ever see, and I've saw many a mad bear. There she squatted and there I squatted, and I couldn't have moved a finger. Then she started down."

Bears don't climb down trees headfirst, like squirrels. Old Susie had to reverse ends to start down. The posture placed her head outside the hollow so that she could not possibly see what was going on beneath her descending rump. Not at all slowly, the rump began wabbling downward, claws feeling for holds.

And now the spell that held Jim fixed was broken. "God-a'mighty!" he yelled. "Git out o' here!"

The yell rumbled and echoed in the deep hollow. The bear was more than startled. She obeyed directions with great alacrity, hauling her body out. Then, balancing all four feet on the rim, she again peered down.

Jim was on his feet now, one hand grasping the rope. He gave it a flap against the bear's nose. She put out a hand, swept the loop from the splinter that Jim had roped, and let it fall at his feet.

Again she reversed ends and began her rearward descent. Again Jim gave his war whoop. He'd been saving his energy most of his life, and now he threw it all into his voice. The bear scrambled out again, and then started down again. Jim was plumb prodigal with his vocal productions. Six times in all the bear retreated before the sounds that Jim sent up. The seventh time she started down she kept coming. Jim hadn't begun to lose his voice; the bear was merely getting used to it. Jim had his knife out, but there was a mighty poor prospect of digging it into a vital spot.

"There wa'n't but one thing fer me to do," Jim afterwards told, "and I done it. When she backed in good reach, I grabbed her by the tail with one hand and give her a good knife-spurring with the other. At the same time, I yelled like nobody ain't never yelled before nor since.

"She started back up again, and this time I was with her. Yes, sir, she set out like Sam Bass's race mare. I had to drop my knife so's to hold on with both hands. She took me up on that tail like a coon pulls crawfish out o' the mud with his'n. When I got to the rim, I made a dive that landed me on my feet. At the same time, that she bear made a dive into the hollow that must of landed her on her head. No, sir, she wa'n't going to make no more rear movements into that holler tree.

"But it didn't hurt her none. While I was a-getting my gun, I heard her talking mama-talk to them cubs. I didn't stop to cipher out exactly what she was saying. I jest pulled my freight fer Jericho. I'd done decided I could go a spell longer without bear grease in the cornbread."

"A gentleman of respectability and veracity" told Elias R. Wrightman, who surveyed lands for the English-speaking colonists in Texas, that he once saw a vaquero run his horse full speed after a bear, cast a loop around the bear's neck, jerk him down and begin dragging him. Thereupon the bear turned over on his back, seized the rope and began crawling up it toward the horseman, who was still making pretty good time. The bear took in the slack sailorwise until he was close enough to reach over and get a handful of horseflesh. At this pass, the vaquero unwound the rope from his saddle horn, threw it to the bear to keep, and dashed away.

But that's not the way a man distinguished — in the story-teller world at least — for something better than "veracity" told it to me.

A long time ago a certain bear that had been offended by a vaquero caught him and ate him up. He liked the meat so well that he took to lying in wait for men. Frequently he was shot at, but no bullet ever seemed to harm him. He bore a charmed life. He had a white spot on his breast that looked like a star, and they called him Star Breast. He haunted a thicket where two roads, or trails, crossed and where travelers sometimes camped, for at this place was the only spring of water in the country and near it was good grass. Finally, the place became so well known on account of the number of people whom Star Breast had made away with here that it was avoided by all travelers.

Now there was one vaquero in the country who was very brave and very desirous of winning fame. His name was Pablo Romero. One day while Pablo Romero and another vaquero were hunting horses on the prairie in the region of the cross-trails, they saw the tracks of Star Breast. Those tracks were so enormous that no one could mistake them for the tracks of another bear.

"Listen," said Pablo Romero, "I'm going to kill Star Breast. I know that it is useless to try to shoot him, and we have no guns anyhow. But I shall rope him and choke him to death the way we rope Indians and choke them. I am riding the best roping horse that a reata was ever thrown from. He has the strength of ten bulls in him. My rawhide reata is new. It would hold an elephant."

Pablo Romero's *compañero* did not take to the idea at all. He pleaded with his companion not to think of such a foolhardy undertaking. "Don't you know," he said, "that if Star Breast is proof against bullets he will be proof against rawhide? He's in that thicket now listening to us and preparing to come after us. Instead of riding on towards him, we must turn and go the other way."

"No," replied Pablo Romero, "in this country lead is not superior to rawhide. A good roper, a good roping horse, and a good rope can conquer anything that breathes."

Pablo Romero would not be turned. His *compañero* finally consented to stay and watch the roping from a distance. They rode on towards the thicket, and, sure enough as they were approaching it, they saw Star Breast emerge. He stood on his hind legs, waved his great hairy arms, rumbled a great roar, and then came on. The horses ridden by the vaqueros were beside themselves with fright, but Pablo Romero, by untying his reata from the horn of the saddle and playing out a loop, persuaded his horse to keep going. A good roping horse can hardly be stopped when he realizes that the rope is being prepared for action. The other vaquero galloped to a little rise.

He saw Pablo Romero fasten one end of the reata to his saddle. He saw him with swinging loop dash towards Star Breast, who had halted, standing up on his hind legs. The loop fell over Star Breast's head, while man and rider dashed on. When the end of the rope was reached, the horse was jerked back and the bear was jerked down. The loop had caught him under one arm and around the neck. Instantly, almost, the horse whirled so that he could get a better pull, and at the same time the bear recovered his upright position.

And now came a desperate maneuver between a gigantic, fierce, powerful and cunning bear at one end of the rope and an expert horse ridden by an expert rider at the other end. Several times the bear was jerked down. Had the loop not been under his arm, the pull about his neck might have choked him. The bear soon learned that by grasping the rope with his hands he could break the force of the jerks. Once he caught the tough rawhide in his teeth to break a jerk. A tooth was jerked out and he howled with rage. He did not catch the reata with his teeth again. He began to go forward up the rope towards the horse. As the length of the rope between the animals grew shorter, the horse had a shorter distance in which to run and therefore could not jerk so hard. He could not jerk the rope out of the bear's hands. He was panting hard.

Pablo Romero was a brave vaquero. He would not quit his horse. He had no gun of any kind to shoot. The rope was knotted so tightly about his saddle horn that he could not loosen it. Apparently he had no knife with which to cut it. Had his *compañero* been very brave, perhaps he might have roped the bear also and have pulled him away from his friend. He was not that brave. Anyhow, this roping contest was against his judgment.

At last, panting and frothing, Star Breast got up to horse and man. Now the vaquero who was watching saw a strange thing. He saw Star Breast reach up and drag Pablo Romero from the saddle. He saw him take the rope off his own neck, coil it up, and tie it to the saddle horn. Then he saw him mount the horse and, with the limp form of Pablo Romero across the saddle in front of him, ride off into the brush. That was the last ever seen either of Pablo Romero or of Pablo Romero's horse.

One time in Montana an old Texas trail hand who had stayed there after helping deliver a herd from Live Oak County gave me a kind of side light on this story. He had been down in California a while, working for Miller and Lux. In 1892, he said, another Miller and Lux man by the name of Jim Reeves roped a big black bear up a tree growing in the San Simeon Valley. The bear jumped before the rope really tightened on him. Jim Reeves spurred, and then for a hundred yards or so it was a race. Jim's horse had to go around a low rocky point and, having a bit of free time here, the bear jumped on top of a rock. Jim reined up and for a minute sat in the saddle admiring the bear, which made a fine sight above him. Then, without a word of warning, the bear sprang upon the horse. Jim at the same time sprang off. For a while that horse went on as spectacular a spree of pitching as ever made a rodeo crowd hold its breath. He sun-fished, worm-fenced, turned around in the air, banked east, knotted his backbone west. He came down with all four feet bunched like a deer's when it is cutting a rattlesnake to shreds, and he came down spraddled on stiff legs. He bawled and he bellered, and there was no rein to check the reach of his head. All the time that bear just hunkered on his back, and then the horse headed for the tall tules.

Jim Reeves saw he was taking the direction to his line camp, about two and a half miles away. His wife was there alone, and Jim set out walking. Jim found her almost scared out of her mind. She had heard a horse running, had rushed out of the cabin, seen a riderless horse dragging something. She supposed it was Jim. But it was the bear, dislodged from the horse's back, probably by the limb of a tree that the horse ran under. All this time the rope had still been around the bear, one end of it tied to the saddle horn. The bear had made his last ride. Jim found the horse not far away; he never was worth anything after that.

Three months later Jim's wife gave birth to a boy that had cheeks and nose shaped like those of a bear.

Old Bill, Confederate Ally

THEY tell me that Jeb Rider's log cabin still stands, about a quarter of a mile up the slope from the spring on Elm Creek. Nobody has struck oil in this part of east Texas yet, and so things out of the past live on there. People still talk about the Civil War, and call up the names of Jeb Rider and certain other Confederates reduced long ago to earth in the little graveyard where wild trumpet vines cover the fence with red flowers all through the summer months and into fall. Old Bill disappeared long before they did, but Jeb Rider's story of Old Bill keeps on blooming with the trumpet vines. This is the way he told it.

When me and my wife married, it was her idear having the house so fur up the slope from where we got water outa the spring on Ellum Creek. She was skeered of floods and strong on a hill breeze. Also, she didn't like bottom land mosquitoes. I was nacherly agin having to tote water so fur, but 'fore long I sometimes wished it were further. I could walk down the trail and set on the cypress log there at the spring and kinder get peaceful. She was always badgering me to clear more land and plant more sweet pertaters and hoe the corn cleaner and keep stovewood chopped up, and put my God-given time in on a lot of other things. I'd always been used to squirreling around with the dogs or jest being quiet and letting whatever was going on kinder soak into me. Stewing about went against my nature.

The best dog I ever had was Old Bill. He was out of a bitch Pa brung from Tinnissee; that is, figgering in several ginerations between. I never can remember whether it was July 13 or July 14 he died, the year before the War started. Anyhow, one cloudy day about a month after he died I was going down the trail to the spring uncommon low in the mouth and was about halfway, kinder unconsciouslike; I heard sump'n behind me. Maybe it was a rustle in the leaves. I didn't pay no 'tention till I heard a low rattle. Then I looked, and I'll be dogged if it wasn't the biggest diamon'back rattlesnake I ever see, right in the trail, not more'n six steps back.

When I stopped and looked, he stopped too and raised his head up in a curious way and looked at me without shaking his tail a-tall. It's that tail-shaking that makes a rattlesnake so fearsome, puts the j'ints in a human's backbone to shaking too. Well, I didn't have a thing along to hit with, not even a water bucket, and when I glanced round fer a stick there wa'n't none in reach. I started on down the trail agin to a dead dogwood I could break off. Then I looked back and that diamon'back was coming on too, keeping a respec'ful distance and looking like he didn't mean no harm.

When I got to the dead dogwood and broke off a stick and drew it back to lam the snake, he looked more harmless than ever. I can't explain it. There he was keeping a respec'ful distance, and all at once he sorter seemed to me like a dog that wants to foller you and be friends but's afraid to come too clost. Well, I stood there a-holding the stick, and he had his head up a little watching me, and his eyes jest seemed to say he understood. They looked a lot charitabler than some human eyes I've peered into.

Then I done clear contrary to nature. I throwed the stick away and started agin on down to the spring. Ever once in a while I'd turn my head and look back. The rattlesnake was still follering, humble and respec'ful. When I set down on the cypress log, he coiled up and kept looking right straight at me. D'reckly I begun to kinder talk to him. I was still youngish and a blamed fool about feeling sorry for myself. And that old snake would nod his head around and look like he felt sorry too.

No telling how long we mighta kept up the conversation if about half a dozen mockingbirds hadn't got to diving at the snake and jabbering and disturbing his peace and mine too. Still, I felt a lot better. When I started up to the cabin, he started too, jest follering like a dog. About halfway up he dropped out, and I didn't see nothing more of him till the next day. I was going down to the spring agin to bring up some water fer Abbie to wash with. Right about the halfway place, he fell in behind me like he'd done the first time, and now his follering seemed jest as nacherl as a dog scratching fleas.

"See here," I says to him after we got settled at the spring, "I'm going to call you Bill. Bill, he was the best coon and possum dog I ever had, and he always understood me. When I wanted to squirrel around, he never had no idears about hoeing weeds out of the yard or putting poles in the fence to keep the hawgs outer the field or anything like that. Yes, sir, you're Bill to me from now on."

And Bill jest nodded his head and looked grateful out of his eyes and shore would've talked if he could of. It was real soothing to be with him, and when Abbie went to squalling fer me to hurry up and bring on the water he acturly winked.

Well, after that we was together lots at the spring. Whenever I went to the store I'd hear talk about the Aberlitionists up North working to take the "niggers" away from us Southern folks and make 'em our equals, and more talk about the Black Republicans. When I got back I'd tell Bill about 'em — sometimes afore I told Abbie — and, by hokey, he'd coil up and look fierce enough to bite a crowbar.

Then the War did come. I volunteered fer Captain Abercrombie's company and traded off some corn and a mule fer a good, gentle horse and bought Abbie a new axe and got all ready to go. The evening afore I was to set out, I went down to the spring to kinder ca'm myself and tell Bill good-by.

It looked like he understood all about the Yankees. I told him to look after things around the spring as best he could and I'd be back someday. The next morning after Abbie got my things all packed and I'd told her good-by and started fer the county seat, I rode to the spring to water my horse.

Well, jest as I was coming out under that leaning ellum over the trail between the house and the spring, I felt sump'n drop acrost my shoulders. It woulda scared me if it hadn't been so nacherl.

"So you want to go to war too, do you, Bill?" I says. He nods.

"I don't know how the fellers in camps would take to you," I says. "They're all Texians, you know," I says, "and got about as much use fer a rattlesnake as a wildcat has for a lost puppy." You see, I hadn't told a soul about Old Bill — not even Abbie. I jest didn't think anybody would understand. But if Bill was so set on going with me, I decided right then I'd try to convert the heathen.

"If you'll promise," I says to him, "not to bother nobody and stay put where I puts you, I'll take you. I'll explain to the fellers and maybe they'll git the idear."

He nods and we rode on.

Some of the fellers seemed to think at first that I was a plain idiot, but they left Bill alone and he left them alone. I shore didn't have no trouble with anybody trying to steal my blankets, and the way Jim Bowie — that's what I named my horse — and Old Bill got to be frenly with each other was a caution. Sometimes Jim Bowie would kinder nose Bill along the back, and many a time when Jim Bowie was a-grazing I've seen Bill crawl out in front of him and scare off devilhorses so Jim Bowie wouldn't accerdently chew one up. You know how a devilhorse, once it's inside the stomick of an animal, can kill it. I fixed up a bag for Old Bill to ride comfortable in, and when we moved, hung it on the horn of the saddle.

Fer months we jest practised marching and squads-righting and squads-lefting and so on. I'd leave Old Bill on the edge of the parade grounds, and I got to noticing how interested he seemed in our movements. When we paraded, he'd get exciteder than the colonel's horse. The band music was what set him up. "Dixie" was his favorite tune, and he got so he could sorter rattle it. It shore was comical to see him histing his tail fer the high notes.

Finally our training was over. We crossed the Mississippi and joined Gin'ral Albert Sidney Johnston's forces. Then when Shiloh opened up, on that Sunday morning in April, we was in it. We fought and we fit all day long, sometimes going forwards and sometimes backwards, sometimes in the brush and sometimes acrost clearings. We didn't know till next day that our gin'ral had been killed. If he'da lived and if we'da had a few more like Old Bill, things would have turned out mighty different.

My regiment was camped on Owl Creek, due north of Shiloh Chapel, and jest before we went into battle that morning I took

Old Bill over to a commissary waggin and told him to stay there and told the driver to kinder keep him. Late evening found us coming back into a long neck of woods that our colonel told us we'd have to clear of Yankees. They'd worked in between us and Owl Creek. We found 'em all right, but they was the deadest Yankees I ever see. At first we was bellying along on the ground, keeping behind trees and expecting fire. Then when we kept finding more and more dead uns, we figgered some other outfit had beat us to 'em. We got to breathing easy, and then somebody noticed that none of the dead Yanks showed bullet marks. It was all-fired strange, and the trees wasn't none of 'em creased neither.

I decided to examine a little closer, and I pulled up the britches leg of one Yank. Jest above his shoetop on the outside, where the ankle vein runs, I noticed a pair of little holes about the size of pin points. I found the same marks on the leg of the next Yank; on another, on another; and then, all of a suddent, I knowed Old Bill'd been there. I told the boys. They went to looking at the dead Yankee legs and couldn't he'p being convinced.

We kep' going through the neck of woods and counting dead Yankees till we got to Owl Creek, a little below camps. My ricollection is that the count run to 417, but it may have been a few less. Course, too, some few might've been counted twicet. I guess the official report would show, if it didn't git burned up at Richmond.

It wa'n't more'n a rifle shot from the near side of the woods to camps. We got in a little before sundown, and there Old Bill was stretched out under the commissary waggin. He looked plumb tuckered out and as gant as a gutted snowbird. Well, the night before one of the boys happened to set a trap fer possum right in camps almost. He went to it as soon as we got in and found a big wood rat. He brung it in alive and put it in front of Old Bill. As a rule, Old Bill never et nothing hardly, but the way he nailed that rat and then swallered him whole was an edicashin in appertite. We all shore was proud of him. After that the boys quit figgering on frying him up fer beef-steak. They took to calling him Diamon' Bill and looked on him as a mascot. Some of 'em said he was the most valuable soldier in the Confederate Army. Why, the Colonel used to git me to send him out on scout duty. No telling how many Yankees he cleaned out of thickets it was dangerous fer a man to enter. He knowed the difference between Confederate gray and Union blue jest as well as Ab Blocker's cow dog knowed the difference between a branded critter and a mav'rick.

Well, 'tain't no use fer me to tell about all the battles we fought in. At Appermattox I was still alive and so was Diamon' Bill. Jim Bowie wa'n't, though, and we rode home on a borrered mule. One day 'way long in the summer I put Bill down at the spring on Ellum Creek, and afore my saddle blanket was dry I was breaking land, putting up the old fences, hoeing weeds out of the patch Abbie had planted, and doing all sorts of work. The dogs was all dead and there wa'n't no time fer nothing else. Lots of days I didn't even think about Old Bill.

Then one day in the spring of '66, while I was going in a hurry down to the spring, I heard something that made my mind whirl back. I wheeled around and saw a big diamon'back running towards me. Afore I could grab fer a stick, I see it was Old Bill. I called out to him, "Bill!" He nodded his head the way I'd seen him do a thousand times. But he made a new kind of motion that says he wants me to foller him. He turns off the trail and I follers.

About a hundred yards off he sidled up to another rattler, and looked back at me. "Mrs. Bill?" I says. He nodded, and the two went on. D'reckly we come to a clearing 'bout the size of our courthouse maybe. Old Bill stopped, raised up like a nacherl-borned commander, and give the durnedest rattle a man ever heard. Then he moved on ahead about ten paces and rared up agin. By that time, squads and troops and companies and battalions of young rattlesnakes was coming out of the brush on all sides. I'm afeared to say how many they was — hundreds, maybe thousands. They come out in regular formations, squads-righting and squads-lefting and fronting-into-line like old soldiers. Bill lined 'em up fer dress parade about the middle of the field. Then he sounded one rattle fer a signal and, keeping a perfect front, they begun advancing towards me, all rattles a-going and every dodgummed one of 'em a-playing "Dixie."

Old Bill knowed what he'd done in the War. The trouble was he was the only rattlesnake in it. He didn't seem to realize the War was over. Here he'd come home and raised this army, and now he was offering it to me. I ricollect how the Confederate boys uster always be quoting Gin'ral Bedford Forrest. He said, you know, that the gin'ral wins who gits there fustest with the mostest. Well, it was jest too late to be fustest. I tried to explain to Diamon' Bill. And that was the last in a military way I ever seen of him.

Part Five

Colonel Abercrombie's Mole

N ow you can talk about cotton acreage in Washington, and Perry McFaddin's muskrat ranch on the Neches, and mole-skin coats in New York. I'll tell you something about cotton and moles right here on the Trinity River."

Uncle Wayne Mitchell had taken the floor. So far as anyone else in the company could recall, not a word had been breathed about muskrats or moles or cotton. Uncle Wayne was so deaf he couldn't hear it thunder, but he read the Houston *Post*, and in his monologues often began with an item in the news. Sometimes he seemed bound to tell a story. Now he took the bridle off.

Cotton was awful high that year. There hadn't been much made during the War; not any to speak of was planted in '65, and in '66 the crop failed complete. But the next year the Trinity bottoms were white, and cotton sold at a boom price. As well as I recollect, it was around two-bits a pound. Rashe McNary — his real name was Horatio but everybody called him Rashe — must have ginned out fifty bales, and Colonel Abercrombie made close to three hundred. After the picking was finished, they shipped their cotton to Galveston on river boats.

Then, carrying their women folks with them, they went down to sell it.

Well, they got a top price, and when they deposited the drafts at the bank, they took out a shot-bag full of gold. It was the first real money either had seen in six or seven years; so you can imagine how good they felt. They told their women folks to buy as many dresses and hats and bustles and carpets and other such trappings as they wanted. Then they set out to act thankful.

There were plenty of places for them to step into, and so, taking a sniff here and a snort there, they kinder grazed out from the main herd. Ever' once in a while, Rashe would suggest they'd better back-trail, but Colonel Abercrombie would say, "A leetle more for thy stumick's sake," or "The freshest grass is fartherest away from the waterhole," or some other sech Bible proverb, and they'd keep on moseying. Along about sundown they found themselves away out on the edge of town.

"Colonel," says Rashe, "it looks like we've strayed clear off the main trail, and I guess we'd better halt and get our bearings."

The Colonel straightened himself up and looked around, and sure enough he was in a part of town he'd never seen. They were just across from a shack with a low door and a patched roof, and they could see a sign over the door. Colonel Abercrombie walked over to read it. It said: FORTUNE TELLING DONE HERE.

"Rashe," says the Colonel, "I'll back you out of having our fortunes read."

"I don't take much stock in these here fortunetellers," Rashe replied, "and I figger they are evil anyway. I mind how the Scripture says that he who useth divination is an abomination unto the Lord. And look what King Saul got from consulting a fortuneteller."

But Colonel Abercrombie had his curiosity up. "There never was a charitabler or a purer man than Joseph," he said, "and remember how he consulted fortunetellers."

It didn't take much arguing to make Rashe give in. They knocked, and a peculiar-looking, dark-complected woman with a red scarf over her head and wickedlike earrings come to the door. She was a Gypsy, I guess.

"Young lady," the Colonel began with a bow. She wasn't very young, but the Colonel was quite a hand for saying nice things to the ladies. He always calculated he'd never seen an ugly woman or tasted bad liquor, though he admitted some was better than others. "Young lady," he went on, "this is my friend Major Horatio McNary and I'm Colonel Abercrombie. We're from Madison County on the Trinity River, and being as we are in Galveston on a visit, we thought we'd like to have our fortunes told."

"Leastwise," Rashe puts in, "the Colonel wants his told. I don't know about it myself yit. I'll see how he comes out."

Well, the Gypsy woman told them to come in and set down. It was darkish inside, but she lit a kerosene lamp on a table covered with red-checkered oilcloth.

Colonel Abercrombie wanted to know how to start the thing off. The Gypsy woman shook her earrings so the light glinted on 'em, and then says, "Cross my pa'm with coin and I'll summon the sperrits."

She stuck out her hand to Rashe first. Rashe wasn't much of a spendthrift; so I expect possibly he gave her four or five picayunes.

She told him his name — like she hadn't got it from Colonel Abercrombie's introduction — and said he had fought through the War and had served in Walker's Division and was now a prosperous planter. That was all true, and Rashe said anybody in Madison County could have told him that without him being out any money. That was about all Rashe got from the fortuneteller.

Then she put her pa'm out to the Colonel, and he crossed it with a two-and-a-half gold piece.

"You are Colonel James B. Abercrombie," she begun. "Enduring the War you were a member of General Longstreet's staff, and you had lots of slaves on your plantation before Mr. Lincoln freed them."

"Anybody could have told the Colonel that without him being out two and a half," Rashe interrupted, but the Gypsy woman went on.

"Enduring the War you and some other Trinity Bottom planters loaded four hundred bales of cotton on ox waggins and had 'em freighted to Brownsville for exporting through Mexico."

The Colonel straightened up a little straighter. "That's right, Rashe, and not everybody could have told me that. Let's see if she knows anything else about that cotton."

"Some of the cotton got lost in the prickly pear and bresh this side of the Rio Grande," the Gypsy woman went on, sorter singsonging like she was in a trance. "I see blood and bandits, and mixed with the red I see bits of white sticking to mesquite thorns all along the road. I see oxen with their tongues out a-laying down, and there's no water."

By now Rashe was as quiet as a little brown wren on her nest.

"But," the fortuneteller continued, "a good part of the cotton got across into Mexico all right and was taken over by an agent in Matamoros to be shipped to England, where the spinners are. It was loaded on a gunrunner."

"That's right, that's right," the Colonel broke in. "Listen, Rashe. Go ahead, young lady."

"The gunrunner escaped the dastard enemy, but, Colonel Abercrombie, you have never heared a word concerning that cotton from that day till this."

"I never have, and I never expect to," the Colonel roared.

"Well, the cotton reached the spinners in the green fields of England," the Gypsy woman resumed.

"I don't doubt it," Rashe exploded.

She kept as ca'm as a Mexican burro eating shucks. "And now, Colonel Abercrombie," she went on, "you say you never expect to hear from that cotton again. Yet it reached an honest buyer, and he has been trying all this time to find out who shipped it. He will learn very soon. Remember the stars have been jostled in their courses."

Here the fortuneteller paused. Colonel Abercrombie said he sure hoped he'd hear something yit, but Rache jest kinder snorted.

The fortuneteller went on, "Well, I see the other gentleman don't have any confidence in the sperrits, Colonel, but you seem more reasonable. Do you believe in what the sperrits have revealed unto you?"

The Colonel said he believed he did.

"I am glad to hear that," the fortuneteller answered. "Yit you will go away and forget what I have told you, or be ashamed and say nothing about it. Nevertheless, on next Saint Patrick's Day, you will receive a letter. In it will be a draft for four thousand five hundred dollars, and it will be from the party in England who bought your cotton. Then you will know that what the sperrits have revealed is true."

Well, sir, the Colonel was sure tickled. "I'm a-going to git that money as sure as we are setting here," he said. "It don't stand to reason that this woman could know all that's already happened without knowing what is going to happen. As sure as shooting, I'm a-going to git that money."

Rashe told him to come on and get away before he went clean out of his head. As they started to leave, the Colonel reached down in his pocket, pulled out a five-dollar gold piece, and gave it to the Gypsy woman. It was her turn to be pleased.

"Colonel," she said, "you have been kind to me and the sperrits are going to be kind to you. If you will ask your friend to step out, the sperrits will reveal to you the whereabouts of forty burro-loads of Spanish gold that for centuries have laid hid from the eyes of man."

Here the Colonel asked the Gypsy woman to let Rashe stay. "I don't mind," he said. "He don't believe in sech things, and so won't interfere by digging for the gold. Go ahead and tell me where it is."

The woman sat back and shut her eyes, and stayed that way for a couple of minutes without saying a word. It was getting darker and darker and the light from the kerosene lamp glinted brighter'n ever on her gold earrings.

D'reckly she started. "Going on two hundred years ago now," she says, "an expedition of Spanish soldiers went up from Mexico City into the Ozark Mountains of Arkansas to hunt gold. They found it — found plenty of it — and mined until they had forty burro-loads of pure gold extracted and melted down. They mistreated the Indians, though, and as a result had to leave. Before setting out, they covered up their shafts, leaving only a line of trees with the tops cut off and a map on a rock to mark the location. It hasn't been located till this good day, though everybody knows about the Lost Louisiana Mine, as they call it.

"But all this don't interest us, and the sperrits appear indifferent to everything connected therewith but the forty burro-loads of gold. The Spaniards started back to Mexico with it, the Indians after them getting thicker and fiercer all the time. They crossed Red River into Texas and took a route right down the Trinity.

"Well, when they reached the land destined someday to be the Abercrombie plantation, the big fight come off and more'n half the Spaniards bit the dust."

Colonel Abercrombie said yes, he'd heard rumors all his life about Spanish gold being buried on his plantation. The Gypsy woman went on.

"The Spaniards surviving this defeat decided their lives were worth more than the gold. After dark they went on the prairie where it was sandy, dug a hole, and planted their whole cargo. They hadn't more'n covered it up and got strung out towards Mexico again before there was another attack. This time not a Spaniard was left."

Rashe forgot himself and put in: "How'll we know where to dig?" he asked.

"I beg your pardon, sir," the Colonel said to Rashe, and then he turned to the fortuneteller. "Jest where is the owner of the Abercrombie plantation going to find that gold?"

"Please be patient," the fortuneteller answered. "Your faith in the sperrits has not been fully proved yet. As I hev said, after you go away and ca'm down, you will be ashamed of this consultation and won't be willing to talk about it. But on Saint Patrick's Day, the seventeenth of March, when you get that draft for forty-five hundred dollars for the cotton that the gun-runner took to England, your faith will be revived and then you will be able to take advantage of the knowledge imparted by the sperrits."

The Gypsy woman shet her eyes and leaned her head back a long time. Finally she said, "You hev a dark shade tree in front of your house, do you not, Colonel Abercrombie?"

"Yes," answered Rashe, "he's got a big umbrella Chiny tree right in front of his house."

The fortuneteller went on, ignoring Rashe. "You love to set under that tree. It's sandy all about there. Well, one day while you are setting there looking down at the ground, you will see the grass and sand moving and a little ridge come up. That will be a mole making his way right at the roots of the grass."

"Yes, it's right sandy there, and I've seen signs of lots of moles on his place," Rashe put in.

The fortuneteller didn't pay him any mind and went on. "You watch that mole. After you watch the dirt move awhile, he will pop out of the ground. Keep your eye on him and follow him. Now mind what I say. After he pops out, follow him clost, for where he digs back in will be the place for you to dig and unearth the forty burro-loads of Spanish gold.

"Now good-by, and keep in mind what the sperrits hev revealed unto you."

Well, Rashe and the Colonel left the Gypsy woman's house. As soon as they got outside, she closed the door and they never saw her again.

"It's funny," Rashe remarked, "that a woman who knows where that much gold is lives in a house like this."

"She deals in things of the sperrit, Rashe. She is not interested in gold." The Colonel spoke with conviction.

"I notice she seemed glad to get the gold pieces you gave her," Rashe sneered.

On the way back to the hotel the Colonel made Rashe promise not to say anything to the women folks about the fortune teller business. "We'll wait till Saint Patrick's Day and see how matters turn out," he said.

Well, time dogtrotted along, and finally Saint Patrick's Day arrived. Madisonville got mail three times a week, and it happened that the seventeenth of March fell on a mail day. Hours before the mail hack was due, the Colonel was setting on the board sidewalk in front of the post office twirling his spurs. Rashe was as clost to him as his own shadder. At last the postmaster got the mail sorted and begun handing it out. There was a letter for Colonel Abercrombie. It was from England. He opened it and saw a draft for forty-five hundred dollars.

The Colonel and Rashe got on their horses and lit out. As soon as they reached the house, the Colonel grabbed two of the rawhide-bottomed chairs that always set on the front gallery and carried them out under the chinyberry tree. The leaves hadn't sprouted yet. It was pretty breezy out there and, I imagine, a little bit early for moles. But they sat till dusk, watching, jest watching. Then Rashe went home. By the time he got back next morning, the Colonel was fairly glued to the rawhide, as vigilant as a hound dog under a treed coon. The watching seemed to have a kind of fascination for him, and before long, Rashe's wife, so they say, got to nagging the daylights out of him for staying away so much and letting everything on their place go to the bowwows.

So the Colonel sat under the tree, Rashe steady by him, all through the rest of March. In April the setting got more pleasant. When the chinyberry and the Cape jessamines put out flowers, you could see the Colonel inhaling deep and enjoying his job. May came, and the setters went to shifting their chairs around so as to keep in the shade. All this time they were having mint juleps as reg'lar as the sun climbs up and goes down.

By now blamed near everybody out from the Trinity River

in Madison County knew how the Gypsy woman had foretold a draft for Colonel Abercrombie's cotton on St. Patrick's Day and how it had come. This don't mean they were expecting the prediction on the Spanish gold to be fulfilled, but the interest in moles that sprung up was a caution to the heathen. There was more talk about moles than about mules or hound dogs. Everybody had seen their tunnels but nobody hardly had ever actually seen a mole itself. Colonel Abercrombie sent off to New Orleans for a set of the *Encyclopedia Britannica* so's to read up on the animal. I don't think he found anything in it more helpful on its habits than what Rashe gave him in a quotation from Shakespeare. Neighbors would ride over and set by the hour helping Rashe and the Colonel watch. They'd argue over whether mint ought to be crushed or not crushed in the juleps, and they'd get scientific over how much sugar is healthiest in a toddy. The darkies were all mole-watching too, though they made a stand at keeping out of sight.

The crops went to weeds, and still the Colonel sat under the chinyberry tree every day and Sunday too, keeping his vigil. It was the biggest-spreading chinyberry in the whole country, and this spring it seemed to be taking its second growth. I lived about twelve miles away, and now and then I'd ride over and set in the afternoon shade. Colonel Abercrombie would be smoking his pipe and stroking an old black cat he kept for luck. He always kept settled down comfortable, but that didn' keep him from cutting his eyes this way and that for the mole.

It was heathenish the way he banked on that black cat, and I told him so. Once in a while an old roustabout they called Uncle Alf would bring out a fresh pitcher of cold cistern water and a demijohn. The Abercrombies made a special good wine out of mustang grapes, and sometimes the Colonel ordered it

When the weather was sultry he'd fan himself with his hat. He wasn't missing any vittles, but it looked to me like he was going short on his naps. He told me he put Uncle Alf to watching one day while he took a siesta and woke up to find him snoring loud enough to scare off all the moles in Madison County. Then he moved his cot from the hallway to a good place under the chinyberry and napped there. I guess he was figuring on the mole making enough noise to wake him up.

I argued that moles don't come out in the heat of the day but work mostly at night. He said he wasn't taking any chances. Jest the same, about this time he took to napping longer after dinner, and he bought five or six new lanterns and hung them up around so any night movement among moles could be detected. When it come to having the wicks trimmed and coal oil put in the lanterns, he was as vigilant as the five wise virgins in the Bible.

Summer went by and cotton-picking time came, and no mole yet. Rashe had kinder give up hope and his wife was keeping him purty reg'lar out in the fields weighing cotton and so on. Late one day about the end of September he rode over to the Abercrombie place, tied his horse to one of them whitewashed hitching posts out in front of the yard, and stepped to where the Colonel was watching. Fall was setting in dampish, and that's the kind of weather moles like best to operate in. It appeared to be pertickerly dampish around the Abercrombie place, for I remember how a honeysuckle covering an old log fence back of the smokehouse kept on blooming.

"It's been nearly a year," Rashe says, "since the fortuneteller woman told us about the mole, and no mole yet. I believe there's been fewer moles this year than ever I saw. . . . I notice you ain't got but one lantern hanging up any more."

It was clost to sundown, and the Colonel called to old Alf to bring some fresh water and mint. The demijohn was on a little table between him and Rashe.

While old Alf was fiddling around with the lantern, Colonel Abercrombie went on talking. "Yes," he said, "it's been a disappointing year for moles. I hate to do it, but tomorrow I'm going to release the guard. I've got to go down to Galveston to see about my cotton, and I think I'll stop by and consult that fortuneteller again. Maybe some way we didn't get her directions straight. You see —"

But just at this instant Rashe jumped up like a shot.

"Good God, Colonel," he busted out, keeping his voice down in his throat and pointing his finger to a spot on the ground about halfway between the house and the chinyberry tree, "there's that mole!"

Colonel Abercrombie threw his black cat down, jumped up twice as excited as Rashe, and nearly run over him getting to where he could see better.

Well, sir, as sure as shooting, you could see a ridge where the mole had come from under the house. He was a-digging his little tunnel along among the roots of the grass—jest scattered crowfoot and grassburs — and he was heading straight for the chinyberry tree. But the racket and the moving around must have scared the little critter. He stopped as still as death and wouldn't budge a hair.

"Jest be quiet," Rashe whispered. "He'll start up again in a minute."

They waited a minute, then five minutes, then ten.

"I'm afraid that mole has suffered a stroke of paralysis," Rashe says, and he wasn't joking. "It looks like he has made his last move. Truly, as the Scriptures say, the ways of the mole are dark."

But about then the sand started cracking again and the grass a-jigging. The mole was still headed for the chinyberry. He moved in jerks kinder, about half an inch at a time. In a little while he stopped again.

By now the women folks at the house and all the help around the place had caught on that the mole was in sight. They were crowding around and tiptoeing up while Rashe and the Colonel, sort of shooing them back, never took their eyes off the mole.

About a step ahead of where he was stopped, a carriage track had cut an inch or so into the turf. Well, d'reckly the mole started tunneling again, and he's making real good time now. Then he come to the carriage track, and there he busted out on top of the ground. By now dusk was turning to dark.

"Goober peas and General Jackson!" Rashe sorter groaned, smothering his voice down. "He's out, and if everybody don't keep quiet he'll get confused and won't go back into the ground at the right place for the forty burro-loads."

"Hush, hush," the Colonel moaned. "Purty soon it'll be dark and then we can't see where he goes down."

A minute later the Colonel sorter whispered, "Somebody bring a lantern! No, don't bring no lantern. The light will blind him!" He went to bending over, sorter skylighting the mole.

Well, I don't guess anybody ever saw anything like it. Rashe and the Colonel were so excited they were dodging their heads this way and that, and the women folks and the darkies were tip-toeing and going around, and meantime the little mole was a-darting hither and yon, now halting and now appearing to be ready to go back in. I always have believed in telepathy, and I always will believe that little mole felt the anxiety everybody around was feeling in trying to figure out where he was going to dig in again. I don't know why the Colonel didn't order the people to clear out.

Once the mole came within an ace of burrowing out of sight, but something undecided him and he took off again. After he had run in every direction there was, and had got four or five steps away from the carriage track where he busted out on top of the ground, something prevented his intentions from ever being revealed. That old black cat the Colonel had kept by his chair and in his lap all spring and summer gave a leap.

Before you could say "Jack Robinson," the cat landed on the little mole, killed it, and gobbled it down. It looked like a kind of jedgment on the Colonel's superstition. I'd remonstrated with him time and again about believing in black cats. He was as bad that way as his old black mammy. Well, after this, there naturally warn't no way in the world to find out where the mole was aiming to dig in. I don't reckon anybody, now, ever will find the right place to dig for them forty burro-loads of Spanish gold.

The Green Powder Keg

IN THE days "before bob-wire played hell with Texas," old man Bostick's cattle ranged over the prairies all the way from San Felipe de Austin on the Brazos River to Eagle Lake against the Colorado. If he wasn't the Bostick who captured Santa Anna and led him to Sam Houston lying wounded under a live oak tree on San Jacinto battlefield, he was no less a man.

He was a Texian out of the old rock, easy-sitting and hard-riding; short in explanation and long in silences; sure of himself in both plan and execution, and just as sure that everybody under him, mostly Negroes, would do the right thing the wrong way. His features were weathered into rawhide; his heart seemed drier than his skin. The pipe he smoked night and day had cased his lungs. He was so tight-mouthed that nobody ever knew what he was thinking.

One day his son Kelly said, "Pa, I've come to get some advice."

Without waiting to hear on what matter, Bostick retorted, "Son, get your own. You won't have to go anywhere for it. You'll always find it a lot handier than somebody else's."

In the manner of old-time range men, he wore a vest summer and winter. No day ever got hot enough to make him shed it. In the inside pocket he carried a little notebook containing all his earthly accounts that needed recording and also a folded

almanac, replaced annually, that was his sole literary require-
ment. Sometimes he wore a white shirt, but never a necktie.
He always drank his coffee an hour before daylight. By daylight, whether he was to ride or not, his horse was saddled and
tied to a certain post. He generally rode.

Old Bostick was as close in other ways as he was with his lips.
There was no call on him, or on anybody else in the country at
that time, for more than a pennyworth of charity. If some people wanted to burden themselves with church buildings and
schools, let them. He felt no need of anything beyond what he
already had; all he wanted was more of the same thing, but he
made no extra moves to acquire it. His house spread out amply
on either side of a great hall, with galleries around half of it

and a stairway through the hall leading to a half story of attics and the bedroom in which his two daughters slept. Every room in the house had a fireplace. The only company old man Bostick ever seemed to care about was the fire.

Anybody who came to this house found a table bountifully supplied with cornbread, butter, buttermilk, fried steak, baked shortribs (in wintertime), blackeyed peas, bacon and greens — when it was greens time — sweet potatoes and Irish potatoes, honey from his own hives, pepper sauce from native Mexican peppers, jars of preserved wild plums and grapes — all in such plenty that half a dozen hounds throve on the daily leavings. There was always a great plenty of not only food and dogs but of Negroes, mules, horses, saddles, wagons, harness, woodpiles, smokehouses, corncribs, rawhide-bottomed chairs and jugs of whisky. Bostick could chamber whisky by the tincupful without being fazed beyond a brightening of his steel-gray eyes.

His two daughters, whose mother had died when they were small and who had been brought up pretty much by a Negro woman, often wanted more money for dresses. Occasionally Bostick humored them. More often he soothed them down with saying, "It's better to be able to buy than to buy," "It's not what you want makes you rich," or something like that. He was fond of these girls in his way, and they of him.

The number of cattle he rendered for taxes was not understood by anybody as being the number that wore the B O S brand. Every year he sold a big string of steers. Twice a year he worked the range close, branding all his own calves and none of his neighbors'. Once in a while he sold off a herd of "shells" — old cows and bulls. He was never known to receive a bank statement. He always took coin for pay when he sold cattle; he always paid in coin for anything he bought. He generally got anything he bought cheaper than other people got it. He loaded his own cartridges with black powder, bought by the keg, and he habitually saved the kegs. They were made of waterproof metal and were painted green. He did not use a great deal of powder, for he never shot for sport — only for meat, and he did not often miss.

What was he doing with his money? Nobody ever asked Old Bostick that question. That was his business. His neighbors, as well as he, knew how to tend to their own business and leave other people's alone.

While this was still the code and while the grass he grazed was still unfenced, Old Bostick lay dying. A cold wet norther beat against the windowpanes, and he seemed satisfied to stay inside. It would not have been like him to pour out at the end what he had kept bottled up on the long road. As he lay on his bed, so placed that he could look into the fireplace coals, eyes asking him the question that lips dared not phrase got back no more answer from his lips or expression than the ashes gave.

After he was buried, still nobody knew what Old Bostick had done with his money. That he had spent it in secret was inconceivable. No will could be found. The two daughters, grown and blooming now, and the son Kelly turned the house inside and out, looked for loose flagstones in the hearth, searched the barns and other outhouses, dug and poked in the yard and lot, but not a sign of hoarded money could they find. They went to Houston, San Antonio, Columbus, Austin and other places where there were banks, inquiring after deposits. Apparently their father had not made any. But the more they figured on how many years he had sold how many cattle and how little he had bought, comparatively speaking, to fill out the homemade and homegrown goods consumed on the ranch, the more convinced they became that there must be a store of money somewhere.

In time they quit looking for it, but speculation about it and anecdotes about the man supposed to have accumulated it persisted in household conversation and campfire talk over the country. The girls married and left the old place. Kelly stayed on, letting everything run down. He was not good at managing either whisky or cattle. Finally he got so tired of the cooking, the dirt, and himself that he proposed selling the homestead and dividing the proceeds. His sisters agreed, and the sale was made. The time came for clearing out the old house and leaving it — and its promise of the Bostick treasure — forever.

On the morning of the appointed day, Old Bostick's children, with the help of two strong-backed Negro men, began pulling forth from the house the accumulations and off-castings of two generations. It was understood as a matter of course that each would take what she or he wanted of the furniture and other goods; the Negroes could have what they wanted of the remainder, and what nobody wanted would be burned. Old Bostick's saving habits on personal items like worn-out boots and on such things as pieces of iron, which belonged in the scrap heap by the blacksmith shop but which lay in boxes and corners and on shelves, had added enormously to the bulk of material to be lugged out.

Finally every part of the house had been cleared but the big dark closet under the stairs, across from the room in which Bostick always slept. In this closet he used to hang his hunting horns, treasure a pair of pistols used in Austin's Colony, hide new axe handles to keep them from running off, save especially long horns from longhorn steers he had raised. It was a hoard of objects ranging from junk to museum pieces — depending on who did the classifying.

The clearing out of the closet brought to light many things

the Bostick children had forgotten: a big box of *Frank Leslie's Illustrated Newspaper* and other magazines their mother had saved, a grandfather's clock that their father had talked of having repaired but never did get to, a sack — or what had once been a sack — of wool, mostly converted into the nests of mice, a buffalo robe that had been used as a rug, a moth-eaten Saltillo blanket worn as a slicker on the Chisholm Trail before slickers were invented, and so on. After the Negroes had pronounced everything out, Kelly decided to have one last look. He had to stoop slightly to go through the door. He struck a match, for the back part of the closet was in thick darkness. The stirred-up dust made him sneeze, and the sneeze blew out the match. He lit a second one, stooping over to protect the flame with his hands.

Thus bent and facing the bottom of the stairs, which sloped the roof of the closet from a height of nothing to twelve feet, he noted some kind of object under the second step. He had to half-crawl to get to it. As he neared it and put his hand on it, he recognized it as one of the old-time metal powder kegs, painted green, a stopper of lead alloy screwed into a bunghole at one end.

Kelly felt, then saw, that the bunghole was closed. He gave the keg a yank; it did not budge. The thing seemed to be nailed down. Bracing himself and pulling steadily at the rim on the keg, he tipped it over. Then it was easy to roll. Rolling it, Kelly heard a clinking.

When he called his sisters, he was alone with the keg in his father's old room, now entirely empty. He shut the door after his sisters came in. He uprighted the keg and unscrewed the metal plate. Gold filled the keg to the rim. They emptied it right there — nothing but gold pieces of twenty dollars, ten, five, and two and a half. They stacked all the twenties in one pile, all the tens in another, and so on. While the girls were finishing this sorting, Kelly went out and brought in three blankets.

Then the three sat on the floor, each with a blanket in front, while Kelly undertook the distribution. "One for you, one for you, and one for me," he began, pitching the twenty-dollar pieces, one at a time, on the blankets. Finally all the coins were distributed. The counting came later. Each had approximately twenty thousand dollars.

One girl tried to get her husband to invest her third. He flatly refused to touch a cent of it, swearing that when he got so he couldn't support his wife she could live on her own money, but that until then she'd have to put up with what he made. For years the bank at Bellville kept a deposit of twenty thousand dollars in her name. The husband of the other girl had no such scruples. He and Kelly bought a ranch over on the Big Bernard. They depended on a whisky bottle to manage it, and the property evaporated faster than uncorked champagne.

All, in the end, that Old Bostick's secret and gold came to was a tale that is told.

In a Drouth Crack

WHILE Texas was still a part of Mexico — though separated by export and import laws — the McNeal brothers freighted a load of general merchandise from the lower Brazos River to Presidio del Rio Grande (in the region of present day Eagle Pass). They sold out at a good profit, receiving pay in silver coins, which they put into stout bags. As there was an export duty on silver from Mexico, they hid the bags from the customs officials. After they had passed, however, the officials became suspicious and sent a detachment of soldiers after them. The McNeals were on a "mesquite prairie" seamed with dry-weather crevices — drouth cracks — when they saw the soldiers coming far off. Hidden from view, they dropped the bags of silver into one of the cracks, took a good look at the landscape and moved on.

The soldiers soon overtook them, searched them, found nothing and turned back for the Rio Grande. The McNeals waited until "all was pacific," as the Mexicans say, and then returned to the drouth crack. "But the cleft was so deep and the ground was so hard they could not dig the money out without picks and spades. These they could not obtain without a trip to the colonies hundreds of miles away. Before they got in, the rains came on, closing the cracks and obliterating their landmarks. If anybody wants to search for buried treasure, there is his chance — if the stuff hasn't gone through to the other side of the world." This is one of Noah Smithwick's stories.

Only two or three times in a century does a drouth dry up the central part of Texas as did that of 1886. . . . Now it was late August. There had been no spring. The cedar elms along Onion Creek were already dropping their leaves. Some oaks were dead. Even the narrow, nonevaporating leaves on mesquites, beginning to take the prairies, had sered. The only winds were whirlwinds — always the sign of more dry weather. The grass roots had died; the bull nettles in the fields were runty and withered. Drouth cracks seamed the black land everywhere.

Fanning his face with his hat, Tobe Pickett sat on the front gallery of his low house, which sprawled out on both sides of an open hall, among live oak trees on Onion Creek, near the Spanish Trail crossing, about eight miles from Austin. He had a way of grumbling to himself, interspersing his phrases with "my-my's" and long sighs, often with a kind of rhyme. He usually ended his soliloquies with a whistling sound that prolonged itself the length of time it took to expire all the air from his thick chest. Now he was going on to himself about the weather.

"My, my, ain't it hot!" he'd say. "Oh, ho, dead doe, how, hmmm! I wonder if it ain't ever going to rain. Rain, rain gone to Spain. Hu, hu, hu" — and then that long, dying whistle.

The only person present to notice his ejaculations and groans and mutterings was his wife, Aunt Mat. She was so used to them that she paid no attention to them now. Wiping the sweat from her face with her apron, she stepped from an ironing board in the hall to the wooden bucket hanging from a rafter of the gallery and dipped out a gourd of water. As she drank, her eyes swept the horizon.

"Seems like them dust-devils get thicker every day," she remarked.

"It's too dry for the dry weather locusts to sizzle," Tobe went on. "My, my, my, looks like it jes' can't rain. Drier'n it ever was before, worser'n it was in sixty-four."

"You don't know how bad it was in sixty-four," Aunt Mat rejoined mildly. "You was stealing peaches in Georgia — between battles with Sherman's Yankees. That Meskin oughta be showing up 'bout now."

"Well," Tobe retorted, "haven't you and everybody else left here during the War told me over and over how the cattle died too poor fer the buzzards to eat? And how the prickly pear took the dry rot and shriveled to nothing? And how half the dogies that didn't starve to death fell down into the drouth cracks? Don't tell me. Dry, dry, dry, and not a cloud to try . . ." — and Tobe was off again on one of his monologues.

The sun was still maybe two hours high. The Mexican hired man came up to the gallery, his feet, in rawhide sandals, touching the ground at each step in a manner of infinite repose.

"Maybe so I go haul the water now?" he queried. "She is more cool."

"Cool!" Tobe exploded.

The Mexican said, "*Sí, Señor,*" and took a restful stand in the shade.

"Ho, hi, hum, whirlwinds till kingdom come," Tobe went on, looking out over the baked land, apparently oblivious of everything else.

"Well, don't jes' set and go on forever," Aunt Mat exclaimed.

"Tell Pablo to get moving and haul the water. When our well went dry, I predicted the last waterhole in Onion Creek would dry up too. If you and Pablo don't fence in that rock waterhole, we won't have any water fit to drink."

"My, my, call it dry! Yes, go on, Pablo, and hitch up that Gotch mule to the sled and haul the water."

As the Mexican made a motion to get going, Tobe added, "And mind out for them drouth cracks. Giles's horse stepped in one yesterday and nearly broke his leg, and his wife said the off wheels of their buggy got into one and they had to drag away down it before it got shallow enough to pull out of. You watch now. Drier than a lime-burner's hat and hotter'n a hot-box in hell. Pablo, maybe a cup of coffee would sorter cool me off."

"*Sí, Señor.*" Pablo went to the kitchen, where he could be heard lifting the stovelid off and raking up coals. After a while he brought out a cup of hot, black coffee. After watching Tobe saucer it, he left to haul the barrel of water.

He did watch out for the cracks. That night he told his wife María he had seen a jack rabbit try to jump a crack and fall into it. He sometimes exaggerated when he talked to María, particularly if other people were around to hear what he said. But very seriously he now added: "When you go to the back side of the field, María, to cut prickly pear for the pigs, watch out that you don't fall into a crack like the jack rabbit. Those cracks — they are a barbarity!"

Late the next day while going across the field to cut prickly pear for the hogs, María saw a crack that really was, she believed, too wide for a jack rabbit to jump. Bending over, she slowly moved along it trying to locate an imprisoned rabbit or something else in its depths. A few feet down, darkness obscured the opening, but presently she saw something that rushed into her memory an old tale known to everybody in the country.

Her eyes made out an iron chest, wedged between the walls of the crack. She could even trace a kind of cable that passed over the lid and through the handle on one uptilted end. That is what she always claimed. Could it be the chest of gold that the Spaniards left so long ago when they were held up on Onion Creek? Many strangers had come to the country looking for that chest. According to some, it was on one side of the creek and according to others, on the other side. As the story went, the Spaniards, when attacked, had thrown it into "a hole." But they hadn't had time to dig a hole. There was no known cave in the vicinity. Some old settlers argued that the hole was a drouth crack, which, of course, had closed with the first good rain, leaving no sign. There were supposed to be signs on rocks and trees in the vicinity.

Thinking of all she had heard, María stood beside the great crack and looked around to make sure that no one had seen her. It was time for Pablo to be coming from Onion Creek with his sled of water. She hurried to the gap, beyond a line of brush, to meet him. A neighbor was with him, however, and her news was for Pablo alone. She went on and cut the prickly pear.

It was after dark before she got an opportunity to talk.

"I tell you, Pablo," she imparted, "that chest has more than gold. Gold, yes, but what riches besides! It is too big. It holds, most certainly, a little saint and a silver cup for the holy wine, and a cross with red jewels in it. Look, it's big like that," and she measured with outstretched arms.

But it was Pablo's opinion that the chest contained nothing but gold. Had not a cousin to his *compadre's* uncle got the story from a priest, who had heard it in a monastery at a town far down in Mexico where another priest had confessed one of the dying bandits who had helped rob the pack train? The Spaniards were on their way to St. Louis with the gold and were right at the Arroyo de los Garrapatas (Ticks) — the old name for Onion Creek — when the robbers attacked them. This *historia*, coming down so directly, told of gold only, in a chest of iron "placed in a hole."

After their children were asleep, Pablo looked out and saw that the big house was dark. "The *patrón* and Doña Mattie are asleep," he said.

Then he lit the kerosene lantern and he and María set out across the field to feast their eyes on the chest in the great drouth crack. They had not gone fifty steps, however, before they heard the strong voice of Aunt Mat asking what was up.

"One *animal*, he catchee the chick," Pablo responded.

"The *animal* has gone and if you don't look out one rattlesnake will bite one Meskin," Aunt Mat's voice came back. "It's too hot for the rattlesnakes in the day, and they are crawling everywhere these nights," Aunt Mat warned. "Get back, I tell you."

The Mexicans put out the lantern. After a while, Pablo wanted to venture forth again without the lantern, but no, María was too afraid of snakes — and only she could lead the way to the chest. "I will show it to you tomorrow," she said.

Pablo speculated how not only poles and ropes, but a team and a derrick might be necessary to get the chest up. He was afraid to let anybody else in on the secret. Yet how was he to haul the great chest out in daylight in an open field without being discovered? Well, he would see the chest in the morning and then settle on a plan.

But the next morning early Aunt Mat put him and her hus-

band to building the fence around the one clear waterhole left in their stretch of Onion Creek. The cattle and horses would have to go on down the creek to the next waterhole. After dinner, instead of taking the siesta that even the lizards in this awful drouth took, Pablo got María to go with him across the field, as if to show her something about the prickly pear thicket. The heat was enough to sizzle the brains of a roadrunner.

The chest, María said, was at a place not visible from the house. But now she could not find it.

"Yesterday when you thought you saw it you were but sun-struck," Pablo accused.

"No, my head was as clear as the water out of Manchaca Spring," María returned. "My eyes were clear. The light down in the hole was clear. I saw the iron chest as clear as the Three Marys come up every evening." And she pointed to where Orion, with his belt of three stars, comes up every summer night.

"You are a fool," Pablo said.

Perhaps the heat was in his head. Quarreling, they went back to their cabin, built in the shade of a great live oak tree. There María bound around her head some fresh willow leaves she had brought up from Onion Creek. Pablo, perversely, placed only mesquite leaves in his hat to cool his head.

After he had had his siesta, María said, "This evening I mark the place, I alone."

When Pablo came in at dark, he asked, "You mark it?"

"Most certainly. I found it exactly, going to bring prickly pear for the pigs. Again I saw the lid and the strong cable going under the handle in one end. On the way back I saw it again and I placed three prickly pear leaves so that one hangs over the hole, just above the box."

"Perhaps the prickly pear will fall in," Pablo said.

"Perhaps the saint in the chest will lift it up on top of the ground," María retorted.

She was hard to argue with. They went on talking for a long time. Was the crack deep on down under where the chest was lodged? It was so deep that the bottom was in darkness. Then if the crack widened another inch, the heavy box might loosen and fall even to *infierno*. This heat and scorching of the world was all coming from that *infierno*.

"Tomorrow in the morning we go without fail," Pablo said. "The fence around the waterhole is finished and I will have time."

"*Mañana* for a surety," María said.

As they talked, they suddenly sensed a breath of freshness in the air. It had the smell that comes only out of clouds. Listen! The "carts of the giants," racing out of the east, were rumbling over their heads. Look! Lightning! Its tongues showed clouds of inky blackness covering the sky. From the big house came a great cry of joy. In fifteen minutes the sky was pouring down barrels, hogsheads, tanks of water; then the downpour turned into an all-night soaker. The next day Aunt Mat told neighbors how Tobe had rushed out into the yard, bareheaded and in his underclothes, and let the rain pour over him, how he had held his mouth open for the water to pound into until he choked, and how he had stretched out his hands and yelled: "The drouth's broke, the frogs croak, green grass, garden sass, slick cows and not a louse!"

Onion Creek boomed down like a regular river and carried away the fence Tobe and Pablo had put up around the rock waterhole. The next day and the next more rain fell. Not a crack was left in the land, the black dirt swelling and sealing up the contractions, leaving only hogwallows. They were little lakes. The sky was still full of water, and all creatures beneath it seemed to know that tomorrow green would be showing everywhere. The old mules were kicking up their heels and the cows were trying to play with their calves. Everybody in the country from the Carolina wren under the bluff on Onion Creek to the Governor of Texas on Capitol Hill was lighthearted.

Everybody but Pablo and María. At daylight after the big night rain, they had floundered together across the field. Deep mud gave the ground uniformity except in the hogwallows, where it was deeper. They couldn't find even one prickly pear leaf to mark the spot where the crack had opened over the chest of gold. María knew where the place was, and yet she didn't know exactly.

"Sakes alive, Pablo," Aunt Mat said when he brought in an armload of stovewood, "you look like you had lost your best friend."

A month later she set out with Tobe on a long-delayed visit to their daughter living on the Brazos River. They had not been gone three hours before Pablo was digging a hole at the spot selected by María.

"How deep you say it was?" he kept asking.

"More deep than you are tall," she would invariably reply. "Better make the hole wide."

Pablo dug one hole fairly deep, though not so deep as he was tall. Then he began shoveling up spadefuls of dirt at other places round about. He worked maybe two hours.

"We wait for signs," he explained to María.

"What signs?"

"Maybe the prickly pear will grow from where it is buried."

"Not if it is buried deep."

"Then a light will show at night. A light always plays in the dark over a place where gold is buried."

Pablo began to take walks at night out to a place where he could overlook the slope across which the great drouth crack had opened and revealed its hoard. He was happy again, like the other animals of the fruiting earth.

"The gold is not destined for us," he said to María.

"Thus it seems," she agreed.

When Aunt Mat and Tobe came back, Pablo told the story — María's story. Aunt Mat told other people.

"Jes' Meskin imagination," was Tobe's only comment when the matter was mentioned in his hearing.

"They're still looking for fox fire to show the right place," Aunt Mat would laugh.

Before long unknown diggers began making holes at one place and another in the Tobe Pickett field. That was back in the nineteenth century. Men, more of them Americans than Mexicans, are still digging holes and telling María's story. And now, whenever it gets dry enough on the old Pickett farm — long since passed into other hands — for the black land to crack, individuals not noted for industry may be seen peering into the seams.

The Stranger of Sabine Pass

ABOUT 1830, an Irishman by the name of Neil McGaffey and his young wife settled on Sabine Pass in what is now Jefferson County, Texas. As a protection against the Gulf storms that periodically sweep in over that country, they built their cabin on Shell Ridge — a kind of inland bar, five or six miles long and hardly, on the average, a hundred yards wide. The house, the only habitation for a long distance up and down the lonely coast, was about two miles from where the western end of Shell Ridge overlooks the waters of the Gulf of Mexico.

The famous Taylor White ranch lay twenty or twenty-five miles to the east. The Broussards had another ranch away off. Already, at this early date, these ranchers were trailing cattle to the New Orleans market. McGaffey began to build up a herd. As the saying went, it cost less to raise a calf than a chicken. Before long, McGaffey had a few hundred head of cattle, along with a faithful old slave named Wash — short for Washington — to help care for them. McGaffey and his wife also had two children, with a good chance for more. Sometimes they went for months without seeing a stranger; when one did appear he was welcomed heartily.

One night, not long after supper, a man called out of the darkness. "My name is Carton," he said, "and I'd like to get food and a bed."

"Get down and come in," McGaffey responded.

"I'm already down. I'm afoot," the stranger responded, advancing to the door.

Being on foot away out from any town or settlement in Texas at that time was a singular condition. But, according to the code, no questions were asked. After an early breakfast next morning, the man who called himself Carton offered to pay for his keep, but of course, nothing would be accepted. He left, without explanation.

That night he came again, was again welcomed, fed, and bedded. Early in the morning he again left. The third night he came once more. The daybreak disappearances and the nightly appearances of the stranger on foot had made him by now an object of suspicion more than of curiosity. The fact that the McGaffeys kept a small amount of money hidden in the house added to their uneasiness.

After the stranger had been given food on this third night, McGaffey point-blank demanded to know his business.

"You have a right to ask," the stranger admitted. "My actions would arouse anybody's suspicions. Yet I have business here. I see that the only way I can carry it out is to make you a pardner."

He paused. Without saying a word, McGaffey listened, gazing at him in the candlelight.

"I have been a pirate," the stranger resumed abruptly. "Three of us owned the ship. We cut loose from Lafitte just before he took up headquarters on Galveston Island. We made good profits — one enormous haul out of a ship loaded with Mexican silver and gold. But the time was up on such doings and we knew it. We were sailing for New Orleans to split with our men and disband when a hurricane caught us. It swept our masts off clean and didn't leave a shred of sail. We were half full of water besides, and the hand-pump had broke down.

"For days and then for weeks we drifted and bailed water. The winds were not steady, and the tides didn't seem to be either. We drifted in one direction and then another. There were thirty-eight of us altogether. When the rations of drinking water got so low there was hardly enough for each man to keep a killdeer alive, half the sailors ganged up and mutinied. Several were killed. That did not give us water. We had a store of wine, and a half-dozen men who broke into it and drank too much went mad and jumped overboard into the sea. Still we drifted on. Some of us had more endurance than others. That's always the way. I saw good men die. We threw their bodies overboard. Then another storm hit us, not so strong as the first one. We caught rainwater and drank. The wind blew us straight in, until our ship grounded at the west end of what you call Shell Ridge.

"Five of us were left alive. One was my pardner. The third owner had died. We came ashore in a small boat and dug a hole in the sand and got water fresh enough to drink. We still had guns, and up a bayou we saw a wild black cow and killed her. After we got a little strength, it was no trouble to keep in meat. It took us six days to get strong enough to work and decide on action.

"We dug a big hole on the side of Shell Ridge, next to the Gulf. Then we brought in a big box from the foundered ship and lowered it into the hole. Next we began putting the gold and silver into the box. We brought the stuff in buckets and just poured it in, bucket after bucket. Of course, we kept enough out to take care of us until we could get somewheres and make arrangements for coming back. After we covered up the hole, we drove brass spikes into two big drift logs half-covered by sand not far from the location.

"The only place to go was New Orleans, and the only way to get there was afoot."

Here the stranger stopped as if to consider something. McGaffey did not say a word, only listened.

"I've told you everything just as it was, so far," the stranger finally went on. "I'll keep the same tack. All five of us, with dried meat enough to last several days, set out for New Orleans. Only two of us got there — the other surviving pardner and myself. The other three never got anywhere, I'm dead certain. We had plenty to buy a sloop with. We bought it and fitted it out and still had money. We didn't mind spending. Then one night an Eyetalian stabbed my pardner down on the levee. He cut me up too, but I paid him his dues. It took me a good while to get well. I had to sell the sloop for expenses. From then on, I had to fight one head wind after another, and me one of the richest men in America. I was barred off from my wealth, like a prisoner from freedom.

"This is not the first time I have been back here, but it was four years from the time we left until I returned — alone, just as I am now. Nobody had settled here, then, but the markers had been washed away or covered up by sand. The wreck of our old boat was gone — not a sign of any kind left. And I can't locate the exact spot now any more than I could the first time I came back. You are the only soul that, drunk or sober, I have ever told the facts to. Help me find it and take half."

"I will help you and we will find it," McGaffey answered.

They searched for weeks, digging into the sand. Occasionally they had their hopes temporarily raised by striking a piece of driftwood deep underground. Finally, along in the fall, McGaffey had to quit to drive some beeves to New Orleans. The ex-pirate, much discouraged, went with him. There he got pas-

age on a ship for New York. He left an address through which
e could be reached should McGaffey find the treasure.

After returning to Shell Ridge, McGaffey went down to the
each one morning with oxen and wagon to haul up a load of
riftwood for the fireplace. A recent storm had brought in an
nusual amount of it. While he was prying one end of a log out
f the sand he uncovered a slab of lumber. He always saved any
ieces of lumber that drifted in, and had a considerable pile of
t at the house. As he worked to get this piece out he discovered
hat it was the lid to a big box.

Suddenly the idea occurred to him that the box might be the
ne buried by the pirates. As he pried the lid off, the description
f "bucket after bucket" of the stuff being poured into the box
ushed to his memory. And there the stuff was. He ran his hand
nto the vast heap of coins and slugs of gold. He threw the wood
ff his wagon so that the oxen could walk home faster through
he sand.

"I've found it! I've found it!" he cried to his wife. "We'll sell
ut and go back to Ireland and build a castle and live like the
ing of Ulster."

Then quickly McGaffey took saw and hammer and nails and
rom the boards of cypress he had been saving made three
oxes. He took them in the wagon to where he had uncovered
he treasure. There he filled them full. Still there was an im-
nense amount of gold and silver in the big box. He buried the
hree smaller boxes, scattering them some distance apart, not
ar from where he had made the find. He rushed back to the
ouse, made two more boxes, filled and buried them. It was
ong after dark before he quit work.

McGaffey's idea, as he explained to his wife, was to scatter
he treasure so that if anybody else found a part of it he would
hink he had found it all. His plan was to gather up all his

cattle immediately, drive them to New Orleans, sell them, bring the money back, dig up what was buried, haul his riches and his family to Galveston, and there ship for Ireland. Sending word to the man in New York who had led him to the wealth was not in his plans.

Before he left with the cattle he told his wife several times that he wanted to take her to the location of the five buried boxes and point them out to her. But each time she refused.

"I don't want to know," she said. "If that strange man comes back and suspicions that you have found the treasure and tried to make me tell where it is, I can't tell if I don't know. I don't want to know."

So she was left alone — and in ignorance — with the children. The faithful old Negro slave went with his master. McGaffey had three hired men to help drive the cattle. In New Orleans he paid them off. Then, after he had sold all the cattle and received payment in coin, he and Wash turned back for Sabine Pass, on horseback. They had a pack horse.

About a day's ride apart, over the road from New Orleans to Texas, were what were called "stands" — each stand consisting of a house where men could get meals and moss mattresses to sleep on, feed for their horses, and a pen for holding their cattle overnight.

Late one evening as McGaffey and Wash were nearing the stand near what is now Franklin, Louisiana, he said to his servant, "Let's ride up. I feel very queer."

They struck a gallop. The man who owned the stand was away, but his wife came out. She had to help Wash get McGaffey down from his saddle and carry him onto the gallery where she made a pallet for him. She got some camphor and went to bathing his face.

"Please don't let the camphor get in my eyes," he said in a weak voice. These were his last words. A few minutes later he was dead.

After a while the owner of the stand came in. He knew Mc-Gaffey and Wash both from stops they had made on other trips. There was nothing to do but bury the dead man. Wash rode on home with the money. If he met any robbers he was to tell them that his master was returning by boat to Galveston. Three men who evidently knew that McGaffey had driven cattle to New Orleans did hold the Negro up, but his story was so plausible that they didn't even examine his pack.

There was no castle in Ireland for Mrs. McGaffey now. Carrying her baby in her lap, while old Wash carried the older child on his saddle in front of him, she rode horseback to her husband's grave. After she had arranged for a tombstone to be put up, she returned to Shell Ridge. She reinvested some of her money in cattle. They were at best worth only a few dollars each in those times.

She did not know where the great treasure was any more than the stranger on foot calling in the night had known. She continued to live on Shell Ridge until she died. Her children grew up and married newcomers in the county. The tradition of the treasure she passed down is still told and believed by her descendants.

During the course of years, hundreds of men have taken high-priced "mineral rods," "plumb bobs," gold "calometers," miners' compasses, mine detectors, and other instruments out to Shell Ridge and prospected up and down and under it. But the sandy earth still holds what it has. Traveling mediums and fortunetellers in Beaumont have for decades answered ques-

tions about the treasure, but no answer of theirs has ever made
the earth respond.

One of the men who searched was Billy Longworth. He knew
all there was to tell about the treasure — and maybe more. I've
merely told his story. I don't know a thing more to tell.

Longworth's Vicey-Versey Map

"THERE's the papers," Longworth said.

He pointed to a stack of manuscripts maybe five inches thick.

"I started collecting leads in 1893," he said. "There's over three hundred accounts of buried treasures and plenty lost mines besides. If I just had a little more backing, my Radio Sleuth would make us rich."

We were long-time friends. He had given me a story for *Coronado's Children*, wherein I had published his San Antonio address and an account of the Radio Sleuth. He claimed to have received over a thousand letters from treasure hunters. Now we were in his room, an island of privacy to the rear of the boardinghouse run by his wife.

My eyes followed Longworth's to a complicated contraption of batteries, wires, microphones, and other parts. Then I began to look over the manuscripts. I could hear Longworth breathing and rolling a brown paper cigarette.

"I see this bullion stored at Olmos Pass has a map to it," I said.

"Yes." Longworth breathed out his words slow with the smoke. "It's a vicey-versey map," he added.

I looked up to question. Longworth was already stringing out.

I had no inclination to interrupt. This is the way he told the story.

There was a Spanish mission on the San Saba all right, but the fort across the river from it wasn't nearly so much to protect the priests as it was to protect the miners. Then in 1756, as the histories tell us, over a thousand Comanches attacked the mission. Where were the soldiers? The histories only say that the Comanches killed and burned without opposition. A lot of the miners had already fled. The soldiers were getting the bullion packed on mules for the retreat.

There were two pack outfits of thirty-seven mules each. The standard load of silver bars for a mule weighed three hundred pounds. I keep up with the price of silver purty well when I'm in town, and according to the quotations in today's San Antonio *Express*, that silver would be worth $157,549.46. Here's the sheet I figgered it on this morning. It's worth more than double what it was when I started out to locate it — all in my favor. That's not a very big treasure compared with some of the others. Still it's not to be sneezed at, and it's dead certain there. Not a flaw in the title.

Well, the caravan set out from San Saba hoping to get within the safety zone of the San Antonio garrison, more'n a hundred and fifty miles away. It was a doomed march from the beginning, but the Spaniards kept shooting the Comanches back until they reached Olmos Pass. That's up in what is now Bandera County. Here along in the afternoon the caravan discovered itself surrounded, bottled up. Hundreds of the Comanches had hurried around through Bandera Pass and blockaded the Olmos Pass trail from the south. Hundreds more closed in from behind. The hills all around were alive with them.

There was and still is a fine spring in Olmos Pass. The Spaniards forted up the best they could. They knew they couldn't carry their freight any farther. It was too bulky to dig a hole for. Them limestone hills are full of caves and fissures. They found an opening already made by nature, stored the bars inside, covered the entrance with rocks, and then made certain markings around to indicate the spot. The stuff was naturally hid out of sight of the main camp. A trusty few did the work.

The Comanches, yelling and helling around, kept them awake all night. Then next morning the massacre begun. Over one thousand warriors. That's of record. The sixty-odd Spaniards had about as much show as a bunch of jack rabbits hemmed up in a corner of wire netting by men three rows deep armed with automatic shotguns.

Comanches in them days didn't scalp so much as they did after they got to fighting Americans. And they were not fighting for the treasure at all. I doubt if they ever even looked for it. They knew where to get all the silver they wanted up in the San Saba country. Years later when Jim Bowie went up there to work the old mine and had that three-day fight with the Indians, he discovered some of them shooting silver bullets from their old muzzle-loaders. Silver was a lot plentifuler with them Comanches than lead was.

Well, after the warriors had made a clean sweep and left the country, one Spaniard who had just been shot in the groin and stunned came to life. He was an oldish man. He got him some water in a gourd and started crawling southeast, towards San Antonio, still forty or fifty miles away. The third day he saw a camp of Lipan Indians. He knew they were friendly and went to them. The daughter of the chief was specially kind to him and nursed him the best she could. Then blood poison set in.

The old herb women and the medicine men couldn't do anything with that.

He knowed his light was about to go out. So he called for a dressed deerskin and some of the red ocher the Indians always kept to paint theirselves with. Then he drawed a map of the Olmos Pass storage and gave the details I have been giving as well as some others. He told the Lipan girl to give the map and its history to a certain priest at the San Jose Mission in San Antonio and to say Gregorio Valdez died praying. Then he died.

I don't know why the map was never properly delivered. I don't know if the Lipans ever looked for the silver storage or not. I guess not. Anyhow they didn't find it. Time went on and the Lipans were still in the country when Seco Robinson went away out there in that Bandera country ahead of anybody else and settled. He had a way of getting along with Indians, and sometimes he'd buy stuff in San Antonio and trade it to them for pelts and deerskins full of honey to sell.

He traded a new Bowie knife for that Spaniard's buckskin map and got its history as handed down among the Lipans. There's one thing about an Indian: he could not read or write, but he could remember. It was the same with Seco Robinson and his descendants.

About this time the Lipans got killed off and run out of the country into Old Mexico. Seco located a section of land around Olmos Pass and built him a cabin right at the spring. I can show you yet some of the shakes he cut out of cypress with his axe to roof it.

Seco begun looking for the storage of the San Saba silver. He had the map, he knowed the country, and he could trail anything from a bee to a buffalo. But the map and the land features wouldn't fit. That pass has got all sorts of crooks and nooks and

corners and little canyons running up from it. Seco was a lot forwarder to hunt deer than bar silver anyhow, I guess. After peering round some, he lost interest. Still he kept the map.

He had a terrible big family. It looked like the older he got the more children he kept begetting. He wore out three wives before he died. One of his last wife's children was kind of afflicted, healthy enough in the body but sick in the head. She was a lunertic, I guess. Her name was Agatha, and about the time they settled down in Olmos Pass she was twelve years old.

Some member of the family used to keep an eye on her most of the time, but, crazy as she was, she knew that rattlesnakes are dangerous and she knew how to keep her directions. They got so they jest let her mosey around by herself. She'd be gone all day sometimes, but she was like a pet pig. No matter where she laid out, she'd come home about sundown. She might have the shed skin of a coachwhip snake looped around her neck, or a bunch of mountain pinks stuck in her hair, or bring in an old armadillo shell heaped full of buckeyes. She'd try to count them, they say, but never could get up to twenty. She was always bringing in things. She was as harmless as a cottontail rabbit. Once she brung in one of them monstrous Spanish stirrups. She said she'd found it covered up in leaf mould at the base of a cedar tree. It was jest another piece of evidence showing the Spaniards had passed that way.

One night at the supper table one of Seco's boys who'd been off working surprised his ma by handing her fifteen silver dollars and telling her he wanted her to go to San Antonio and buy herself some fixings.

That loco girl when she seen the silver grabbed it across the table and said, "Oh, brother, where'd you get this?"

He told her it was money he had earned.

Then she says, "I know where there's lots of heavy stuff like that. . . . Why," she goes on, "it's ricked up like wood in pieces that long." Then she measures with her hands about the length of a old-timey silver bar.

"I tried to bring a piece home once," she says, "but it was too heavy and I dropped it down in a crack."

Then all the family was at her to tell where she'd found the silver.

"Back there in the cedars," she says. "It's in a hole the gophers use, just big enough for me to crawl into." That country is jest covered with cedars, you know.

The family kept prodding her for details. Then they seen she was getting excited like she did sometimes, and they didn't question her any more that night. When she got excited that way, she was as crazy as a bedbug.

The next morning she seemed fairly ca'm, and her brother took her out to show him the rick of silver bars. She started off running. Then d'reckly she stopped and went to imitating a roadrunner bird, going crut-crut-crut thataway. The long and short of it is that she never could be made to fasten her mind on locating the storage of San Saba silver. She died years ago and is buried under an ellum tree about a hundred yards out from the spring.

Now, not a sane court in the world would take the evidence of an idiot girl. But here's a piece of evidence any court would take. After Seco Robinson was gone and his family scattered to the winds, a charcoal burner from the hill country come into San Antonio one day and after selling his charcoal and buying some groceries went up to the office of a doctor named Cattermole. The doctor pronounced his trouble an old rupture.

"How much will the operation and the hospital fee be?" the charcoal burner wanted to know.

The doctor told him. Then the charcoal burner told him he

didn't have a thing to pay with except a bar of metal he thought might be silver down in his wagon. The doctor dropped everything and went down to examine the bar. He made a fine operation, and when the man was cured got him to lead him to the spot where he'd found the bar.

That spot was beside a trail leading down into the Olmos Pass. In my mind it was the bar the idiot girl found too heavy and dropped. I undertook to trace that bar down and found where Old Dan Sullivan's bank give Cattermole close to five hundred dollars credit for it. Yes, sir, I found the entry — and the bank didn't lose anything on that deal. Doctor Cattermole got well paid for his operation all right. He bought up three or four sections of land around Olmos Pass and built what he called a country home. He looked for the storage cave for years.

One other thing. About the time the country begun to fence up with bob wire, people up in the hills turned to cutting cedar posts and selling them. Lots of families still make a living that way. Three or four of Seco Robinson's sons became regular cedar-cutters. One day three Mexicans showed up and asked the Robinson boys if they'd ever noticed anything of an iron spike driven into a Spanish oak round there. They hadn't. The Mexicans camped and spent several days looking round. One said something about this having been the range of the Lipan Indians. Then he let out his people had knowed the Lipans in Mexico. In fact, he said he had Lipan blood in his own veins.

The Mexicans went away and more'n a year later while one of Seco's boys was hunting wild turkeys and squatting under a Spanish oak trying to call up an old gobbler with a caller made out of a quill, he felt something sticking him against the shin. He kinder moved and put his hand down, at the same time watching for the gobbler. He felt the spike.

It was at a tree he had seen a hundred times and cut posts all around. The limb with the spike in it had rotted off. He could see the stub it had fallen from, but he couldn't tell which way the spike was pointing when the limb was in place.

Well, that's the way things go. The boy brung the spike in, but it didn't do him any good. The Mexicans were gone to nobody knows where, and the Spanish oak didn't seem to fit the map.

When I got hold of that map, back about the time the depression hit and bargains was plentiful, the first thing I done was to hunt up the owner of the Olmos Pass land and arrive at a clear understanding. We're under a fifty-fifty contract, but he's quit staking me to anything. I made my camp at the spring and went to inspecting the land, strip by strip, as thoroughly as my wife clears a winderpane of fly specks. Still I couldn't make the map fit.

Then I took to follering the method of the old Spanish prospectors. They slept by day and watched by night for a rainbow-colored light to play up over the ground. That's jest the blossoming on the surface of mineral gases formed below. Nothing supernatural about it at all. It's nature's signpost to silver and gold. But that was a terrible dry year and the cedars there are so thick you can't cuss a cat in 'em.

Of course, I'd examined first thing all the crevices and gopher holes, but it stands to reason that all the old openings filled up long ago with sediment washed down from above. It was jest an accident anyhow that after the Spaniards closed the entrance to their cave a gopher opened it up a little for the idiot girl to crawl into.

I made trip after trip into that country. On the last one I suddenly got the key to the map. It was thisaway: I decided on the policy of sorter playing like I was the idiot girl and going out jest so far from the spring each day. I'd mosey along and maybe spend two hours watching an armadillo dig up roots. I've had one smell the toe of my shoe. I'd spend an hour dogging a ground squirrel and then prod a beargrass stalk down his hole. I'd watch a horned frog flattened out motionless on the ground waiting for a fly to come by. Then if the fly got away and flew off, I'd foller it. Sometimes I'd get down on a grassy opening and press the grass down and then watch it raise back up or maybe I'd lay down on the grass, as still as an old rusty lizard asleep, and under my hat watch a buzzard show up and wheel and wheel over me. They say a buzzard waits the will of God. I'd notice which direction the buzzard took off and then scout out that way. I was waiting on the will of God too.

You can't expect anything out of Old Man Chance in cutting down cedar posts or raising cotton, but in this game of finding a lost mine or a lost storage, you can. I was jest kinder turning myself over to Old Man Chance.

Now I don't believe in mediums or fortunetellers or clairvoyants or anything like that. I don't believe in Spanish dip needles, wiggle-sticks, doodlebugs, magnetic finders and such frauds. I do believe in that Radio Sleuth I have perfected. It is based on scientific principles, like the torsion balance test used in oil fields. But my Radio Sleuth has to get pretty close to metal before the broken wave current is detectable. Here is where a good map or some sort of reliable waybill comes in.

Well, as I was saying, I tried to wander around and imitate the habits of Seco Robinson's idiot girl. I'd been out all day, and the next morning I had to come back to San Antonio to tend to gover'ment business. I was laying there on the pallet, my eyes kinder half shet, thinking how little a needle is in a big haystack, when I seemed to hear a voice as ca'm and clear as a fieldlark's morning call.

I can't describe how low and cautious it was also. I say I *seemed* to hear it. Mind, I'm not superstitious, though there are some things in this world I don't know. I opened my eyes and raised up. The stars made a good light, and right there by my pallet I saw — or maybe I had better say I seemed to see — that afflicted girl. I didn't even feel funny, the whole thing was so natural.

She says to me in that same low, cautious, clear voice, "I can't lead you, but if you'll read the directions vicey versey on the map, you'll find the bullion."

That's all she said, and then she wasn't there.

She'd said enough. I didn't even have the map with me, not depending on it any longer. As I've said, I had to come back home the next day. As soon as I got home, I pulled the map out and begun studying it. Then it was as plain as day to me that if a body was to go east where the map says to go west and vicey versey, things would fit a lot better. It's a vicey-versey map all right, and why that interpretation didn't come to me before, I don't know. The Spanish were reg'lar coyotes at throwing their followers off the scent, and of course this map made by a Spaniard was meant to be interpreted by a Spanish priest.

That drawing you see on the paper is just a copy. I don't show the original to many people.

Longworth got up, went over to an old-fashioned leather trunk, unlocked it, raised the lid, and lifted up a folded buckskin. The ocher markings on it had faded out entirely in places, but some were plain. I noticed one marking that looked like a tree: The plainest marks on the buckskin were a cross, and, under it, the blurred name: **Greg r o V dez 756.**

Before Longworth left on what was to be his last trip to

Olmos Pass, I bet twenty-five dollars on Old Man Chance. Longworth didn't have time enough left to make the vicey-versey map work. He had already experienced all the golden streets and pearly gates there are in the folklore of eternity.

Guarded by Rattlesnakes

UNTIL the day of his death there was not a gray streak in Longworth's Indian-black hair or a blot on his golden hope. He was tall and lank, deliberate and earnest. He wore a long black mustache that drooped like the ends of a pair of horns on an antiquated Texas steer. His eyes and soft voice seemed to have absorbed all the dreams of the *más allá* — the farther on — that had lured him for a lifetime.

I first met him in San Antonio, where so many stories and storybook characters are always waiting. He had been working off and on for years, with financial backing from a San Antonio lawyer, to clean out "an old tunnel" in the San Saba River country for the two thousand bars of silver stored there from the Lost San Saba Mine.

This is one of the many stories Longworth gave me not long before he died — effortlessly, as befitted his life. It came to him from an old one-armed sheepherder named Pedro Hernandez in the Uvalde country. Pedro was a good shot, and while he was out with his flock he used to carry a brass-bellied .44 Winchester, using the stub of his arm to support the barrel when he aimed.

One evening while he was on a knoll watching his sheep graze down a wide draw, he noticed the leaders of the herd suddenly wheel and start up it. He knew they had scented danger. Not far below the place where they had turned, a second draw emptied into the main one. Pedro's good eyes made out a coyote slunk down close to a low cliff at the junction of the draws. He fired.

When the smoke cleared away — for he used old-time black powder — he could not make out any coyote, dead or alive. He was sure he had hit the animal; the bottom land was so open that not even a jack rabbit could hide there. Puzzled as to how the coyote had disappeared, he walked to investigate. In the rocky cliff at which he had seen the coyote, but out of view from the knoll from which he had shot, he discovered the low, narrow mouth of a cave, into which coyote tracks pointed. Noiselessly he peered within but saw only darkness. He knew that if he remained silent, the coyote would, if not dead, soon come out. He took a stand where he could watch the opening and waited. Before long, the coyote's head appeared. Pedro downed him in his tracks this time. Then he scalped him, for there was a bounty on coyotes. It was summer and the pelt was worthless.

Many times Pedro had passed up and down these draws, but he had never before noticed the cave, the small entrance concealed by a jut of rock and a bush. He had matches, and now, having gathered some dried sotol leaves for flares, he went inside to look around. The farther back he went, the higher and wider he found the room. Finally, lighting matches and burning sotol leaves, he made out a pile of something on the level floor in the middle of the cave. As he got close to it, it looked like a pile of dirt. It was so far back that by now the circle of light marking the mouth of the cave looked no bigger than a tin plate.

Right at the piled-up object, he could not make out what it was. He kicked it, and the kick broke open a kind of fiber sacking. Gold coins poured out on the dusty floor. The dust was as dry as a lime-burner's hat. There were several sacks. The fiber matting, or sacking, had long ago lost all life. Pedro tried to pick one of the sacks up, but where he caught hold of it, it pulled apart and the gold jingled to the ground.

As anybody would do, Pedro now began to fill his pockets with coins. He was moving mostly in the dark, for dry sotol leaves quickly burn up. He pulled off his shirt and tied knots in the sleeves at the wrists in order to use them as bags, but the shirt sleeves had so many holes in them that he was not making much headway in bagging the gold when all at once he heard the buzzing of rattlesnakes. The buzzing sounded all around him. He dropped the shirt, and the buzzing stopped. He lit matches and looked around, but not a snake was in sight. He picked up the shirt and made two steps toward the opening of the cave. The buzzing set up again. He retreated to the pile of gold — so that he could stand on top of it and be clear of the snakes. He again dropped the shirt, and the buzzing again hushed.

Leaving the shirt where he had dropped it, Pedro again started for the opening. The rattlesnake whirring became louder and more angry in warning than ever. That sound can run needles into the spine of a man looking at a rattler in broad daylight, a safe distance off. In darkness, near at hand, it is paralyzing. But Pedro was not too paralyzed to jump back to the pile of gold. Instinctively he cast the coins from his pockets — every coin he had picked up.

The den, the cave, became as silent as the darkness was deep. Pedro lit a match and burned his last flare of sotol leaves. Not a snake, not even a snake's trail, lay on the dusty floor. When Pedro headed for the mouth of the cave this time, he heard nothing. In the sunlight at the entrance, once he was outside, he stopped and looked back. There, a few feet away in the sandy floor-covering at the mouth of the cave, he could see his own tracks and the tracks of the coyote — but no snake tracks.

Rattlesnakes do not den up in summertime, though during the day they keep in coolish places. At that time of year they do not come together in great numbers as they do to hibernate. Pedro knew this well. He knew he had seen a fortune in gold. He wondered if he had imagined the rattling. He had not, after all, seen a snake or smelled the strong rattlesnake smell. Rattlesnakes when aroused give off an odor as strong as that of excited javelinas casting musk from the back gland.

No sheepherder is avaricious, but Pedro was in need of some money. He stepped around the point of the draw, looked up it, and saw that his dog was watching the sheep. Then he gathered a big handful of dry sotol leaves and did what not one Mexican sheepherder out of a thousand would have done. He went back into the cave. When he got to the sacks and began gathering his pockets full of the gold coins, he forgot all about rattlesnakes. Soon he had all he could carry and started briskly towards the light.

At the first step a sound of rattling went up that seemed to fill the cave. He stopped dead still, dropping what money he held clutched in his one hand. The rattling continued. He lit a match, and there in front of him the biggest rattler he had ever seen was reared up waist-high, ready to strike. It is hardly necessary to say that he backed up to the sacks and emptied the last coin out of his pockets. The rattling died down. He was too weak for a while to attempt walking. Finally he got his breath, and the blood began to circulate in his body again. When he lighted a sheaf of sotol leaves and held it high so as to illumine wide spaces, he could not see a snake. He said he did not know

whether he walked or crawled or ran out of the cave. Once out, he had to lie down and rest before he could make it to where he heard the bells on his sheep.

Pedro Hernandez told Longworth that he believed the snakes were evil spirits guarding the money. If they had been real snakes, he said, they would have left trails in the powdered earth on the floor of the cave and would have smelled.

"Did you ever go back in the cave again?" Longworth asked him.

"No, *Señor,* and not for all the gold in the world would I go back."

"Will you make the sign of the cross, Pedro, and swear that you are telling me the truth about the sacks of gold?"

And Pedro made the sign of the Holy Cross and solemnly said, "I tell only truth."

He told Longworth he would guide him to the mouth of the cave — that far and no farther. One day Longworth set out from Uvalde for the ranch on which Pedro lived, but his car burned out two bearings and he had to give up the trip. Sometime after this, during prohibition days, a friend of his went to the ranch to get Pedro's guidance, but the rancher ran him off. The rancher didn't explain, but Longworth found out he had a still located on the draw not far from the rattlesnake-guarded cave. No doubt the cave is still there.

The Apache Secret of the Guadalupes

SINCE that new day for two worlds on which Spaniards plunged into the Americas after gold and silver, white men have believed that Indians know where the precious metals are but won't tell. No Indian has ever profited by revealing precious metals to the takers of his land. Yet all secrets leak, and belief in many a lost mine is fortified by a tradition of some Indian's parting with his secret.

Journeying west to survey the new international boundary that resulted from the conquest of Mexico by the United States, John R. Bartlett recorded in his diary: "The bold head of the Guadalupe Mountain has been before us eight or ten days. We were more than a hundred miles off when it was discovered. Even then its features stood out boldly against the blue sky."

Any bold stretch of earth — the Bad Lands of the Dakotas, the mighty chasm of the Colorado River between Arizona and Utah, Death Valley in California, the Guadalupe Mountains of Texas and New Mexico — is significant not only for what it reveals but for what it hides. Tradition of Apache knowledge of gold in the Guadalupes goes back to the century of Coronado's Expedition.

No other character has been so vividly connected with the tradition as Ben Sublett. Derided as a "crazy prospector," he would disappear into the vastness of the Guadalupes at a time when other men would not penetrate them except in bands to fight the Apaches. How he lived or where he went, nobody knew. He had a "hunch." According to legend, he had also a friend among the hostiles who told him a tribal secret. One day in the eighties he drove his rickety rig up to the Mollie Williams Saloon in Odessa, east of the Pecos, got out, strode inside, and in a triumphant voice called for drinks all around. The barkeeper, remembering past credits, hesitated; the loiterers, some of whom had paid Sublett's bills, remained loitering. But when the prospector threw a buckskin pouch stuffed with gold nuggets on the bar, all hands came to life.

"Boys," he cried, "Old Ben Sublett has been poor, but he ain't poor no longer. Drink!"

They drank. Old Ben Sublett drank too. "Boys," he gloated, "I hev found the richest gold mine in the world. I can build a palace of Californy marble and buy up the state of Texas for a back yard for my children to play in. Drink till the likker runs out yer ears."

Ben Sublett brought back other nuggets — they say. He never built even a shack or bought so much as a quarter-section of greasewood alkali. The golden secret kept him happy. Men trailed him, waylaid him, tried to worm into him; he never revealed a direction or a landmark. "If anybody wants my mine," he said, "let him go out into the Guadalupes and hunt fer it like I did." At the end, after demanding that his body be buried naked, he died swearing that he'd go to hell with the secret locked inside it.

I shall not repeat the stories of Ben Sublett and other seekers of Guadalupe gold told in *Coronado's Children*. When I wrote that book I was not acquainted with John C. Cremony's *Life Among the Apaches*, published in 1868. His translation of gold into silver is not unusual among traditional tales of eluding riches. "If you can't get a redbird, jaybird'll do."

One Apache well known to Cremony bore a name meaning Quick Killer. He seems to have been a Bluebeard among women and an axe-man among warriors. He hunted, slept, ate, killed, lived alone. For "some unaccountable reason" he became attached to Cremony and related to him many of his experiences. He had very long black hair, which he kept plaited, and the plait hanging down his back was ornamented with thirteen silver conchos, graduating in size from a saucer down to a circle about twice the diameter of a silver dollar. He was extremely vain of these ornaments on his luxuriant hair. Cremony supposed that they had been taken from the saddles of Mexican victims.

One day, touching the conchos, he asked, "Did you have a hard time taking these?"

"You mistake, Tata," Quick Killer replied. "These are not off Mexicans. I found silver and beat it out myself into the conchos."

"Where did you find it?" Cremony asked.

"In the Guadalupe Mountains. I was with other warriors going to the Llano Estacado to hunt buffaloes. While we were climbing the mountain to look out upon the plains and make sure they were clear of Comanches, I caught hold of a bush on a canyon wall to pull by. It gave way, and I saw a bright lump where its roots had been. I picked it up. It was heavy like the *plata* on saddles of rich Mexicans. I found more lumps and later beat them out into shape. This was many years ago. I have never been back to the place."

When John C. Cremony heard this story, he was a major in

the United States Army and was stationed at Fort Sumner, New Mexico. The year was 1863. Three or four months later he received orders to make a scouting expedition to the south. With Quick Killer as guide and with thirty-three other men, he headed for the Guadalupe Mountains. At evening camp the day they reached the Guadalupes, Quick Killer told his friend that they were near the silver and that he would guide him to it tomorrow. The next morning the whole detachment rode to a canyon. There it was halted and left in charge of a sergeant, while Major Cremony and Quick Killer rode on, the Apache leading. After they had gone about a mile and a quarter, Quick Killer gave the signal to halt. They tied their horses to a tree and, taking a short-handled pick, walked on.

In Cremony's stuff-shirted prose, "We ascended about three hundred feet until we reached a bold and unmistakable mineral ledge, thickly shrouded with underbrush and stunted trees. Quick Killer stopped a moment, examined the place well, and proceeded directly to where he wanted to dig. He unearthed, only a few inches down, several magnificent specimens of virgin silver. I was satisfied, and, possessing myself of a goodly lump, we retraced our steps to the command, none of whom were made cognizant of these occurrences."

When Cremony wrote his narrative in 1866, the Guadalupe Mountains were still held by Apaches, but he considered that the "wood, water and grass" abounding in the region of the silver would someday facilitate mining. He seems to have been one of those greedless individuals to whom knowledge means more than possession.

The way to get evidence on ghosts is to tell about seeing one — and ghosts don't die. Not long after *Coronado's Children*,

with its chapter on Ben Sublett's lost mine of Guadalupe gold, was published, a chiropractor in San Antonio furnished me this yarn, which has also been applied to the Lost Nigger Mine of the Big Bend.

In the year 1926 an old Mexican, stove-up all over and as deaf as a post, came into the chiropractor's office. He gave his name as Policarpo Gonzales — called Poly for short. He spoke fair English, but seemed as out of place there as a sandhill crane in a chicken coop.

All he wanted, he said, was to be able to hear music. He began taking treatments, and after one about three weeks later asked permission to rest a while in the office before going home. While he was resting someone turned on the radio.

Crying out, "I hear music! I hear music!" Policarpo began to dance. His steps and rhythm were so unusual that the chiropractor asked him where he had learned this dance. "From the Apaches," he answered. His face was gleaming, and when he said good-by he was swinging his hands and humming with the music.

The next day he returned, very grave, and said: "Doctor, you have done much for me. I hear now the delightful music. Last night on the plaza I could hear the accordion and the guitar. But I have no money to give you. It is true that I did not promise money, but I owe. I must pay somehow. Listen. . . .

"When I was eleven years old my mother gave me to Colonel Boone. That was while he was stationed at Fort Stockton to fight the Apaches. Sometimes I went to school with the children of the officers. Often I rode with the men on scouts. One summer night, while only fourteen of us were camped away to the south towards the Chisos Mountains, more than fifty Apaches attacked. They were all yelling. We fought. I know not how many were killed on either side. In the end I found myself wounded in the leg and captured.

"Yet I was not afraid. My mother had told me that Indian blood is in my veins. In my heart I am *puro Indio*. The Apaches often captured Mexican children and trained them to be good tribesmen. They were kind enough to me. I learned to shoot the bow and arrow with the other boys. I learned their language and to dance.

"Also, I learned where the Apache gold in the Guadalupes is. The Guadalupes were our stronghold. Sometimes I would go into the cave with men and help them break off chunks of the ore. Certain Apaches friendly with the Mexicans who came from New Mexico to catch mustangs or from Chihuahua to haul salt from the salt lake south of the Guadalupes would trade this ore for guns and ammunition. There was no other use for the gold. More than one stranger stealing into the Guadalupes to hunt it was caught and killed. The Apaches did not want the gold. All they wanted was to be left alone in their own land.

"All the time the white men kept coming nearer. At last nearly all the warriors had been killed. Some had gone to join Geronimo's band to the west. Then one day the chief called together all who were left and told us that we could hold the land no longer. He told us to fill up the entrance to the cave so as to hide the gold.

"It was within reach of a spring. We rolled and carried rocks for two days; we covered up all sign of the cave. Then the chief called me to one side. He said I was to go back to white people. He and the other Apaches were going to Arizona to surrender, or maybe into the Sierra Madre. He told me if ever I found one white man to trust I might show him the gold. Soon after that we parted. I was eighteen years old."

After this talk, Policarpo walked the floor several minutes, muttering what the chiropractor took to be Apache words. Then he continued: "In all these forty-nine years I have been in many places, known many men. You are the first I have found it in my heart to tell. I owe you for something better than gold. If you will take me, I will show you where the gold is. Like the Apache, I myself want little."

Within twenty-four hours the chiropractor had supplies and Policarpo in his car and was driving for the Guadalupes. They left the car at a ranch that furnished horses. Then, with a blanket apiece and a few provisions, they rode to the spring which Policarpo said had been the Indian camping ground. They came to it in the late evening and after Policarpo dismounted and got the stiffness out of his knees, he made a speech in Apache, seemingly, to his departed people and his own departed years. "If I could call them back," he said in English, "I would be young again."

There were plenty of deer in the country and that night, after eating venison, Policarpo told stories of his youth — stories so definite and circumstantial in detail that there could be no doubt of his having lived with the Apaches, but stories not pertaining to the gold. In the morning he said he wanted to go alone.

While the chiropractor waited, a doe looked at him and then drank from the spring, a javelina came into view, gave the danger signal and wheeled back into the underbrush, an eagle screamed overhead.

When the sun was maybe three hours high, Policarpo called. After the man he trusted reached him, he led the way down a rough slope. Then he stopped and sat on a rock.

His voice was pleasant and happy and his face was bright as he said, "We Indians never forget. I remember everything as well as if it had been yesterday." He was silent a little while. Then he got on his knees, locked his hands together, and put them, knuckles down, on the ground at the point of his knees.

"Forty-five feet down, pure gold," he said.

He loosened a big rock and showed how the Apaches had rolled boulders to fill up the mine entrance. "When we Indians hide anything," he said, "no white man can find it."

Back at the spring Policarpo showed where his lodge and the chief's lodge and other shelters had been. The only thing to do now was to return to San Antonio and prepare for excavation and mining. Men, tools, pack outfit, and other expensive necessities would be required.

Within a few weeks old Policarpo, who had done all that could be expected of him, died. A year later the chiropractor returned to the Guadalupes and camped at the spring for a month. He easily found the spot over "pure gold, forty-five feet down." He marked it well — and then came away. "There's an old saying," he explains, "that it takes a mine to work a mine. I'm waiting for that first mine."

The Indian who as a favor tells a secret of hidden gold is not obligated to prove anything. I'm not either. In 1941 I helped Mr. J. D. Talley celebrate his eighty-eighth birthday, in Austin, Texas. He was a refined old gentleman of marked neatness and did not look or talk as a cowboy who had ridden the open range and trailed longhorn herds to the wild cow-towns of Kansas is supposed to look and talk. That evening he told this tale.

When his people moved to Hays County — the county of the beautiful San Marcos River — in 1870, they became neighbors to an odd character named Reece Butler who had been on the frontier a long time. He had a few cattle, farmed a little, hunted whenever he wanted to, was a blacksmith, carpenter, and furniture-maker and could do anything. He made a wagon out of bois d'arc wood he got up on Red River. He made fiddle keys out of the wood of Mexican persimmon. He made charcoal for the forge in his blacksmith shop out of mesquite wood. He claimed that mesquite charcoal produces a hotter fire than cedar charcoal, which is more commonly used. He made crucibles from clay found on the Colorado River near Austin.

Reece Butler had fought the Indians, but he had also been friendly to some of them, and one time an Indian whose life he had saved guided him to a deposit of silver and gold ore somewhere in the Llano River country — where the Lost San Saba Mine is sometimes placed by hunters who can't find it on the San Saba. About once a year Reece Butler would yoke six oxen to his homemade bois d'arc wagon and pull out alone. A month or so later he would come back with a heavy load of black-looking ore. What he did with it was no secret, but the place where he got it was. One time a man tried to follow him; the man did not come back.

He would unload the ore at his blacksmith shop, pound it into small pieces no bigger than acorns, place them in one of his clay crucibles and then use his bellows and mesquite charcoal to melt the metal. The extract from a wagon load of ore would amount to a hunk about as big as Reece Butler's two burly fists. It was mostly silver, but anybody could see streaks of gold in it. This hunk of gold-tinged silver he would take to Austin and sell to a jeweler named Bahn.

In the course of nature Reece Butler died, and with him died all knowledge of the ore deposit shown by one Indian to one white man.

O. Henry's Treasure Hunt

AUTOBIOGRAPHICAL facts never inhibit the art of a true story-teller any more than any kind of facts hobble hope in a genuine treasure-hunter. In "Buried Treasure," O. Henry wrote:

"I had been every kind of a fool except one. I had expended my patrimony, pretended my matrimony, played poker, lawn tennis, and bucket-shops — parted soon with my money in many ways. But there remained one role of the wearer of cap and bells that I had not played. That was the Seeker after Buried Treasure."

"Bexar Script No. 2692" — which first appeared in O. Henry's *Rolling Stone*, published at Austin, Texas, and read mostly by Austin people — brings in "the well-known tradition of a buried treasure on Shoal Creek west of the city," and "three young men" who dug there "last Thursday night with great diligence."

One of these young men was William Sydney Porter, later to be known as O. Henry. They dug in 1894. Two years later, the treasurer of Travis County, of which Austin is the seat, killed himself over this treasure. He had advanced over forty-five hundred dollars of county money to a pair of crooks who claimed to be spending it to get a "correct chart" to the treasure. The day that his books were to be audited, the treasurer relieved his bondsmen by taking his own life. Every once in a while somebody still digs on Shoal Creek, following a tradition that, long before Sydney Porter came to Texas, two Mexican generals entertained in the home of Governor Pease gave him, as a token of appreciation, a waybill to the treasure.

That was not the waybill, however, that O. Henry dug by. I will tell the story as I set it down years ago at the dictation of a veteran newspaperman named Vic Daniels. He knew O. Henry well in Austin and shared his literary aspirations. His brother Dixie Daniels was for a time O. Henry's partner on the *Rolling Stone*.

The velocity of the *Rolling Stone* was hardly perceptible to the naked eye and O. Henry was yearning for a wider outlet when he learned that the *Hatchet*, a humorous weekly published in Washington and regarded by some as a peer to *Life* or *Judge*, could be bought for twenty-five hundred dollars. Major George W. Littlefield, the chief banker in Austin, talked hospitably about the venture and expressed an anxiety that "Texas get more notice in a literary way," but he would not put up any money.

Then the appearance of a character far removed from the financial world made O. Henry believe — for an hour — that he was about to have money to throw at the birds. When he came to Texas from North Carolina, he lived long enough on a sheep ranch down towards the Rio Grande to learn "cowpen Mexican." Later, while he was working in the Texas State Land Office at Austin, he returned to the region to inspect state-owned lands. One night a rancher leasing state land told him a treasure story that had been told him by a *pastor* (shepherd) named Enrique.

The next day O. Henry ate *frijoles* with Enrique in camp and made him glad by listening. According to the Mexican's story, while Santa Anna's armies were trying to put down the revolting Texans in 1836, the paymaster and the general of one division colluded to steal the pay money that had, after much delay, arrived for officers and men. The plan of the thieves was to hide it and leave it until an opportunity arrived for getting it out of the country. They considered it wise to store the money where white men seldom went.

With seven privates to aid him in transporting and burying the gold, the paymaster turned away from the San Antonio and Nacogdoches road, on which the army was camped, for the "mountains" up the Colorado River. On the way two of the privates hatched a scheme for securing the wealth to themselves. In the night they slit the throats of the paymaster and the five other privates, saving a canteen of their blood. They were in the vicinity of what is now Austin, at the edge of the Colorado hills. They buried the money on a creek running into the Colorado River, not far above the junction. Then they poured the blood over the buried treasure as a "warden." Next, according to the nature of greed — and to a plot that was traditional when Chaucer made "The Pardoner's Tale" into the finest treasure story ever written — one of the two murderers killed the other. He made a chart to keep. Meanwhile, the guilty general had gone on with Santa Anna's army to San Jacinto, where he was killed. The surviving murderer was now the lone master of a fortune.

But he could not possibly get out of the country with it alone. He could not rejoin the army. What saved him was the defeat of the Mexicans and their disorderly retreat. The avenging Texans drove out of the country many Mexicans who had not taken a military stand. The thief-murderer got across the Rio Grande, but was afraid to come back for his fortune. His wants had never been educated, anyhow, and, according to an old Spanish proverb, "He who wants little has all."

As years went on, he began to talk of the buried fortune. Most who heard him did not believe; nobody who believed had ambition enough to risk the long trip and the terrible *Tejanos*. "He who wants little has all." As a boy the ancient *pastor* now pouring his story into O. Henry's ears heard it from the man who had himself poured human blood over the money in the ground. The *pastor* believed the story. O. Henry believed it also.

But the *pastor* did not have the chart. To get it he would have to go far into Mexico and secure it from the son of the man who made it, now dead. He offered to get it and deliver it for one hundred dollars. O. Henry advanced twenty dollars on the deal — all he could muster at the time — and promised the other eighty dollars upon delivery of the chart. Then O. Henry returned to Austin and became absorbed in his new literary plaything, the *Rolling Stone*. He had almost forgotten about the *pastor* and the chart, and he and Vic Daniels were figuring in every direction how to raise money to take over the Washington *Hatchet* when a letter — written by an *evangelista*, a scribe for illiterates — arrived from the *pastor*.

The *pastor* said that he had made the journey back to his old home, located the chart, and now was very sick, too sick to travel. If the *patrón* would send him forty-five dollars more, he would dispatch the chart by his son, who would not only deliver it but interpret it. O. Henry scraped up forty-five dollars and sent it. Vic Daniels scoffed, saying that he would never see Mexican or chart. "Yes, I will," O. Henry declared. "You don' know how faithful and reliable an old Mexican like that *pastor* is."

Three months or so passed, and then one day the son of the *pastor* arrived in Austin on a poor, sore-backed, red roan pony and found his way to O. Henry. He delivered the chart and re ceived the remaining thirty-five dollars due on it. It called for a live oak tree on a creek west of what is now Capitol Hill. Shoal Creek runs down just west of the main city of Austin into the Colorado River. The trunk of the live oak could be located by two eagle wings cut into it. Here the interpreter of the chart said that the wings should be flying up the creek. Forty-five varas from the tree, north, up the creek, lay the gold, four and one-half feet underground, near the bank.

There were supposed to be sixteen thousand doubloons in the chest. O. Henry and Vic Daniels figured that at $16.66 each, the total value would be close to $260,000. Such a great sum sounded unreasonable, but when they figured the number of men in Santa Anna's army, the pay of the soldiers at the rate of $1.50 a month, the pay of the officers, and the fact that the pay had been accumulating over a period of six months, the money in the pay chest should have totaled just about a quarter of a million dollars. O. Henry secured the opinion of a professor of geology in the University of Texas, who estimated that since 1836 there had been a deposit of about fourteen inches of soil along the bank of Shoal Creek. That would mean that the chest was down five feet, eight inches.

With such details in hand, the two Daniels boys and O. Henry made a reconnaissance. They found a live oak tree with what appeared to be a pair of eagle wings carved on it. The bark of the tree had been scaled off and the wings cut into the bole. The marks were so barked over that unless one had been looking for them they would never have been detected, and it took imagination to translate them into eagle wings. With a borrowed surveyor's chain, they measured off forty-five varas to a likely-looking spot for digging.

On the evening after these preliminaries were finished O. Henry hired a livery rig with the understanding that if it were not returned that night the liveryman might look for it at Manchaca on the road to San Antonio. The treasure hunters were keeping their activities and plans secret. If they dug up the money, they were going to take it to San Antonio and put it in a bank. The livery rig was loaded with spades, grubbing hoes, and a lantern.

About dark, having hidden their buggy in the brush, the treasure hunters began digging. After going a foot or so through soil that had apparently never been disturbed, they came to a pocket of soft earth, about four feet long and three feet wide. Earth once loosened and put back in a hole always retains a certain loose texture — so regular diggers claim. The hunters were getting down to about the four-foot level and were intensely absorbed, their lantern adjusted so that its rays would not spread beyond the hole, when the most unearthly yell imaginable arose from the undergrowth along the creek, seemingly not forty yards away. It sounded like the whoop of a drunk man turned into a fiend, the scream of a panther and the scalp yell of a Comanche, all combined.

The hunters froze in their tracks. A minute later the yell was repeated from another direction. Then from another. Vic Daniels blew out the lantern and reached for an old Navy six-shooter he had brought along. But the others would not allow him to shoot. After a silence of several minutes, the lantern was relit and the diggers were at work again. But only for a short time was there peace. The unearthly yells, here, there, all around, were resumed. The fortune seekers drove back to town.

The next morning the Austin *Statesman* had a headline story on the escape of a maniac from the Insane Asylum into the brush along Shoal Creek, where he let out yells awful beyond description until his pursuers "bayed" him by surrounding him and giving back yell for yell.

With lingering but dampened hope, O. Henry went back to the hole soon after daylight. Nobody disturbed him while he dug until the soft ground played out and he struck limestone that had evidently never been penetrated. He quit, satisfied that the $260,000 had never been buried. Not long after this episode he ran away from Austin to South America to escape trial for embezzling bank funds. He returned and was sent to a prison that gave him the opportunity to associate with his own imagination and write. His treasure hunt furnished material for two or three treasure stories that followed.

Where Did Sam McFarland
Cross the Colorado?

A~T THE~ beginning of this century Samuel Louis McFarland was selling Singer sewing machines in the hill country of Texas drained by the San Saba, Llano, and Colorado rivers. In youth he had taught a country school in his native Kentucky. He had preached, tried sheep-raising, and, like Audubon and Grant, kept a store. After he got among a remote population in Texas he practiced obstetrics before he turned to sewing machines. He had a faculty for making money and likewise for losing it, but he always lit on his feet. The great knack of hoping never decayed within him.

After McFarland settled in Burnet, amid hills of legendary lost silver lodes, he took to carrying a pick in his buggy. As he drove over the country with his sewing machines, he wasn't exactly prospecting, but went prepared to prospect should anything likely show up.

On a hot, dry day in the summer of 1902, while returning home, he halted at the Colorado River ford to let his horses drink and cool off. The water was only a few inches deep at the ford and it was clear. He dipped up a cup of it, and while he was standing there by the buggy drinking, he noticed, a

little to one side, a dark streak, or seam, in the rocky bottom of the river. He was curious.

He pulled off his shoes and socks, rolled up his trousers, got his pick from under a sack of corn that he always carried in the back of the buggy, and while his horses gratefully let the water drip from their lips, dug into the formation. He dug out between twenty and thirty pounds of chunks, put them in his buggy for a test, and then with cheerful feelings drove his cheered horses on into Burnet.

A man who had been "a kind of mining engineer" out West was living there at this time, and the next morning Sam McFarland showed him a chunk of ore about the size of a man's fist.

"What kind of ore is this, anyway?" he asked.

The kind of mining engineer seemed very much excited. "Why, this is horn silver," he exclaimed. "Where did you get it?"

"Out of the Colorado," Sam McFarland replied.

The mining engineer misunderstood him and in a disappointed tone said, "Yes, they have lots of it out in that state."

"No," Sam McFarland said, "I don't mean Colorado state. I mean the Colorado River here in Texas."

The engineer was more excited than ever. "I'll go in partners with you," he said, "and we'll start taking out the ore. That ore will make us as rich as cow yards — if there's enough of it."

"From the looks of the vein," Sam McFarland said, "there's plenty of it."

"Just where'd you say you saw it?" the engineer asked.

He had a reputation for being slick. "I didn't say," was the only answer he got.

The discoverer of the silver had another partner in mind. His daughter Gertrude was marrying Hugh Furman, whom he liked very much. He showed Hugh a chunk of the ore, told him how and where he had found it, and wanted to go after it at once. But Hugh was busy on another project. He was a kind of *mañana* man, anyhow, his father-in-law thought. Meanwhile, Sam McFarland was expanding, looking as usual for new pastures. Word came that he had been awarded a contract for grading a stretch of roadbed for a railroad building into the Rio Grande Valley.

He left the hills and rivers where Jim Bowie looked for silver and where, almost from the day that Bowie died in the Alamo and carried all his secrets to another world, generations of men have been looking for the "Lost Bowie Mine." For several years Sam McFarland's enterprises flourished and he made money. Then one winter day as he was boarding a train he slipped on the icy steps and severely injured his back. Financial reverses followed the injury. In 1925, at the age of seventy-one, he went to live with his daughter Gertrude and her family in

Maryland. He had plenty of time now for memories, and a seam of ore in the bed of the Colorado River down in Texas became a very bright one.

One day he told his story to his grandson Harold Furman, who was still in school. The gleam of the silver under water took his eye also. In the spring of 1927, youth and grandfather went to Texas and to the crossing of the old Burnet-San Saba wagon road on the Colorado River. The river was on a rise, and they could see nothing. Things seemed changed anyhow. While waiting for the river to run down and for summer drouth to lower the flow to the minimum, the two drove on south visiting relatives. Finally, in August they headed back north out of Corpus Christi for the Colorado crossing. They had driven only a few miles when a car smashed into them, breaking old Sam McFarland's leg. He had to go back to Maryland on a stretcher. He died the next January without having recovered.

In 1930 the grandson came again, alone this time. "The water was very deep." He found nothing. All he knows is the story that his grandfather told him, his father's distinct recollection of holding a chunk of heavy ore in his hand, and his mother's recollection of seeing more chunks in their Burnet home. He gave me the story after a series of dams on the Colorado River had formed lakes that submerge all the old fords for many miles.

The *Mezcla* Man

Elojio Juarez of the Rancho de Los Olmos and I were riding in the big pasture of open hills on the south side of the Nueces River. He knew all that country as intimately as any of the thousands of deer and javelinas knew the trails through their own thickets. Its traditions had come down to him through generations of vaquero people. He was quiet and had laughing eyes, and no better vaquero ever roped an outlaw Brahma steer in the chaparral.

Fine September rains had fallen that year. Calves, tails stretched out, were running around their grazing mothers. Bulls had mats of mud on their heads from butting gully banks. Our horses seemed to feel as fresh and free as the white-tailed deer showing us their flags as they bounded into the mesquites. Elojio and I felt fresh and free too. When we came up on a high ridge where we looked across the San Casimero — 20,000 acres in one pasture — to the Casa Blanca hills, towards San Diego, we instinctively stopped and got down on the green-turfed ground. Elojio rolled a shuck cigarette, I filled my pipe, and the horses went to chopping off mouthfuls of mesquite grass.

"Know you," Elojio said, "that all this land down the Nueces and far to the south used to be in sheep?"

"I have heard so," I answered.

"There was the *brasada*," he went on, "but between the thickets was all prairie, where mustangs ran and the flocks of sheep moved slow and white, like clouds from the Gulf of Mexico with morning sunshine on them. It was the time of rich, rich *hacendados* and poor *pastores*" — the owners of haciendas and peonized sheepherders.

And then, for we were in no more of a hurry than the floating Gulf clouds, Elojio told this story.

There were no banks in the country then, and so when the rich rancheros sold their wool and sheep, they brought the money home. It was gold, with some silver. They had secret holes in the rock walls of their houses for hiding away the money. Often they buried it in the floor. The floors were of dirt cemented with bull blood to make it hard. They had secret places for gold under the fireplace rocks. Sometimes they put it in holes outside the houses, maybe close to the corrals. There were many places to hide the gold.

There were robbers, too, who came down from the north, and bandits who raided up from the other side of the Rio Grande. And always there were the Indians, the Comanches and the Lipans, but they were not after gold; they took horses and children and girls.

Now, one ranchero had more sheep and more wool and more *pastores* and *vacieros* than any other. Each *vaciero* superintended several shepherds and kept them supplied with food, for they could never leave their flocks. This old rich ranchero had more gold also than any other man, and he was very cunning. He lived in the high hills of the Casa Blanca country west of San Diego. His house was a kind of fort, with walls higher than the flat roof and loopholes in the walls to shoot through. He kept a guard up there on the roof day and night.

One time after he had sold thousands of sheep and had conducted a caravan of carts loaded with wool to San Antonio, he brought home more gold than he had ever had before. But now instead of hiding it in his house, he carried it in secret to the highest hill on his ranch. It was not far from the house. People still call it Cerro del Rico — Hill of the Rich One. On the upper slopes of this hill and on top of it black chaparral and catsclaw and other thorned brush grew so dense a javelina could hardly squeeze through it. The top of the hill was flat; perhaps it still is, and here in the middle of the thicket was a small natural clearing. The trail up to this clearing was very dim and thorny, for hardly anybody but the wildcats ever traveled it.

The cunning old *rico* knew it though. He went up alone with his gold. It must have been right after a rain, for he found mud. There in the middle of the clearing he made a great big man out of *mezcla*, which is a mixture of mud and straw or little sticks, the same as adobe. Big sticks supported the legs and neck and arms of the *mezcla* man. He was as big as a giant, and he was natural like a picture. His head was thrown back, and his mouth was wide open. He stood with his arms stretched to the east and to the west, and across his chest was this writing:

DIG OUT TO THE EAST AND THE WEST
THE WAY MY HANDS ARE POINTING
AND YOU WILL FIND
THE GOLD

Oh, but this *mezcla* man was strange-looking, and his stomach was so big that anybody who looked at him would have to laugh. Perhaps Sancho Panza looked like him.

After the cunning old *rico* had finished making the *mezcla* man there in the middle of the thicket on top of the hill where nobody ever went, and had written on his breast that waybill to the gold, he kept his secret. He raised more sheep and the shearers sheared more wool for him and he got more gold and hid it. All he paid out was coppers. He was like two millstones grinding out gold from the people under him and around him. They say that when he snored at night his snores said, "*Más oro, más oro.*"

Then one night while he was snoring for "more gold, more gold," the bandits came as quietly as the owl flies and choked the guards before they could shoot or cry out and went into the snoring room. They grasped the cunning old *rico* while he was still on his back.

"Your gold," the chief of the bandits said.

"There is none," the *rico* replied.

"You had better say," the *bandido* said.

"There is none," the *rico* repeated. That is all he would say.

"Hang him," the chief of the *bandidos* ordered.

The others tied his hands behind him and took a hair rope, so that it would not cut his skin too much, and noosed him by the neck. Then they drew the other end of the rope over a beam and pulled him up until his feet were kicking nothing but air. When he went to breathing like a lassoed wild horse choking down, they lowered him.

"What is the name of the dance you were doing for us?" one of the bandits laughed.

The *rico* said nothing.

"Now say where the gold is," the leader ordered.

"There is none."

"One more chance you have," the leader said.

"There is none."

"All right," the leader cried, "hang him up again."

Again he danced and again he strangled, but the dance was weaker and the sound of the little air passing through the tight noose was shriller. The bandits let him down again.

"For the last time," the bandit chief said, "I ask where is the gold."

The *rico* was purple in the face and coughing, but he wheezed out, "There is none."

"May you go with God!" one bandit called as he tightened his hand on the rope to pull.

"And all you to the *infierno*," the *rico* gasped back.

"That's where you will snore now for more gold," another bandit taunted.

After the *rico's* legs had made their last jerk, the taunter observed, "He loved his gold better than his life."

"It was his pride that he loved," the bandit chief said — "even better than the Holy Virgin."

Then all went to searching. They looked in his bed and under his bed and all the other beds, paying no attention to the crying women and children. They got bars and dug into the floors and pried up rocks of the fireplaces. They found the store of candles and had the rooms all lit up while they tapped and hammered on the walls searching for secret little holes fitted with money boxes. They pried up the lid of the big leather chest. They looked everywhere there was to look inside the house and found not one piece of gold, but they knew plenty of it was somewhere.

When daylight came they went to digging holes at certain places under mesquite trees and around the big corral. They were many and well armed, and they impressed all the *peones* to dig for them. They were as cunning as the old *rico* himself, and some rode around looking for signs. One found the trail going up through the brush on that hill and followed it and came to the *mezcla* man. He could not read the writing on the *mezcla* man's breast, but he knew it meant something. He came back yelling, "Now it is found, now it is found."

All the bandits went up the hill. The leader read out aloud the words on the *mezcla* man's breast: "Dig out to the east and the west the way my hands are pointing, and you will find the gold." What joy they had! Quickly they dug under the hands of the *mezcla* man, but the packed earth had never been softened by digging. The directions did not say how far out

to dig, and now the bandits ran east and west the way the
hands pointed, looking for likely places to dig. Perhaps it is
here, perhaps it is there, perhaps it is over yonder. They dug
and dug. They were in a hurry, not only from eagerness for
the gold but from knowledge that before long honest people
would find out about the murder of the *rico*, a very important
man, and begin trailing them down.

With all the travel up and down the hill, from digging to
water and food and from water and food to digging, the trail
became as plain as the road to Laredo. On the afternoon of the
second day the bandits heard horses galloping. They left the
country.

When the ranchmen who were after the bandits came to the
thicket and saw the strange *mezcla* man and read that writing
on his breast, they forgot all about murder and justice. They
thought only of finding the gold. Nobody was after them, and so
they could dig as deep and as far out as they wanted to. They
would sight along the *mezcla* man's shoulders and along his arms
and out his forefinger and out his middle finger and out his little
finger, trying, trying to locate the right place on the ground to
dig for the gold. They even sighted out to a hill five miles
away and dug a hole there. They cut paths through the brush
east and west. But after they had dug and dug and found nothing, they became disgusted and quit.

Then the *pastores* began grazing their sheep up to the Cerro
del Rico. Each had a shepherd dog with his flock. The way
to train a dog to guard sheep is to take him away from his
mother before he opens his eyes and let him suck a ewe. When
he grows up, he thinks he is a sheep and will not let a coyote or
anything else bother his kinspeople. These *pastores* would leave
their dogs to care for the sheep and go up the hill and dig
all day long. They dug new holes and they dug the old holes

deeper. But they did not find anything, and after a while they became disgusted and quit coming.

Only one old *pastor* did not quit. He was more wise and had more knowledge than any of the other *pastores*. He knew what it meant when the coyotes howled on top of the hills after sunup instead of in the valleys before daybreak. He knew what it meant when the bullbats were thick in the evening air. He knew what it meant when rattlesnakes crawled around in the middle of a hot summer's day instead of remaining asleep in the shade of bushes. He said that when a *paisano* (road-runner) stopped suddenly while running down a trail, stood on one leg, and bowed his head, he was praying — praying for rain, perhaps. He could make better medicines than anybody else out of the leaves of the gray *cenizo* plant, the bark of the huisache tree, and the roots of the leather weed. He could read in the stars, and also, it was said, he could read an almanac. He was very astute, very wise.

So he kept on coming to that high hill and digging. Every morning he would put his gourd of water down at the *mezcla* man's feet, take his grubbing hoe and spade, and then for hours dig, dig, dig. He made some of the old holes deeper and he put down new holes. Meanwhile his shepherd dog kept the sheep out on the prairie.

One hot day after he had been working very hard and was very thirsty and tired, he came in from his digging to drink from the gourd. He took the stopper made of shucks from its mouth and, while his head was raised up to receive the water, his eyes fell again on the writing upon the *mezcla* man's breast. He had read it many times, but he read it again out loud: "Dig out to the east and the west the way my hands are pointing and you will find the gold."

After he had done drinking, the *pastor* regarded the writing for a long time. He read it again, over and over. At last he said, speaking to the man of mud and sticks in front of him:

"Why, the robbers came here and found you and read what you say and dug out to the east and the west, and they did not find any gold. Then all the rich and important rancheros in the country came. They had confidence in your word, and they dug out to the east and west, and they did not find gold. Then after they quit, the *pastores* still believed you, and they dug more holes and made the old holes deeper. But they did not find any gold. And I! Well, here I have been listening to you and digging my arms off for over a year, and I have never found so much as a copper *centavo*.

"Why, you are just an old billy goat of a liar!" Then he slapped him on his big mouth.

The *pastor* was very indignant. "Shameless one," he said, "it is not with your mouth that you deceive. Right now your lying to honest people will end."

He seized his spade and hacked off the head of that *mezcla* man with his wide-open mouth. Then he chopped off the right arm, which pointed to the east, and then the left arm, which pointed to the west. And then, *wow!* he came with all his might down through the words on the *mezcla* man's breast and into his enormous stomach.

And when he did, the gold coins and some silver coins too just poured out on the ground. They were so heavy that the *pastor* could not carry them all. You see, the cunning old ranchero had built the man to hold plenty, and then he had fed him through his open mouth until he was full.

"Elojio," I asked when he thus ended his story, "what did the *pastor* do with so much money?"

"Oh, he gave his master some of it, and he kept the rest, and he never had to herd sheep any more. He went back on the other side of the river into his own country, and there he lived *muy contento* all the rest of his life."

And very contented I now rode on with Elojio.

Notes and Credits

Notes and Credits

I see no valid reason for repeating in notes information given in the main text. The Bowie knife narrative demands proof, and so it is annotated *ad taedium*. I wish, above all, to give credit to the storytellers who have told unto me.

Part One

CORN DODGERS AND SAN JACINTO CORN

Of homesteading on the Tombigbee River in Mississippi, in 1818, Gideon Lincecum wrote: "Soon all the families had houses, and all hands went to work, cutting down and clearing the maiden forest to make fields to plant corn in. I cut down six acres of the canebrake that jammed itself almost down to the place where I built my house. I burnt off the cane on the 5th of May, and planted it with a sharp stick on the 6th. Twice while it was growing I cut and beat down the young cane that sprouted up from the old cane stumps. That was all the work the crop got. The bear and raccoons ate and destroyed a good deal of it, and yet I gathered 150 bushels of good corn." — *Autobiography* of Gideon Lincecum, *Publications* of the Mississippi Historical Society, Vol. VIII, 1904, 471-472.

The story of the biscuit cartwheels was a common story, in varying forms. "During the time I was without bread, a man stayed all night with us who had just come to the country. He had some crackers and gave the children some. My son took his out in the yard, made a little wagon and used the crackers for wheels." "Reminiscences of

Capt. Jesse Burnham," *Texas Historical Association Quarterly*, V (1901), 13-14.

A. W. Eddins contributed "The First Corn Crop in Texas" to *Legends of Texas*, edited by me for the Texas Folklore Society, 1924, 236-237. Somebody whose name I have forgotten gave me the incident of the little girls and pigs, which I have added to the narrative of a typical family of settlers.

The San Jacinto corn episode is in *The Life of Sam Houston, The Only Authentic Memoir of Him Ever Published*, 1855, and in subsequent biographies by Crane (1884), Bruce (1891), Marquis James (1929). W. A. Craddock, whom I quote on corn raised from the grains given out by Sam Houston, was a solid, genuine man, with strong historical interests, even if mightily opinionated.

THE WILD WOMAN OF THE NAVIDAD

"The Reminiscences of Mrs. Dilue Harris," *Texas Historical Association Quarterly*, IV, 97-108, include details about the African who ran away from an owner on the Brazos and made his way to the Navidad.

The "Reminiscences" of Samuel C. A. Rogers are in manuscript form in Archives of the University of Texas Library.

Martin M. Kenney's manuscript was first published by his daughter, Mrs. Margaret Kenney Kress, of the University of Texas, in *Legends of Texas*.

Victor M. Rose, *Some Historical Facts in Regard to the Settlement of Victoria, Texas*, Laredo, Texas, 1883, 71-72, gives a cursory sketch of the "wild woman" and assigns the date of her appearance from 1840 to 1850.

Under the title of "The Wild Man of the Woods," a number of fabricated letters, over the name of Mose Evans, "contributed by Swante Palm," are in *A Texas Scrap-Book*, compiled by D. W. C. Baker, New York, 1875, 361-366. In a letter to Sam Houston from his wife, dated May 8, 1848, Mrs. Houston notes: "Your friend Mose Evans 'the wild man of Texas' has become a baptist and a very pious man." (Marquis James, *The Raven*, Indianapolis, 1929, 368.) For full treatment of the character, see "Mose Evans: the Wild Man of the Woods," by Donald Day, *Publications* No. XVIII (*Backwoods to Border*) of the Texas Folklore Society, Austin, 1943, 89-104.

After being captured, according to Victor M. Rose, as cited above, the Negro was named Jimbo and sold by his captors to P. T. Bickford, of Refugio County. "Jimbo would run away when work assigned him was not to his taste, and spent the greater part of his time in the woods, a refugee from justice. He could give no account of himself whatever, and the general supposition is that he was one of a cargo of slaves brought from Africa to Texas by the notorious Monroe Edwards and was lost in the woods while too young to remember the history of his captivity. May we suggest that he might have been one of the lot of Africans that escaped from the Bowie brothers? . . . He was a fetich worshipper and with a jackknife carved his gods from a shingle. Freed by the Civil War, he finally gravitated to the ranch of Mr. Tijerina, a Mexican gentleman residing on the San Antonio River, where he died in the year 1881."

"Wild man" and "wild woman" stories got into fiction, as witness the "wild man" clapped into Captain Marryat's *Narrative of the Travels and Adventures of Monsieur Violet in California, Sonora and Western Texas* (1843); "The Wild Girl of the Nebraska" and "The Texan Huntress" that Charles W. Webber brought into his *Tales of the Southern Border* (1868) and *Wild Scenes and Wild Hunters* (1852) respectively; R. M. Ballantyne's *The Wild Man of the West* (1863); and the satiric "Wild Man of the Woods" by Frederick Gerstecker, in *Western Lands and Western Waters* (1864). "It is certainly a peculiar circumstance that the rumor of 'wild men' . . . should exist in Western Forests," says Gerstecker, "in spite of the fact that seldom, or never, such a thing comes to light. Frequently, after being quiet for months, the rumor breaks out afresh, and one hunter or the other declares he has found the trail of the wild man and traced him to his home in some cave or hollow tree on the mountains." Under the heading of "Wild Man of the Woods" the Galveston *Daily News*, November 2, 1878, reported that a wild man had been caught, probably in Kentucky, and taken to Louisville to be exhibited. Long before this the Galveston *Weekly Journal*, May 26, 1851, reprinted from the Memphis *Enquirer* the report of a long-haired giant, with a footprint thirteen inches in length, loose in the Arkansas woods. Many other such reports could be cited.

See "Big and Little Foot," by Mrs. S. J. Wright, *Legends of Texas*, 242.

THE DREAM THAT SAVED WILBARGER

The chief and the most reliable account of the Wilbarger scalping, and of the dreams, or visitations, that followed, is in *Indian Depredations of Texas*, by J. W. Wilbarger, Austin, 1889, 7-13. "We have stated the facts," says J. W. Wilbarger, "as received from the lips of Josiah Wilbarger, who was the brother of the author of this book, and confirmed by Wm. Hornsby, who still lives, and others who are now dead."

John Henry Brown, who knew Wilbarger well, contributed an account of the incidents to the *Texas Almanac*, 1861, which was reprinted in Baker's *Texas Scrap-Book*. In his *Indian Wars and Pioneers of Texas* (n. d.) Brown extended the account. A version derived from a descendant of the Hornsby family is in *Pioneer Women of Texas*, by Annie Doom Pickrell, Austin, 1929, 58-68. A vivid but inaccurate version is in A. J. Sowell's *Life of Bigfoot Wallace*, printed as a pamphlet in 1889 and reprinted, also as a pamphlet, by *Frontier Times*, Bandera, Texas, 1927; see pp. 13-14 of reprint for the Wilbarger story.

Many descendants of the Hornsby family living in Travis County and elsewhere in Texas have versions of the story. Following Wilbarger in the main, I have incorporated what other details seem valid.

BIGFOOT WALLACE AND THE HICKORY NUTS

The most delightful book on Bigfoot Wallace, who kindled imagination more than any other Texas ranger, is *The Adventures of Bigfoot Wallace*, by John C. Duval, 1870, several times republished. Herein Bigfoot lives with gusto and tells his yarns with superb naturalness.

The primary sources on Bowie's early life are two sketches by his brothers. That by John J. is more extensive and detailed. It was contributed by "Dr. Kilpatrick, of Trinity, Louisiana," who evidently rhetorized it somewhat, to *De Bow's Review*, New Orleans, October, 1852, 378-383. Rezin P. Bowie's letter, dated from Iberville, Louisiana, August 24, 1838, reprinted from the *Planters' Advocate*, appeared in *Niles' National Register*, Washington, D. C., Vol. V (September, 1838–March, 1839), 70. Both are fully quoted, with negligent and unclear references, in *Bowie Knife*, by Raymond W. Thorp, University of New Mexico Press, Albuquerque, 1948. This work, though lacking in orderly arrangement of materials, assembles much scattered and recondite material bearing on the Bowie knife.

The Bowies and Their Kindred: A Genealogical and Biographical History, by Walter Worthington Bowie, Washington, D.C., 1899, has considerable about the Bowie knife.

In 1931 I contributed an essay entitled "Bowie and the Bowie Knife" to the *Southwest Review*, XVI, 351-368. In a slightly changed form and with a new title, "The Knife That Was Law," it was syndicated by the New York *Herald Tribune Magazine*. Edward Gay Rohrbough read the newspaper version and came to the University of Texas to write a thesis on Bowie under my direction. His unpublished *James Bowie and the Bowie Knife in Fact and Fancy*, University of Texas, 1938, is replete with knife lore.

The statement "At twenty paces . . ." concerning Rezin P. and Jim Bowie's prowess comes from J. O. Dyer, "A Truer Story of the Bowie Knife," Galveston *News*, March 21, 1920.

A score or so of accounts of the so-called Sandbar Duel have been published. One in the Fontaine Papers, copied from the *Concordia Intelligencer* of March, 1860, seems to be reliable. The fight was in Concordia Parish of Louisiana. "A History of Rapides Parish, Louisiana," by G. P. Whittington, *Louisiana Historical Quarterly*, Vol. 16 (1933), 628-634, is good on details. So is "The Sandbar Fight," a section of "A History of Concordia Parish," by Robert Dabney Calhoun, *Louisiana Historical Quarterly*, Vol. 15 (1932), 638-643. This contains a statement made in 1880 by Dr. Maddox, one of the participants, and a letter from Col. Robert A. Crain, another participant, dated Oct. 3, 1827, soon after the fight. Both of these accounts specify Bowie's big knife. "Bowie and His Big Knife," by Meigs O. Frost, *Adventure* magazine, June 15, 1935, 110-116, explains particularly well the hostility between Bowie and Norris Wright.

On circumstances leading to making of the knife see John S. Moore to W. W. Fontaine, in Fontaine Papers, Archives, University of Texas Library; also in Galveston *News*, Sept. 8, 1875; Theresa M. Hunter, reporting the testimony of another Bowie, "Grandson's Own Story of the Bowie Knife," Dallas *News*, Jan. 12, 1930, and in an article in the Austin *American*, Aug. 14, 1927; Homer S. Thrall, *A Pictorial History of Texas*, 1879, 502-503.

Some accounts of varying smiths supposed to have wrought the knife are in the following: an article by J. Marvin Hunter, "Who Invented the Bowie Knife?" in *Frontier Times*, Bandera, Texas, Vol. 19 (November, 1941), 39-41, wherein the New York *Star* of May, 1836, the *Red River Herald* of Nachitoches, La., and other sources are cited; an undated clipping from the Washington *Post*; Annie M. Bowie, in the Galveston *News*, March 31, 1890; William M. Newsom, *Whitetailed Deer*, New York, 1926, 249-254; an article in the Natchez *Free Trader*, May 17, 1861, as reprinted in the New Orleans *Picayune*, April 26, 1925; *American Notes and Queries*, I (June 2, 1888), 49-50, with credit to the San Francisco *Chronicle*, and VIII (Dec. 12, 1891) with credit to the Cincinnati *Enquirer*.

The Dan W. Jones manuscript with the Arkansas classic concerning James Black lay unpublished for years before it was printed in the Arkansas *Gazette*, Nov. 20, 1919, since which time it has been reprinted in various places, among others in Herndon's *Centennial History of Arkansas*, I, 982-986. Raymond W. Thorp in his *Bowie Knife*, as cited, bolsters the narrative.

Allsopp, Fred W., *Folklore of Romantic Arkansas*, New York, 1931, II, 72, gives the story of the knife's cutting a silver dollar.

For information on Sowell the blacksmith see Sowell, A. J., *Rangers and Pioneers of Texas*, San Antonio, 1884, 126-127; also 107, 118, 124.

For Smithwick's story of the duplicate he made see Smithwick, Noah, *The Evolution of a State, or Recollections of Old Texas Days*, Austin, 1900, 135-138, 114.

For the wild story of the Spaniard in Cuba see letters by P. Q. in the Baltimore *Commercial Transcript*, June 9 and June 11, 1838, as reprinted in Raymond W. Thorp's *Bowie Knife*, 93-99—my source. The lies in the letters, which other newspapers copied, infuriated

Rezin P. Bowie, whose reply to them has been cited. The story of shooting the Spaniard, from the Jacksboro, Texas, *Echo*, May 25, 1877, is credited to Wilkie's *Spirit of the Times*.

Perhaps the original Spaniard story is in Alger, William R., *Life of Edwin Forrest*, Philadelphia, 1877, I, 118-123, 247-248. An article in the San Antonio *Express*, July 8, 1888, p. 6, credits a confirmatory account to Charles Durang, whose *History of the Philadelphia Stage* ran serially in the Philadelphia *Sunday Dispatch* in 1868. I have looked through a microfilm of the series without locating the Bowie story. With credit to the San Francisco *Chronicle*, the story is in *American Notes and Queries*, I (June 2, 1888), 49-50.

The naked fight in the dark room is in a scrapbook of newspaper clippings given me by Mrs. Georgia Stenger of New York in 1928. An unidentified clipping attributes the yarn to the Pittsburgh *Dispatch* of 1887. The story of a duel with knives in a dark room has been affixed to numerous characters, as exemplified in G. W. Featherstonhaugh's *Excursion through the Slave States*, London, 1844, II, 55-58, and in *The Lives and Adventures of the Desperadoes of the Southwest*, by Alfred W. Arrington (who wrote under the name of Charles Summerfield), New York, 1849, 67-72.

Same unidentified clipping mentioned in the preceding paragraph gives the story of the across-the-log duel.

Bowie's rescue of young Lattimore is told in a lengthy article, by "an aged correspondent," published by the *Record-Union* of Sacramento, California, and reprinted in the Galveston *Daily News*, March 6, 1880. A variation of the story, in which Bowie hands over to a bride the fortune her groom has lost to a Mississippi River steamboat gambler, is told in Wilkie's *The Spirit of the Times*, XX (July 13, 1850), 243, with a credit line to the New York *Sunday Times*. The same story appeared in the *Democratic Telegraph and Texas Register*, Houston, June 20, 1850, reprinted from *Noah's Sunday Times*. The story is repeated in Major Ben C. Truman's *The Field of Honor*, 1884, 290-296.

For the story of the contract-marriage rescue, see Linn, John J., *Reminiscences of Fifty Years in Texas*, New York, 1883, 302-304.

For the Henry Clay story, see *The Texas Monument*, La Grange, Texas, March 22, 1854, with credit to *Quarterly Review* (n.p. or date); Alger, *Life of Forrest*, 1877, as cited; John Henry Brown on Bowie, in his *The Encyclopedia of the New West*, Marshall, Texas, 1881, 433-438; *American Notes and Queries*, III (July 27, 1889), 155.

Freeing the slave is described by "an aged correspondent" in the Sacramento *Record-Union*, as reprinted in the Galveston *Daily News*, March 6, 1880; also in John Henry Brown's sketch on Bowie cited above.

Chief authority for the Sumner Bacon story is John S. Ford, *Memoirs*, manuscript in Archives of the University of Texas Library, II, 332. The story is in part confirmed by William S. Red, *The Texas Colonists and Religion, 1821-1836*, Austin, 1924, 137, 84n.

The story of the Methodist preacher comes from "an aged correspondent" in the Sacramento *Record-Union*, as reprinted in the Galveston *News*, March 6, 1880; James Hatch, also "aged," of San Antonio, to J. Frank Dobie, May 4, 1928; typewritten pamphlet by Hatch, in my files; *American Notes and Queries*, I, (June 2, 1888), 49-50, with credit to the San Francisco *Chronicle*; Morrell, Z. N., *Flowers and Fruits in the Wilderness*, Dallas, 1886, 84-85.

John S. Moore's claim to the original knife is in Fontaine Papers, as cited.

The story of the knife's being left by the butchered deer is in John S. Ford, *Memoirs*, manuscript in Archives, University of Texas Library.

For self-important claimants to possession of Bowie's knife, see *American Notes and Queries*, II (March 23, 1889), 25, and VIII (Dec. 12, 1891); *Longhorn Magazine*, University of Texas, Austin, Feb. 1922.

I heard the popular story of the knife, the judge, and the six-shooter told, I forget by whom, before I read any of the skimpy forms of it in print. If one man does not tell a story—as a story—the way it should be told, the next man is under artistic obligations to improve it. One version is in John Henry Brown's *Indian Wars and Pioneers of Texas*, Austin, Texas, n. d., 407-408, quoting a speech on Williamson made in the Texas Senate in 1891. Duncan W. Robinson, *Robert McAlpin Williamson*, Austin, 1948, 160-162, quotes variations.

THE ROBINHOODING OF SAM BASS

The facts about Sam Bass are established by Wayne Gard in his biography *Sam Bass*, Boston, 1936. The best thing written about him, which takes into account popular attitudes as well as facts, is a long article entitled "Sam Bass, Texas' Beloved Bandit," by Walter Prescott Webb, in the Dallas *News*, Jan. 2, 1927. Webb also contributed "The Legend of Sam Bass" to *Legends of Texas*, 226-230.

Among numerous people who supplied me with anecdotes about Sam Bass, some are now dead. I am especially indebted to Mrs. Alice M. Elliott, Irving, Texas, and to the following other individuals, all of Texas: L. D. Bertillion, Mineola; Wes Burton, Austin; Dr. John C. Graves, Kilgore; —— Hoffman, Denton; —— Jackson, Van Horn; L. Marchand, San Antonio; E. T. Simmang, Giddings; Betsy Walton, Fort Worth.

One anecdote was derived from a manuscript of reminiscences by W. C. Cochran in the Archives of the University of Texas Library.

I doubt that Sam Bass "always tipped the brakemen and porters" of trains he took a hand in robbing, but Mrs. Henry Harrison Beck says so in *On the Texas Frontier*, St. Louis, Mo., 1937, 191-192. I doubt a lot of things.

Bass's six-shootering initials into a live oak is an example of what Frost Woodhull called "folklore shooting." See his essay on that subject in *Publications* No. 9 of the Texas Folklore Society, 1931.

Part Two

NORTHERS, DROUTHS AND SANDSTORMS

Sources: the population of Texas.

FROZEN INSIDE A BUFFALO HIDE

The body of this folk yarn is in *Twenty-Seven Years on the Texas Frontier*, by Captain William Banta and J. W. Caldwell, Jr. (first published in 1893), Council Hill, Oklahoma, 1933, 36-37. Versions of the story are in *A Texas Ranger*, by N. A. Jennings, New York, 1899, 21-23; *Wild Sports in the Far West*, by Frederick Gerstecker,

New York, 1860, 306-307; *The Old Santa Fe Trail,* by Colonel Henry Inman, Topeka, Kansas, 1916, 205-206; "Some Reminiscences of an Old Lawyer," by Judge W. R. Chambers, Lebanon (Tennessee) *Democrat,* Aug. 20, 1931.

In Allen, J. Taylor, *Early Pioneer Days in Texas,* Dallas, 1918, 415-416, a barrel instead of a buffalo hide imprisons the victim. A rollicky variation of the yarn, in which a buffalo tail gets through the barrel bunghole, is in "Cowboy Lore in Colorado," by Honora DeBusk Smith, *Southwestern Lore* (*Publications* No. IX of Texas Folklore Society), Austin, 1931, 34-37.

THE COLD-NOSED HOUNDS

This is one of Jim Ballard's stories. He lives at Beeville, Texas, and is an artist at storytelling. "The Cold-Nosed Hounds" was published in the *Atlantic Monthly,* January, 1944, and then included in *The Pocket Atlantic,* edited by Edward Weeks, Pocket Books, Inc., New York, 1946.

HONEY IN THE ROCK

H. B. Parks, my chief creditor for these tales about wild honey, gave me a manuscript for publication by the Texas Folklore Society but, after some editing, he and I decided to give it to the *Southwest Review,* in which it appeared, summer issue, 1930.

The account of Andrew Sowell, bee hunter, is taken from A. J. Sowell's *Rangers and Pioneers of Texas,* San Antonio, 1884, 121-122.

For Gustaf Wilhelm Belfrage, see a sketch of him by Samuel W. Geiser in the *Southwest Review,* Vol. XIV (1929). Belfrage is quoted on Round Rock by E. T. Cresson in an introduction to "Hymenoptera Texana," *Transactions* of the American Entomological Society, Vol. IV (November 1872).

Part Three

THE TEXAS BLUEBONNET

"An Indian Legend of the Bluebonnet," by Mrs. Bruce Reid, in *Legends of Texas,* 1924, was the first appearance in print, so far as I know, of this myth. It has been retold many times and is now well known over the state. The sacrifice motif is as ancient as the hills. It is hard to keep sentimental banality out of the tale, but the public does not mind it.

THE HEADLESS HORSEMAN OF THE MUSTANGS

Patrick Burke's account of tying a scarecrow on a mustang stallion and then turning him loose to stampede other mustangs is in *A History of Bee County*, by Mrs. I. C. Madray, Beeville, Texas, 1939, 5.

The Bigfoot Wallace-Creed Taylor narrative is from Warren Hunter's "The Headless Horseman," in *Frontier Times*, Bandera, Texas, I (1924), 12-14.

A RANCH ON THE NUECES

In *The Longhorns*, *The Mustangs* and elsewhere I have retold incidents told me by Rocky Reagan, rancher of Live Oak County. Years ago, while he had the Ray Ranch leased and was living on it, he told me this story.

DESPERATE RIDES

"Ad Lawrence's Leap" is from D. W. C. Baker's *Texas Scrap-Book*, 1875, 342-344. One night about twenty-three years ago while we sat in quietness, all traffic in bed, on the porch of a café-store at the corner of Twenty-third Street and Guadalupe, in front of the University of Texas, Railroad (R. R.) Smith of Jourdanton, Texas, down in the brush country — my country — told me the story of John Booth's ride. He was a lawyer and believed in free intellectual enterprise; he was a man of infinite repose, rich in lore of characters and happenings of old times. He had cultivated the art of storytelling and was a wonderful talker. Often I remember him and salute his ghost. I wrote a narrative-essay entitled "The Saga of the Saddle" for the *Southwest Review* (January, 1928), in which I put John Booth's ride and two other stories Railroad Smith told me. In 1936 they were included in my book, *The Flavor of Texas*, now long out of print.

THE PLANTER WHO GAMBLED AWAY HIS BRIDE

This tribal tradition was told me in the summer of 1951 by Sigmund Engleking, a civilized character, at his home out from Comfort, Texas.

Part Four

THE PANTHER'S SCREAM

The story of the woodsman who mocked a panther is from James K. Greer's *A Texas Ranger and Frontiersman*, Dallas, Texas, 1912, 57.

The Hall County pioneer who placated a panther with wild turkey carcasses is in Inez Baker's *Yesterday in Hall County*, Memphis, Texas, 1940, 146-147. One of my students at the University of Texas gave me the Jim Buckner story; it is paralleled by one in John Mortimer Murphy, *Sporting Adventures in the Far West*, London, 1879, 91-92.

Jeff Ake's yarn is abridged from *They Die But Once*, by James O'Neil, New York, 1935, 215-217.

The panther tales handed down by "Queenie," Sam Shaffer's wife, were furnished me by one of her descendants, Mrs. Faye Davidson, a student of mine in the University of Texas, 1940.

The panther-smoothing iron episode is from *History of Pioneer Days in Texas and Oklahoma*, by John A. Hart and others, n.p., n.d., 57-58.

Wayman Hogue's tale is condensed from his *Back Yonder*, New York, 1932, 171-181. The Texas version of the same story, by Grandma Adams, is from Bess Kennedy's *The Lady and the Lions*, New York, 1942, 23-24.

The frontier woman who cut off the panther's paw was the grandmother of Mrs. J. E. Boyd, of Texarkana, Texas, who told me the story. Mrs. Ada Payne, who gave me her grandfather's story of being covered up by panthers, lives at Thalia, Texas.

BEARS ARE INTELLIGENT PEOPLE

The old-time Negro cook's story of a bear that fattened his pork was told me by the late Worth Ray, of Dallas and Austin. Frank Bryan of Dallas gave me the Jim Ingram story.

Elias R. Wrightman's asseveration is in Mary S. Helm's *Scraps of Early Texas History*, 1884, 187. The elaborated parallel yarn of Pablo Romero was told me years ago by Bob Snow, of the Texas Game, Fish and Oyster Commission. I published it in *On the Open Range*, Dallas, 1931, from which it has been lifted, with my own permission. I can't recollect the name of the old trail driver in Montana who told me the Jim Reeves story, but he told it.

OLD BILL, CONFEDERATE ALLY

This story was told me by the late Charles W. Ramsdell, Professor of History in the University of Texas — an authority on the Confederacy. I wrote it down for the *Junior Historian*, published by the Texas State Historical Association, and then it was published in the *Atlantic Monthly*, October, 1943.

Part Five

COLONEL ABERCROMBIE'S MOLE

Bill (W. H.) Kittrell of Dallas, prince of storytellers, gave me this tale in 1932 — wrote it out after I had heard him tell it. I tinkered with it a little, and upon a request from the editor of *Holland's Magazine* sent it to him. He sent a check for fifty dollars, which I turned over to Bill Kittrell, telling him that the next time I used the story I would keep the riches. To me it is the best buried-treasure story I have ever heard. Partly from force of habit, I have tinkered with language and details since the story was published in *Holland's*, February, 1933.

THE GREEN POWDER KEG

My friend Houston Wade, who made a living by working in the post office at Houston and spent his life gathering the lore and history of old-time Texas, gave me this story. His published works, *Notes and Fragments of the Mier Expedition*, *An Early History of Fayette County*, etc., are as far away from his daily-bread work as the *Essays of Elia* are from the ledgers that Charles Lamb kept.

IN A DROUGHT CRACK

This tale is made over from a version contributed by Mrs. Lida M. Lee of Austin to the Austin, Texas, *American*, Oct. 25, 1925.

Noah Smithwick, *The Evolution of a State or Recollections of Old Texas Days*, Austin, Texas, 1900, pp. 52-53, has the quotation in my second paragraph describing the cleft.

THE STRANGER OF SABINE PASS; LONGWORTH'S VICEY-VERSEY MAP; GUARDED BY RATTLESNAKES

One might make a whole book from the tales about lost mines and buried treasures told by W. M. Longworth, to whom I owe these three. The tales written out in longhand that he gave me not long before he died, in January, 1937, amount to 808 typewritten pages — towards 250,000 words, enough to fill two books larger than this one. The genius that possessed him made him more interesting than any story he ever told — and I have failed to reveal him.

THE APACHE SECRET OF THE GUADALUPES

The chiropractor who told me the latter part of this pieced-together tale has switched to another lost mine and no longer lives in San Antonio.

O. HENRY'S TREASURE HUNT

V. V. Daniels told me this story in Corpus Christi, where he was on the editorial staff of the *Evening Times*, September 14, 1925. The Dallas *News*, August 9, 1931, published a piece by him entitled "O. Henry on a Treasure Hunt." The details in it are pronouncedly different from those he gave me.

WHERE DID SAM MCFARLAND CROSS THE COLORADO?

Sam McFarland's grandson, S. H. Furman of Glen Burnie, Maryland, gave me this tale in 1949.

THE MEZCLA MAN

Right after my vaquero friend told me this *cuento*, on Los Olmos Ranch, owned by my Uncle Jim Dobie, in La Salle County, I wrote it down. That was going on thirty years ago. I included it in *On the Open Range*, 1931. Thanks to an improved memory, I have about doubled the length of the story by putting in certain details that Elojio Juarez and I both forgot to put in at the time of our tellings. Carl Hertzog of El Paso printed the remade tale into a delightful-appearing pamphlet that Bertha McKee Dobie and I sent out as a Christmas remembrance for 1954.

One time along in the 1930's, while Carl Sandburg was in Austin, I told him the story. He said, "Someday I'll put this mud man into a pome and call it *B-E-L-L-Y G-O-L-D*."

Index